Emissions
from
Combustion Engines
and
Their Control

D. J. Patterson

Associate Professor
Mechanical Engineering
University of Michigan

N. A. Henein

Associate Professor
Mechanical Engineering Science
Wayne State University

 ann arbor science PUBLISHERS INC.
P.O. BOX 1425 ● ANN ARBOR, MICHIGAN 48106

© copyright 1972 by Ann Arbor Science Publishers, Inc.
P.O. Box 1425, Ann Arbor, Michigan 48106

Library of Congress Catalog Card No 72-77313
ISBN 0-250-97514-9
All Rights Reserved
Printed in the United States of America

Preface

Studies of engine emissions and their control have spanned more than twenty years. Already a new generation of low emission engines has been developed for automotive propulsion. Concern for the environment is leading to more stringent requirements, and legislation will cover a broader range of combustion engines and vehicles. This in turn demands that engineers become even more sophisticated in their emission control solutions.

This book delineates the fundamentals of combustion and emission formation in both homogeneous and heterogeneous combustion systems. The emphasis is on the gasoline and diesel engines. However, the same fundamentals may be applied to other homogeneous combustion systems such as the Wankel engine or to other heterogeneous combustion systems such as gas turbine, steam or Stirling engines. These fundamentals are used in a consistent manner to examine the emission control techniques which have been applied successfully to control hydrocarbon, aldehyde, carbon monoxide, smoke and oxides of nitrogen emissions. The emphasis is on the concepts rather than the mathematical formulations. In many cases the reader is referred to cited literature for more detail.

Since experience shows that emission control tends to be unique to individual engine types, the book does not illustrate ready-made solutions. Rather it has been our objective to acquaint the reader with the underlying principles and control methods so that he may bring them to bear upon his own emission problem. Numerous figures and tables have been included to graphically portray key aspects.

The book is intended as an introductory text in combustion engine emissions and their control. It is designed for the engineer, research worker or student who is concerned with the theory and practice of engine and vehicle emission control. In particular the design engineer will find a detailed account of how theory can be applied to the development of hardware. The research worker will find an overview of the entire problem, the fundamentals needed for its study and a complete list of the pertinent published papers in the field. The instructor will find that the book is suitable as a text at the senior or graduate level. It can be used in a three credit hour single semester course or in a continuing engineering education course.

Chapter 1 discusses the role of the automobile in air pollution, the course of regulatory emission legislation and the general progress made in controlling automotive emissions over the years. Included in this chapter is a discussion of smog chamber results and the concept of hydrocarbon reactivity.

Chapter 2 highlights fundamental aspects of reciprocating engine design, operation and fuels and the relationship between engine and vehicle performance. This chapter is intended as an introduction to the reader who is not acquainted with engine and vehicle theory or as a refresher. Particular attention is given to topics which affect emissions.

Chapter 3 discusses combustion and flame propagation in enclosed volumes and engines. The temperature distribution in the chamber is examined. Heterogeneous combustion is covered in Chapter 8.

Chapter 4 details the mechanisms of formation of hydrocarbons, aldehydes, carbon monoxide and oxides of nitrogen in homogeneous mixtures and gasoline engines. Topics include the phenomena of wall quenching, effect of dilution and spark timing on combustion limits and the mechanisms of nitric oxide formation.

Chapter 5 discusses the effect of gasoline engine design and operating variables on emission formation and reduction. Topics include the effects of mixture, ratio, ignition timing, charge dilution and surface-to-volume ratio.

Chapter 6 treats the effects of fuel composition and fuel system design on evaporative emission losses from carburetors and fuel tanks. Several numerical examples illustrate key points.

Chapter 7 details features of current emission control systems for gasoline engines and discusses advanced system concepts such as charge dilution and catalytic or noncatalytic exhaust treatment.

Chapter 8 deals with the mechanisms of combustion and emission formation in both direct injection and indirect injection diesel engines. Topics include fuel injection, spray combustion and emission formation in swirling gas and the effects of design and operating variables on emissions. Emission characteristics of the diesel such as odor and smoke particulates are studied. Comparisons are made between the emissions of the different reciprocating engines.

Chapter 9 describes exhaust gas instrumentation: nondispersive infra-red, flame ionization, gas chromatographic, and chem-iluminescent. Chapter 10 describes the theory and use of the constant volume sampling system for vehicle emission measurements. A discussion of 1975 and 1976 U.S. Federal test procedures is included.

The authors express their appreciation to the publishers of the several technical publications cited for permission to reproduce figures, particularly to the Board of Directors of the Society of Automotive Engineers for permission to reproduce many figures from the Progress in Technology Series books, Volumes 6, 12, and 14. These were found to be an excellent source of detailed material. Further we wish to acknowledge the Ford Motor Company Technical Education Program for their continued encouragement in the development of this material. Also, we wish to thank Miss Ruth Howard for typing the draft. Finally, we wish to acknowledge the cooperation and patience of our wives and families during the preparation of the manuscript.

Ann Arbor   D. J. Patterson
Detroit   N. A. Henein
June 4, 1972

CONTENTS

1. Automotive Emissions and Air Pollution   1

2. Engine Fundamentals   39

3. Combustion and Homogeneous Mixtures   97

4. Emission Formation in Homogeneous Mixtures and
   Gasoline Engines   117

5. Effect of Design and Operating Variables on Gasoline
   Engine Exhaust Emissions   143

6. Hydrocarbon Evaporative Emissions   181

7. Present and Future Emission Control Systems for
   Gasoline Engines   197

8. Diesel Engine Combustion Emissions and Controls   231

9. Emission Instrumentation   305

10. Federal Automotive Exhaust Emissions Test Procedures   335

Symbols and Abbreviations   349

Index   351

AUTOMOTIVE EMISSIONS
AND AIR POLLUTION

"The day may soon come—if it's not already here—in which the individual automobile can no longer be tolerated as a convenient form of transportation, simply because of its adverse effects on the health of people, not just the aesthetics of the atmosphere."
— Dr. John Middleton, June 1968

Part I Introduction

The relationship between automobile exhaust emissions and air pollution has been established largely as a result of studies of the air pollution problem in Los Angeles, California. Initially it was thought that the Los Angeles problem might be similar to that experienced in London since the Middle Ages, that is, a combination of smoke and fog, or smog. However, this was not the case.

As early as 1943 serious air pollution was detected in the Los Angeles area. This air pollution caused plant damage, eye and throat irritation, cracking of stressed rubber, and a decrease in visibility. By 1947 the problem was severe enough that civic groups aided by the news media took action. As a result, in 1948 the state legislature passed a law permitting the formation of air pollution control districts with the power to curb emission sources. An air pollution control district was established in Los Angeles county that year.

Initial efforts were aimed at reducing particulate emissions by controlling both industries such as steel mills and refineries as well as open burning. These efforts reduced dustfall by two-thirds to a level that prevailed in 1940, before smog became a serious problem. While this effort improved visibility, eye irritation and other smog symptoms remained. Consequently, a research program was undertaken to define the cause or causes of this apparently new type of air pollution problem.

One major difference between Los Angeles smog and that found in London or New York was that the atmosphere of the former was often strongly oxidizing in nature because of the high ozone content. This was opposed to the reducing atmosphere normally as-

1

sociated with the SO_2 emissions from powerplants and home furnaces. No significant industrial release of ozone into the atmosphere was occurring in the Los Angeles area. Thus some form of atmospheric reaction was suspected. The research of Professor A. J. Haagen-Smit at the California Institute of Technology, first published in Industrial and Engineering Chemistry, June, 1952,[1] demonstrated that in the presence of sunlight and NO_2 hydrocarbon compounds reacted to form a variety of oxidation products, one being ozone, that could account for the observed effects.

Because it was thought that the automobile might be a major hydrocarbon contributor, the Automobile Manufacturers Association formed the Vehicle Combustion Products Committee in 1953 to further define the problem and search for potential automotive solutions. Simultaneously in California a concentrated effort was made to reduce hydrocarbon emissions from stationary sources, mainly refineries, in the Los Angeles area. Losses at these refineries were reduced from 400 tons/day in 1951 to 85 tons/day by 1964.[2] However, by 1958 with smog still a serious problem, it was apparent that some type of automotive hydrocarbon emission control would be required for Los Angeles. This was implemented in 1959 when the California legislature added a requirement for air standards to the health and safety code. The air quality standards adopted are shown in Table 1.1.

Most significant of these is the oxidant standard − 0.15 ppm.

Table 1.1

Air Quality Standards°

Pollutant	Parts per million for one hour		
	"Adverse" level	"Serious" level	"Emergency" level
Carbon monoxide		120	240
Ethylene	.5		
Hydrogen sulfide	.1	5	
Sulfur dioxide	1	5	10
Hydrocarbons Nitrogen dioxide Oxidant Ozone Aerosols	.15 on "oxidant index"	not established	not established

°Air-quality standards adopted by California set three levels of pollution: "adverse," at which sensory iritation and damage to vegetation occur; "serious," where there is danger of altered bodily function or chronic disease; "emergency," where acute sickness or death may occur in groups of sensitive persons. (Data from Reference 2.)

Half of the population experiences eye watering at this level and plant damage is also noticeable. The standard also set 30 ppm by volume for 8 hours as the maximum allowable CO concentration. At this level 5% of the blood hemoglobin is inactivated. In addition it was stipulated that these levels should not be exceeded on more than four days a year. The object was to reduce pollution to the 1940 level, a level not deemed objectionable. (In Los Angeles the average oxidant level from 1964–66 exceeded 0.15 ppm for 1 hour on 120 days a year, whereas in New York the average carbon monoxide level from 1964–66 exceeded 15 ppm for 8 hours on 36 days a year).

To implement the air quality standards, the California Motor Vehicle Pollution Control Board was created in 1960. Its function was to set specifications on vehicle exhaust and evaporative emissions and to certify that future vehicles sold in that state were in fact meeting such specifications. To meet the air quality goals by 1970 it was estimated that an 80% reduction in hydrocarbons and a 60% reduction in carbon monoxide would be required. Thus carbon monoxide emission was added to that of hydrocarbon as a prospective subject for automotive exhaust emission regulation.

The first automotive emission requirement dealt with crankcase blowby. The California Motor Vehicle Pollution Control Board (CMVCB) adopted a resolution requiring blowby control devices on all new cars sold in California beginning with the 1963 models. In 1961 the automotive industry began installing positive crankcase ventilation systems (PCV) to control blowby on cars sold in California. In 1963 these were installed nationwide on new cars.

Exhaust emission control was subsequently proposed by the CMVCB for 1966. The requirements for vehicles whose engines exceeded 140 CID were 275 ppm HC and 1.5% CO. These levels represented a 70% reduction in HC and a 57% reduction in carbon monoxide from the exhaust of an uncontrolled vehicle.

The Federal government began its involvement in the air pollution area in 1955 by empowering the Department of Health, Education, and Welfare to provide research and technical assistance to problems relating to air pollution. This was further implemented by the Clean Air Act of 1963 which was designed to stimulate state and local air pollution control activity. An amendment to the Clean Air Act in 1965 specifically authorized the writing of national standards for emissions from all new motor vehicles sold in the United States. The result has been the requirement of exhaust emission control devices on automobiles nationwide beginning with the 1968 models.

Initially, both in California and nationwide, exhaust emissions were measured on a concentration basis, as parts per million by volume (ppm) or mole per cent. The vehicle was placed on a chassis dynamometer and operated over a prescribed driving cycle. The driving cycle used in California to certify 1966 and newer vehicles and by the Federal government to certify 1968–71 vehicles has commonly been referred to as either the California Cycle or Federal Test Procedure (FTP).[15]

Because air pollution depends upon both the concentration of pollutant emitted and the volume, the 1970 and 1971 Federal standards[16] were based upon a calculated mass emission rather than just concentration. The FTP driving cycle was used but average vehicle emission concentrations were multiplied by a total cycle calculated exhaust volume which varied with vehicle weight according to a predetermined formula. This pseudo mass emission assessment was an interim step in a true mass emission measurement. A true mass emission measurement procedure has been developed for use in certifying 1972 and newer cars. The new procedure, discussed in detail in Chapter 10, employs variable dilution sampling, often termed constant volume sampling (CVS), and includes a new driving cycle. For 1972–74 vehicles, a single gas sampling bag is employed and the cycle has been termed CVS-1.[17] For certification of 1975 and 1976 vehicles three sample bags are employed to better assess the proportion of warmed up to cold engine emission. This version has been termed CVS-3.[18] Table 1.2 provides a summary of Federally required emission standards for automobiles.

It is interesting to note that NO_x control began in 1971. This recognized the importance of NO_2 in the photochemical smog reactions as well as effects on health. Particulate emission control has been proposed for 1975 primarily for health and aesthetic reasons. In addition reduction of particulate emissions makes possible more sophisticated exhaust control systems such as catalysts which may be required to meet the 1975 HC, CO, and the 1976 NO_x standards. Evaporative emission control systems were installed on vehicles sold in California beginning in 1970 and were installed nationwide beginning with the 1971 model year. Evaporative emissions of hydrocarbons were regulated to 6.0 grams per test until 1972, and thereafter to 2 grams per test. The 1975 and 1976 standards are effectively identical to those suggested by the Panel on Electrically Powered Vehicles[3] as the ultimate feasibility in automotive emission reduction.

Table 1.2

**Past, Present and Future Federal Automotive
Exhaust Emission Standards**

Year	HC	CO	NO$_x$	Partic-ulates	Federal register reference
FTP Cycle					
1968	275 ppm (3.2 g/mi)°	1.5% (33 g/mi)°	–	–	Vol. 21, No. 61, Pt. II, Mar. 30, 1966.
1970	2.2 g/mi (180 ppm)°	23 g/mi (1%)°	–	–⎫	Vol. 33, No. 108, Pt. II,
1971	2.2 g/mi	23 g/mi	4.0 g/mi^c	–⎭	June 4, 1968.
CVS-1 Cycle					
1971	4.6 g/mi	47 g/mi			
1972	3.4 g/mi	39 g/mi	4.0 g/mi⎫		Vol. 35, No. 219, Pt. II,
1973–74	3.4 g/mi	39 g/mi	3.0 g/mi⎭		Nov. 10, 1970.
CVS-3 Cycle					
1975	0.41 g/mi	3.4 g/mi	3.0 g/mi	.1 g/mi^p⎫	Vol. 36, No. 128, Pt. II,
1976	0.41 g/mi	3.4 g/mi	0.4 g/mi	.1 g/mi^p⎭	July 2, 1971.

Evaporative losses: 6.0 g per test in 1970 in California, and 1971 nationwide, and
2.0 g per test beginning 1972 nationwide.
° equivalent for a 4000 lb vehicle.
c: California requirement only.
p: proposed

AUTOMOTIVE EMISSIONS AND THEIR ROLE IN AIR POLLUTION

The emissions from gasoline-powered automobiles consist largely of unburned hydrocarbons, carbon monoxide, oxides of nitrogen, oxides of sulfur, and particulate matter including smoke. Of the total hydrocarbon emissions from an uncontrolled automobile, 20–25% arises from blowby from the crankcase, 60% from the exhaust and the remainder from evaporative losses from both the carburetor and the fuel tank. Direct measurements in urban centers have demonstrated what the automobile contributes to air pollution.

Figure 1.1 shows morning time variation in urban CO levels just before and just after a change to daylight saving time. The

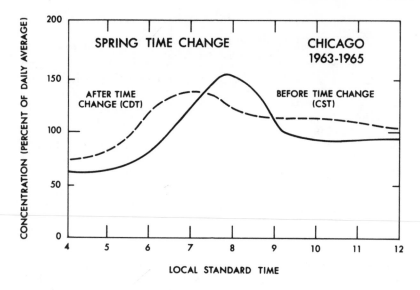

Figure 1.1. Time shift of morning peak carbon monoxide levels. (Figure from Reference 3.)

shift in the peak CO value corresponds to the shift in rush hour traffic.

Figure 1.2 shows weekday HC, CO and NO versus Saturday and Sunday levels. The 8:00 a.m. peak almost disappeared on Sunday morning. Sunday afternoon peak concentrations of CO and NO were lower than those on weekdays. Nonmethane hydrocarbon concentration, the portion emitted primarily by motor vehicles, exhibited a similar reduction on Sunday.

Figure 1.3 shows atmospheric oxidant levels resulting from the photochemical reactions of HC and NO_2. Note that the peak oxidant level correlates most closely with maximum solar radiation. Apparently reduced automotive emissions on Sunday morning do not affect overall atmospheric concentrations enough to reduce materially the Sunday oxidant build up. It should be recalled that at 0.15 ppm oxidant half the population experiences eye watering.

On a nationwide basis the Department of Health, Education and Welfare has estimated that automobiles contribute about 48% of all the carbon monoxide, 4% of the sulfur dioxide, 32% of the oxides of nitrogen, 59% of the hydrocarbons and 8% of the particulate matter in the atmosphere. The values are shown in Table 1.3. It must be pointed out that tonnage figures do not reflect

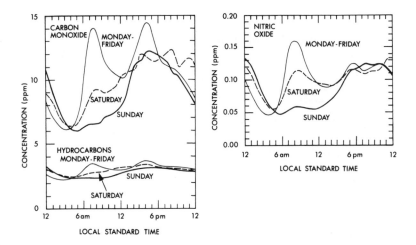

Figure 1.2.   Chicago weekday vs. weekend levels. (Figure from Reference 3.)

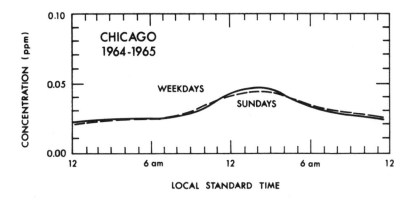

Figure 1.3.   Weekday-Sunday oxidant levels, May–October only. (Figure from Reference 3.)

pollution severity. For example, in terms of health effects a ton of SO_2 is worse than 25 tons of CO.

When the items listed in Table 1.3 are quantified in terms of air pollution severity, the contribution of the automobile may be judged on effects rather than tonnage.

AIR POLLUTION SEVERITY

Table 1.3 lists the estimates by weight of major pollutants added to the atmosphere in the United States. From these figures

Table 1.3

H.E.W. Estimate of Total U.S. Emissions
(Millions of tons/year)

	Carbon monoxide (1968 est.)	Hydrocarbons (1968 est.)	Sulfur dioxide (1966 est.)	Oxides of nitrogen (1968 est.)	Particulates (1966 est.)	Aldehydes per cent (1963 est.)
Transportation						
Motor Vehicles						
Gasoline	59.0	15.2	1.0	6.6	1.0	40.8%
Diesel	0.2	0.4		0.6		1.6
Aircraft	2.4	0.3		nil		0.8
Railroads	0.1	0.3		0.4		} 5.3
Vessels	0.3	0.1		0.3		
Non-highway	1.8	0.3		0.3		
Stationary[a]						
Coal	0.8	0.2	15.0	4.0	4.0	10.1
Fuel oil	0.1	0.1		1.1		
Natural gas	nil	nil		4.7		
Wood	1.0	0.4		0.2		
Refuse Disposal	7.8	1.6	1.0	0.6	1.0	35.0
Industry	9.7	4.6	9.0	0.2	6.0	5.6
Miscellaneous[b]	16.9	8.5[c]		1.7		0.8
TOTAL	100.1	32.0	26.0	20.7	12.	100%
Auto %	59.0	47.5	3.9	31.8	} 8.5	40.8
Diesel %	0.2	0.7		2.9		1.6

a: includes space heating.
b: includes emissions from forest and other fires.
c: includes organic solvent evaporation and gasoline marketing.

one readily concludes that the automobile is the nation's largest pollutor—43% by weight. The chief compound emitted by the automobile is carbon monoxide. However, compared to the other pollutants, carbon monoxide is relatively harmless. A more meaningful assessment of pollution severity can be made by considering the harmful effects of the pollutant in addition to the quantity emitted. In effect, weighting factors can be developed for each constituent.

One scheme for assessing air pollution severity termed "Pindex" has been proposed by Babcock.[5] This method considers the contribution to air pollution of particulate matter, sulfur oxides, nitrogen oxides, carbon monoxide, hydrocarbons, oxidant, solar radiation, and particulate-sulfur oxides synergism. Each compound is assigned a weighting or tolerance factor which in the Pindex system is based upon air quality criteria. Tolerance factors range from a low of 214 for oxidant (not much tolerance) to a high of 40,000 for carbon monoxide (high tolerance). This means that 214 pounds of oxidant have the same health effect as 40,000 pounds of carbon monoxide.

Figure 1.4 shows a schematic of the Pindex method. First the atmospheric concentration of each emitted compound is calcu-

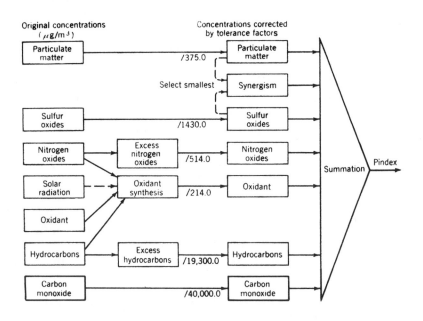

Figure 1.4. Pindex calculation scheme. (Figure from Reference 5.)

lated in terms of micrograms per cubic meter, $\mu g/m^3$:* 1 $\mu g =$ 10^{-6} g. In addition, hydrocarbons, oxides of nitrogen and oxidant are converted to $\mu mol/m^3$. For this calculation, hydrocarbons are assumed to be methane, oxides of nitrogen NO_2 and oxidant O_3. Next it is assumed that oxides of nitrogen and hydrocarbons react with sunlight to form additional oxidant. The assumption is made that one mole of hydrocarbon reacts with one mole of nitrogen dioxide to form one mole of oxidant. The amount of additional oxidant assumed to be formed is calculated by multiplying the molar concentration ($\mu mol/m^3$) of nitrogen oxides of hydrocarbons, whichever is least, by 6×10^{-4} and this product by the solar radiation in cal/cm²-day (average value 375). The original concentrations of hydrocarbon and nitrogen oxides are corrected by subtracting the moles of each which have reacted to form oxidant. The value of 6×10^{-4} was estimated from atmospheric data and reflects the observed balance between hydrocarbons, oxides of nitrogen and oxidant.

Next the corrected concentrations are divided by tolerance factors. Then the particulate matter-sulfur oxide synergism term is calculated. This term recognizes that both constituents together are more harmful to health than each separately. The synergism term is assumed to be the smaller of either of the particulate matter or sulfur oxide concentrations corrected by the tolerance factors as suggested in Figure 1.4. Finally the sum of the seven terms is computed. This sum is the Pindex rating.

Figure 1.5 shows a sample computation. Table 1.4 shows air quality data for several U.S. cities and the calculated Pindex levels. As a point of interest the air quality standards proposed by the Environmental Protection Agency in 1971 are listed in Table 1.5. The Pindex value provides a ready means for ranking air pollution severity.

While the above discussion focuses on the Pindex computation it is apparent that other similar schemes can be formulated based on a different set of assumptions. Obviously the principal value of such computations is to quantify the relative contribution to air pollution from each emitted constitutent. For example using this scale, the automobile's contribution to air pollution is slightly less than 20% rather than the aforementioned 43% based on weight

---

*For gases: Concentration in $\mu mol/m^3 =$ PPM $\times$ P/$\bar{R}$T. Concentration in $\mu g/m^3 =$ PPM $\times$ MW $\times$ P/$\bar{R}$T, where: PPM is gaseous concentration in parts per million; MW is molecular weight of compound; $\bar{R}$ is universal gas constant, 82×10^{-6} atm m³/g mole °K; P is atmospheric pressure, atm; T is atmospheric temperature, °K.

Given information

Particulate Matter	(PM) =	$143.0 \mu g/m^3$
Sulfur Oxides	(SOX) =	123.0
Nitrogen Oxides	(NOX) =	136.0
Carbon Monoxide	(CO) =	7250.0
Hydrocarbons	(HC) =	2157.0
Oxidant	(OOO) =	43.2
Solar Radiation	(SR) =	$400.0 cal/cm^2 day$

Convert reactants to $\mu mol/m^3$

NOX = 136.0/46.0 = 3.0 $\mu mol/m^3$
HC = 2157.0/16.0 = 134.5
OOO = 43.2/48.0 = 0.9

Determine limiting reactant for oxidant synthesis (NOX or HC): NOX is limiting

Create Oxidant
OOO = 0.0006 × SR × (limiting reactant)
OOO = 0.0006 × 400.0 × 3.0 = 0.72 $\mu mol/m^3$

Determine total oxidant and excess HC and NOX:
OOO = 0.9 + 0.72 = 1.6 $\mu mol/m^3$
HC = 134.5 − 0.72 = 133.8
NOX = 3.0 − 0.72 = 2.3

Convert reactants back to weight basis
OOO = 1.6 × 48.0 = 77.3
HC = 133.5 × 16.0 = 2140.0
NOX = 2.3 × 46.0 = 105.0

Apply tolerance factors
PM = 143.0/ 375.0 = 0.381
SOX = 123.0/ 1430.0 = 0.086
NOX = 105.0/ 514.0 = 0.204
CO = 7250.0/40000.0 = 0.181
HC = 2140.0/19300.0 = 0.111
OOO = 77.3/ 214.0 = 0.361

Determine synergism term (SYN)
SYN = SOX or PM (whichever is smaller)
SYN = SOX = 0.086

Sum terms to determine pindex
Pindex = PM + SOX + NOX + CO + HC + OOO + SYN
Pindex = 1.41

Figure 1.5. Sample calculation. (Data from Reference 5.)

only. The major objection to this method is the difficulty of accurately assigning values to tolerance factors and other parameters involved in the computations.

OXIDANT PROBLEM IN THE UNITED STATES

The oxidant level of the atmosphere is directly related to the hydrocarbon and oxides of nitrogen content. This relationship is discussed in Chapter 1, Part II. Figure 1.6 shows the number of days on which an oxidant level of 0.15 ppm was exceeded for 8

Table 1.4

Air Quality Data for U.S. Cities*

	PM ($\mu g/m^3$)	SO$_x$ (ppm)	NO$_x$ (ppm)	CO (ppm)	HC (ppm)	Oxidant (ppm)	
Chicago	124	0.14	0.14	12.0	3.0	0.01	
Cincinnati	154	0.03	0.06	6.0	3.0	0.02	
Denver	126	0.01	0.07	7.9	2.4	0.03	
Los Angeles	119	0.02	0.13	11.0	4.0	0.05	
Philadelphia	154	0.08	0.08	6.8	2.0	0.01	
Saint Louis	143	0.04	0.07	5.8	3.0	0.04	
San Diego	69	0.01	0.05	3.0	6.0	0.03	
San Francisco	68	0.01	0.14	3.2	3.0	0.02	
San Jose	92	0.01	0.12	5.0	4.0	0.02	
Washington	77	0.05	0.07	6.0	3,0	0.02	
Pindex Levels							Total
Chicago	0.47	0.42	0.56	0.38	0.11	0.10	2.04
Los Angeles	0.34	0.06	0.52	0.34	0.15	0.50	1.91
Saint Louis	0.42	0.14	0.26	0.18	0.11	0.36	1.47
Philadelphia	0.49	0.24	0.32	0.21	0.07	0.10	1.43
San Jose	0.26	0.03	0.48	0.16	0.15	0.30	1.38
Denver	0.35	0.03	0.29	0.25	0.09	0.29	1.30
Cincinnati	0.44	0.09	0.24	0.19	0.11	0.20	1.27
San Francisco	0.19	0.03	0.56	0.16	0.11	0.20	1.25
Washington	0.26	0.15	0.28	0.18	0.11	0.20	1.18
San Diego	0.19	0.03	0.20	0.09	0.22	0.30	1.03

*Annual averages (approximated from 1962 to 1967 data).
Data from Reference 5.

Table 1.5

Federal Air Quality Standards

	April 28, 1971	
	Federal standards*	
Substance	Primary	Secondary
Oxidant	0.08 ppm (1 hr.)	0.08 ppm (1 hr.)
Carbon moxide	9.0 ppm (8 hrs.)	9.0 ppm (8 hrs.)
	35 ppm (1 hr.)	35 ppm (1 hr.)
Sulfur dioxide	0.14 ppm (24 hrs.)	0.10 ppm (24 hrs.)
	0.03 ppm (annual)	0.02 ppm (annual)
Particulate	75 $\mu g/m^3$ annual	60 $\mu g/m^3$ annual
	260 $\mu g/m^3$ 24 hrs.	150 $\mu g/m^3$ 24 hrs.
Nitrogen dioxide	0.05 ppm (annual)	0.05 ppm (annual)
Hydrocarbons (less methane)	0.24 ppm (3 hrs- 6–9 a.m.)	0.24 ppm (3 hrs.- 6–9 a.m.)

*Original standards were $\mu g/m^3$.

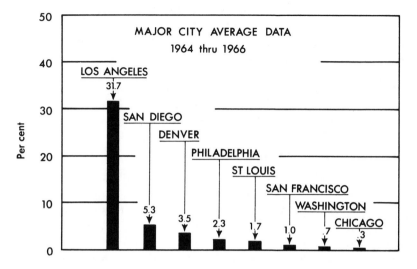

Figure 1.6.   Smog indication: per cent of days on which oxidant standard of 0.15 ppm was exceeded for 1 hour. (Data from Department of Health, Education and Welfare.)

hours at several locations. At a level of 0.15 ppm oxidant, approximately 50% of the population experience some eye watering. In 1971 the Environmental Protection Agency set 0.08 ppm as the maximum 1 hour exposure level permissible (Table 1.5). Consequently 0.15 ppm is not a desirable level. It is appalling to see that in Los Angeles photochemical smog and the attendant eye irritation was experienced on roughly 120 days of the year, or 32% of a year. Table 1.3 indicates that automobiles contributed 59% of the hydrocarbons and 32% of the nitrogen oxides nationally. Because of the judicious clean up of other sources in the Los Angeles area, the automobile there contributed nearly 70% of the total hydrocarbons and organic compounds in the atmosphere. There is no doubt that the hydrocarbons emitted from the automobile are now the single largest remaining organic contributor to the Los Angeles smog problem.

In reviewing Figure 1.6 the next worst city is San Diego with 19 or 20 days per year, then Denver at 13 days per year, and finally Chicago with one day per year. There is almost an order of magnitude difference between the smog problem in Los Angeles and that in the rest of the country. Thus in terms of photochemical smog, Los Angeles represents a somewhat unique situation. The major problem arises there because of (1) the large automotive population, which is of the order of 3 million cars,* (2) because of the presence of strong sunlight, which is necessary for the photochemical reactions, and (3) because of the lack of ventilation of the Los Angeles basin, arising from geographical and meteorological factors.

Let us view this oxidant level data as being one point on a curve of the significance of automotive hydrocarbon and nitrogen oxide emissions to the local and national air pollution problem.

CARBON MONOXIDE PROBLEM

Figure 1.7 illustrates the national and local carbon monoxide picture by showing the per cent of days on which the carbon monoxide level averaged above 15 ppm for 8 hours. However, present California Board of Health recommendations are that a person should not experience more than 30 ppm CO for 8 hours. And in 1971, the Environmental Protection Agency recommended 9 ppm as an 8 hour exposure limit. In light of this, 15 ppm does not represent a particularly desirable air quality.

The most significant aspect of the carbon monoxide problem is that it is more widespread than the photochemical smog problem which results from hydrocarbons and nitrogen oxides. In New York 30% of the days averaged 15 ppm or greater of carbon monoxide. It is apparent that the carbon monoxide problem in New York in terms of days per year is about equal to the hydrocarbon problem in Los Angeles. The next most severely affected city, Chicago, had 20% of the days per year with excessive CO. And there are two cities that experienced 15 ppm for 8 hours on 36 days of the year. Table 1.3 shows that 48 % of the carbon monoxide is estimated to arise from vehicle exhaust. Therefore, it must be concluded that CO is the most widespread automotive air pollutant. Let us consider this data as an additional point on the curve of the relative national and local significance of automotive generated air pollution.

While this is admittedly an incomplete picture of the importance of automotive emissions to the total air pollution problem, there has been enough evidence of this type to cause the Federal government to initiate nationwide controls on hydrocarbons, nitrogen oxide, and carbon monoxide emissions from automobiles.

---

*The Los Angeles Basin has 3 million cars in an area of 1500 sq. miles or 2000 cars/sq. mile. Compare this to the state of Michigan with 3.6 million cars and 60,000 sq. miles or 60 cars/sq. mile. This comparison assumes that the emissions in the state of Michigan are distributed over the entire state rather than a limited region.

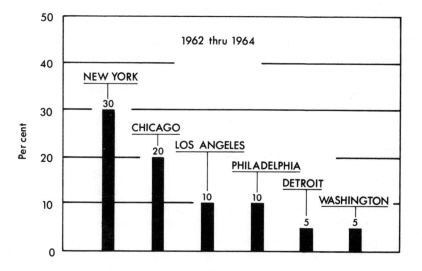

Figure 1.7. Carbon monoxide measurements: per cent of days CO averaged above 15 ppm for 8 hours. (Data from Department of Health, Education and Welfare.)

SUMMARY

In summary, emissions from automobiles do contribute significantly to air pollution in some areas. Much has been accomplished, however, by the automotive industry to reduce emissions. Table 1.6 summarizes the past and projected reduction in emissions for a typical vehicle. In 1961, crankcase blowby contributed 113 g/day of hydrocarbon. Today this has been reduced to zero. Exhaust emissions were 354 g/day or 900 ppm based on concentration. This was reduced by 70% to 108 grams (275 ppm) in 1966 in California and nationwide in 1968. In 1970, evaporative control was added for California. This reduced evaporative hydrocarbon losses from 100 g/day for an uncontrolled vehicle to 12 g/day. Nationwide, an additional 33% reduction was achieved in exhaust hydrocarbon emissions in 1970. In 1971 total vehicle hydrocarbon loss was reduced to 84 g/day nationwide—an 85% reduction from the 1960 vehicle. Likewise carbon monoxide emission was reduced nearly 60% in 1968 and by 70% in 1970. Thus the initial California emission reduction targets have been exceeded for individual new vehicles.

The Clean Air Amendments Act of 1970 called for a further reduction in HC and CO of 90% by 1975. As a result, for 1975 models, HC and CO emissions from the typical vehicle will have

Table 1.6

Calculated Vehicle Emissions-Grams/Day/Car
Based on Federal Standards (33 mile trip)

| Year | Crankcase | Hydrocarbon | | | Carbon Monoxide Total | Oxides of Nitrogen Total | Particulates Total |
		Exhaust	Evaporative	Total			
FTP Cycle							
1960	°113	°354	°100	°567	2590	128	—
1963	0	354	100	454	2590	128	—
1968	0	108	100	208	1112	°192	—
1970	0	72	100	172	777	230	—
1971	0	72	12	84	777	130	—
Overall reduction from 1960 vehicle				85%	70%	—	
CVS-3 Cycle							
1970	0	135	100	235	1120	130°°	—
1975	0	14	4	18	112	99	3.3
1976	0	14	4	18	112	13	3.3
Overall reduction from 1960 vehicle				98%	97%	90%	—

°Data from Reference 4.
°°1971 vehicle

been reduced by about 98% and 97% respectively as Table 1.6 shows.

Prior to specific control, oxides of nitrogen rose somewhat as a result of the lean mixtures used to control hydrocarbon and carbon monoxide emissions. In 1971 California required that oxide of nitrogen emissions be reduced to essentially the level of an uncontrolled 1960 vehicle — 4.0 g/mi. This became a Federal requirement for 1972 vehicles. An additional 90% reduction has been required nationally for 1976.

It must be noted that the reduction in emissions from the entire vehicle population will occur considerably slower than Table 1.6 suggests. This is because an average vehicle has a lifetime of approximately ten years and 100,000 miles. Thus at any time the vehicle population consists of lower emission new cars and higher emission older cars. Moreover, the total number of vehicles increases each year.

Table 1.7 lists currently required and proposed standards for diesel and gasoline heavy duty trucks. Eventually it is anticipated that emission standards will be set for all combustion engines, from those powering lawnmowers to locomotives.

Part II Photochemical Smog

Photochemical smog is a form of air pollution which arises from the action of sunlight or hydrocarbon compounds and oxides of nitrogen. Smog, which is highly oxidizing in nature, is known by its results—cracking of stressed rubber, eye and throat irritation, odor, plant damage, and decreased visibility.

The chemistry of photochemical smog is very complex. It is characterized by extremely dilute concentrations of reactants and correspondingly slow reaction rates in many cases. The atmospheric hydrocarbon compounds number in the hundreds, with as many as 200 distinct hydrocarbon compounds found in the automobile exhaust. Many of these hydrocarbon compounds, such as the paraffins, are relatively inert in the atmosphere. Others, such as the olefins, are extremely reactive and combine readily with NO_2 in the presence of sunlight to form smog products.

Table 1.7

Past and Proposed Federal Nonpassenger Car Emission Standards

	HC	CO	NO	Truck smoke opacity
Diesel engines				
1971–72	–	–	–	Accel 40%, Lug 20%
1973–p	3 g/ bhp-hr	7.5 g/ bhp-hr	12.5 g/ bhp-hr	Accel 20%, Lug 15% max. any mode 50%
Gasoline engines				
1971–72	275 ppm	1.5% CO	–	–
1973–p	160 ppm	0.8% CO	2000 ppm	–

p: proposed

Smog reactions are initiated by sunlight in the ultraviolet region below 4000A. Because of the extreme complexity of identifying the reactions and rates of reaction directly in the atmosphere, "smog chambers" have been built to simulate the atmosphere, but under controlled conditions. Banks of high intensity lamps, designed to provide a light spectrum and intensity similar to sunlight, are used. Figure 1.8 shows a "smog chamber" built by General Motors Research. Initially the chamber is charged with an atmosphere containing concentrations of hydrocarbons and nitrogen oxides similar to those found on smoggy days in the Los Angeles area. Usually one hydrocarbon compound is added for each test, with various hydrocarbon and NO concentrations being tested. After the chamber is charged and well mixed, the lights are turned on and the reactions commence.

Figure 1.8. This 300 cu. ft. "smog chamber" at the General Motors Research Laboratories simulates the Los Angeles daylight atmosphere. Exhaust from vehicle in adjacent room (left rear) is diluted with air and pumped into chamber (right) where 247 special fluorescent lamps irradiate it. At bottom is inside view of stainlese steel tank with its forest of fluorescent lamps.

The result is shown in Figure 1.9 and is typical. The chamber was charged initially with 1 ppm propylene hydrocarbon and 0.4 ppm nitric oxide. Immediately after the light was turned on, a large concentration of nitrogen dioxide was rapidly produced from the existing NO. After a significant amount of NO_2 was formed, a noticeable decrease in hydrocarbon concentration commenced and oxidant products began forming. The NO_2 concentration then dropped rapidly to approach a final equilibrium value. The reactions shown in Figure 1.9 reached completion after about 3 hours.

The most significant oxidation products are ozone and peroxyacyl nitrates (PAN) both of which cause severe eye irritation. Oxygenated hydrocarbons (aldehydes) as well as organic nitrates

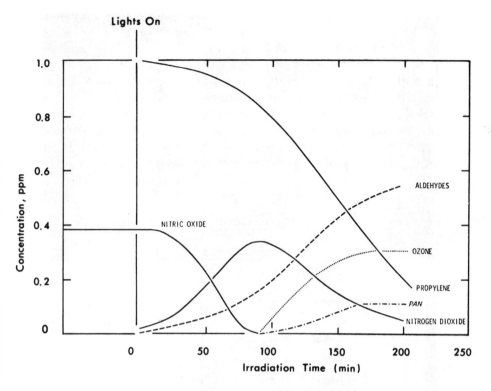

Figure 1.9. Typical concentration changes in a photochemical smog reaction (PAN = peroxyacetylnitrate). (Data from Reference 4.)

are the predominant organic products. Visibility-decreasing aerosols are observed also in these smog chambers.

CHEMISTRY OF SMOG FORMATION

Dr. John Caplan of the General Motors Research Laboratories has proposed a detailed explanation of how hydrocarbon compounds and NO react in the atmosphere to form smog products.[6] His explanation, which is particularly relevant to the automobile emission problem, is discussed below. The proposed reactions as well as other atmospheric reactions involving nonautomotive emissions may be homogeneous gas phase reactions, gaseous reactions at surfaces of suspended particles, adsorbtion and reaction on surfaces of suspended particles, or liquid phase reactions in aerosols.

Thirteen equations thought to govern smog formation are listed in Figure 1.10. Hydrocarbons and nitric oxide are the vehicle-produced reactants. The reactions occur simultaneously and in many instances the products of one reaction furnish the reactants for another. In some cases these reactions regenerate some of the original species to give a chain reaction.

Of the two vehicle-contributed components, hydrocarbons are involved in 2 and nitric oxide in 6 of the 13 reactions. The manner in which nitric oxide and nitrogen dioxide react is responsible in part for the complexity of the system and the unexpected effects

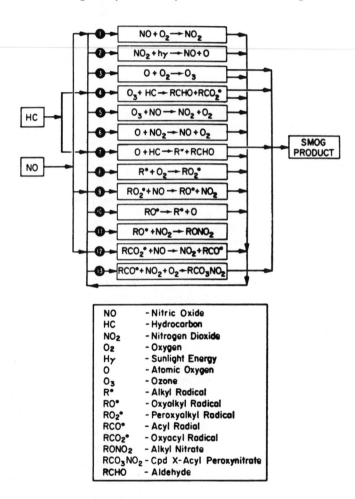

NO	- Nitric Oxide
HC	- Hydrocarbon
NO_2	- Nitrogen Dioxide
O_2	- Oxygen
$H\gamma$	- Sunlight Energy
O	- Atomic Oxygen
O_3	- Ozone
$R^\bullet$	- Alkyl Radical
$RO^\bullet$	- Oxyalkyl Radical
$RO_2^\bullet$	- Peroxyalkyl Radical
$RCO^\bullet$	- Acyl Radial
$RCO_2^\bullet$	- Oxyacyl Radical
$RONO_2$	- Alkyl Nitrate
RCO_3NO_2	- Cpd X- Acyl Peroxynitrate
RCHO	- Aldehyde

Figure 1.10. Route of photochemical smog formation tracing the reactions of hydrocarbons and nitric oxide in the presence of oxygen and sunlight. Thirteen equations are involved. (Data from Reference 6.)

that changes in nitric oxide concentration have in altering the rate of smog formation. Nitrogen dioxide is two-faced; it is the compound in reaction 2 that absorbs sunlight to trigger smog formation, yet in reaction 11 it reacts with oxyalkyl radicals to form an alkyl-nitrate which terminates the chain and ends the reactions. Thus, nitrogen dioxide both starts and stops smog formation.

Products usually associated with photochemical smog emerge from four of the reactions: ozone from reaction 3, aldehydes from reactions 4 and 7, and compound X from reaction 13. The last product is believed to contribute to eye irritation.

Reaction 1 starts the entire chain. This reaction proceeds very slowly when no light is present. For example, in the absence of light only 2% of the NO would be converted to NO_2 after 24 hours, and it would take 1600 hours to convert 97%. With light NO is converted to NO_2 relatively quickly, 90 minutes in the case of the data shown in Figure 1.9. Thus reaction 1 is primarily a photochemical reaction.

In the absence of hydrocarbon compounds, reactions 2, 3, and 5 would then reach an equilibrium at which an extremely low level of ozone would be produced. However when HC is present, reaction 7 proceeds, leading (via reaction 8) to the oxidation of NO to NO_2 in reaction 9. This reaction outruns reaction 5, thereby using up the NO which normally would reduce the O_3 in reaction 5. Moreover a negligible *net* consumption of 1 occurs in reaction 7 because of reaction 10. At this point we are left with reaction 3 producing ozone but reaction 5 in which ozone is reduced being bypassed. Consequently a large ozone buildup occurs as shown in Figure 1.9. Reaction 11 is a chain termination step which becomes dominant at high NO_2 concentrations, late in the reactions. It inhibits the overall reactions. Reactions 4, 12, and 13 illustrate possible routes for formation of smog products yielding the eye irritants, aldeydes and PAN.

WHAT TO CONTROL–THE NITRIC OXIDE CONTROVERSY

Since both hydrocarbons and NO are necessary reactants in the 13 smog equations, a reasonable assumption might be that a reduction of either would reduce smog. Laboratories do confirm that this is the case with hydrocarbon compounds. This conclusion is the same whether based upon the oxidation rate of hydrocarbons, the oxidation rate of nitric oxide to nitrogen dioxide, or the formation of smog products such as aldehydes, ozone, and PAN.

On the other hand, the effect of an NO reduction is not as clear. Laboratories do not agree on the potential benefits of NO reduction. Some smog chamber data suggest that almost any reduction of NO, short of complete elimination, would increase smog products. There is agreement that NO reduction would lead to lower atmospheric NO$_2$ concentrations and thereby reduced coloration of the atmosphere and plant damage; moreover, because NO$_2$ is toxic, a reduction is thought to be beneficial to health.

General Motors, the State of California, and the U.S. Public Health Service have all presented results from their smog chamber tests. A discussion of these follows. In viewing these data, however, one must keep in mind that the present imperfect understanding of atmospheric chemistry makes somewhat tenuous the extrapolation to the atmosphere of these controlled experimental results.

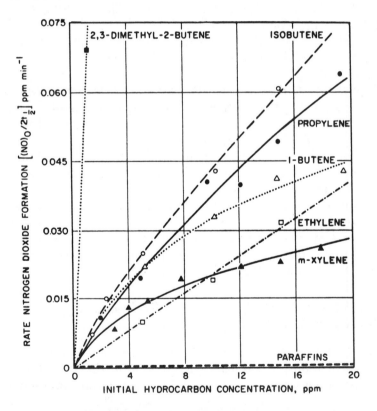

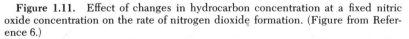

Figure 1.11. Effect of changes in hydrocarbon concentration at a fixed nitric oxide concentration on the rate of nitrogen dioxide formation. (Figure from Reference 6.)

A. General Motors

Figure 1.11 shows the effect of changes in hydrocarbon concentration at a fixed nitric oxide concentration on the rate of nitrogen dioxide formation for several hydrocarbons. From this result, two important observations can be made:

(1) In every case a reduction in hydrocarbon concentration reduces the rate.

(2) Hydrocarbons differ widely in their reactivities in forming smog.

The effect of changes in atmospheric nitric oxide concentration on smog formation is shown in Figure 1.12. Here the rate of hydrocarbon oxidation is shown as a function of initial nitric oxide concentration for three concentrations of propylene. At every nitric oxide concentration, reduction in hydrocarbon concentration from 2 to 1 to 0.5 ppm reduced the rate. On the other hand, whether a reduction in nitric oxide reduced the rate depended upon the starting point and how great a reduction was involved. For all three propylene concentrations, the rate first increased and

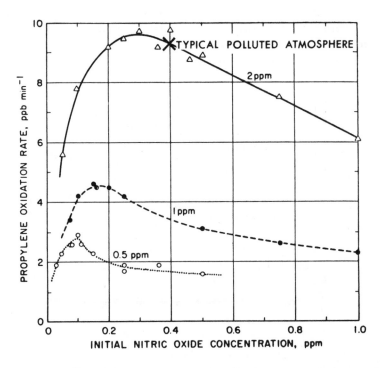

Figure 1.12.   Effect of changes in nitric oxide concentration on propylene oxidation rate for three propylene concentrations. (Figure from Reference 6.)

then decreased with decreased nitric oxide concentration. More-over, the nitric oxide concentration which resulted in the max-imum rate for a given hydrocarbon concentration decreased as the hydrocarbon concentration itself decreased.

In addition, one must consider the situation that would prevail with a 1 ppm hydrocarbon concentration and 0.4 ppm nitric oxide concentration.* This may arise in areas such as Los Angeles and its environs with additional control of the hydrocarbon emissions. At this lower hydrocarbon level, the effect of reducing the nitric oxide concentration is even more unfavorable when considered in terms of smog formation rate.

Further evidence of the adverse effects of NO reduction found by General Motors is shown in terms of equilibrium ozone prod-uct in Figure 1.13. These data show that reduction of atmospheric NO to as low as 0.15 ppm continuously increased the level of ozone in the smog products.

B. State of California

Romanovsky[11] reports smog chamber results from studies con-ducted by the State of California, Department of Public Health. Tests were run with nitric oxide concentrations up to 4 ppm and hydrocarbon concentration up to 8 ppm. Propylene was the hydro-carbon compound used in the tests.

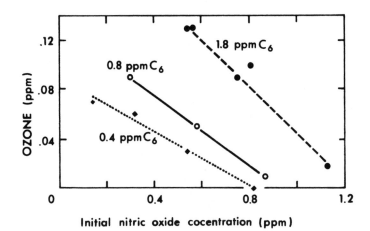

Figure 1.13. Effects of initial nitric oxide and hydrocarbon concentrations on ozone yield. (Data from Reference 4.)

---

*A concentration of 2.0 ppm propylene and 0.4 ppm NO can be taken as typical concentrations in polluted atmospheres.[8]

Figure 1.14 shows the effect of varying NO and propylene concentrations on the resulting oxidant concentration. The oxidant is primarily ozone. Results show that combined reduction of HC and NO reduces oxidant yield. However, reduction of only one constituent may not, depending upon the starting point.

For example, at a NO concentration of 1 ppm, reducing propylene from 8 to 4.5 ppm actually increased oxidant formation. Further reduction reduced the oxidant. This deleterious effect of HC reduction is of academic importance since it occurs at higher than usual atmospheric concentrations. At a concentration of 2 ppm or less, hydrocarbon reduction is clearly beneficial. On the other hand, Romanovsky confirms the G.M. findings that reduction in NO first increases then decreases smog products. For example, at a propylene concentration of 2 ppm reducing NO from 4 ppm first increased the oxidant to a maximum of about 0.45 ppm at an NO concentration of 1.5 ppm. Further reduction of NO then reduced the oxidant level. This conflicts with Figure 1.13 which shows no maximum.

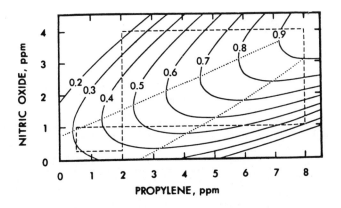

Figure 1.14. Effects of varying concentrations of propylene and nitric oxide on ozone yield. (Figure from Reference 11.)

Romanovsky's main thesis is that both NO and hydrocarbons should be reduced together. He draws lines (dotted in Figure 1.14) at the nitric oxide and propylene minima, respectively. Within the sector bounded by these lines, oxidant reduction results from both NO and hydrocarbon reduction. However, at very low hydrocarbon concentration, NO must be reduced to virtually zero before a smog benefit is realized. The lower left-hand corner of this figure may be compared with Figure 1.13.

Figure 1.15 shows the effect of varying NO and propylene on nitric oxide half life. This figure, which may be compared to Figure 1.11, shows that reducing propylene concentration uniformly decreased the rate of NO disappearance and hence the rate of NO_2 formation. However, at a fixed hydrocarbon level, reducing NO increased NO_2 formation rate.

Figure 1.16 shows the effect on propylene disappearance rate. The lower left-hand corner of this figure may be compared to Figure 1.12. For example, at 1.5 ppm propylene the rate was a maximum at about 0.5 ppm and decreased at both higher and lower NO concentrations. Finally, Figure 1.17 shows the effect of NO and propylene concentration on nitrogen dioxide yield. In general, reducing NO reduced atmospheric NO_2 levels.

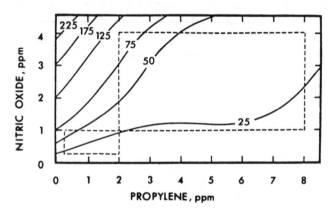

Figure 1.15. Effects of varying propylene and nitric oxide concentrations on nitric oxide half life in minutes. (Figure from Reference 11.)

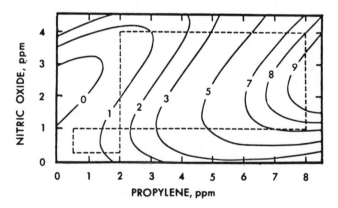

Figure 1.16. Effects of varying propylene and nitric oxide on the maximum rate of propylene disappearance in pphm per minute. (Figure from Reference 11.)

C. U.S. Public Health Service

Korth, *et al.*[12] studied the effect of hydrocarbon to oxides of nitrogen ratio on automobile exhaust in a smog chamber using diluted automobile exhaust. Figure 1.18 shows their smog cham-

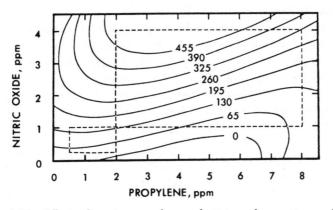

Figure 1.17. Effects of varying propylene and nitric oxide on nitrogen dioxide (ppm) normalized over 260 minutes. (Figure from Reference 11.)

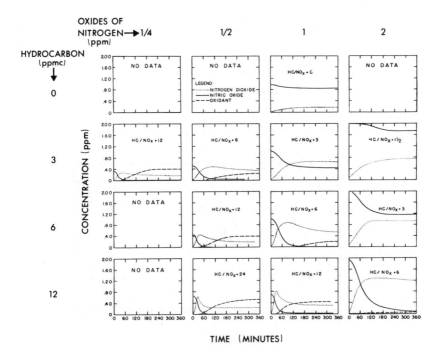

Figure 1.18. NO–NO$_2$ oxidant reactions (120 minute average irradiation time). (Figure from Reference 12.)

ber concentration results as a function of time. Hydrocarbons are
reported as ppm carbon (ppmc). Thus to compare with the other
data presented, the hydrocarbon concentration of the previously
discussed data should be multiplied by the number of carbon
atoms in the molecule. For example 2 ppm propylene corresponds
to 6 ppmc propylene.

Figures 1.19, 1.20, and 1.21 show Korth's results. Figure 1.19
shows the NO_2 formation rate for varying initial HC and NO
concentrations. At 6 ppmc HC, which corresponds to 2 ppm as
propylene, the maximum rate of NO_2 formation occurred at 1 ppm
NO, and decreased as NO was reduced. At 3 ppmc (1 ppm as
propylene) a maximum was not reached as low as 0.5 ppm NO.

Figure 1.20 shows equilibrium oxidant concentration for varying initial NO and hydrocarbon levels. This curve shows that the
oxidant continued to increase as NO was reduced to 0.25 ppm at 1
ppm propylene equivalent. This result agrees well with Figure
1.13. Figure 1.14 suggests the turnaround concentration was about
1.0 ppm NO.

Figure 1.21 shows average NO_2 concentration resulting from

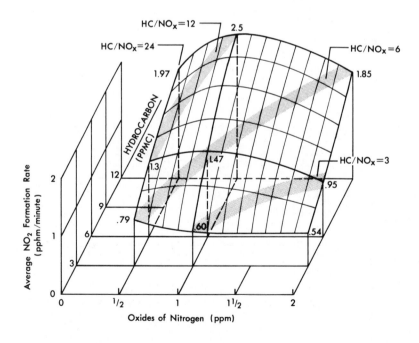

Figure 1.19. Average NO_2 formation rate vs. hydrocarbon and oxides of nitrogen concentration. (Figure from Reference 12.)

the smog reactions. A decrease in NO decreased atmospheric NO_2 concentrations. At 1.0 ppm NO a decrease in hydrocarbons first increased then decreased NO_2 concentration. This result is in agreement with the result shown in Figure 1.17.

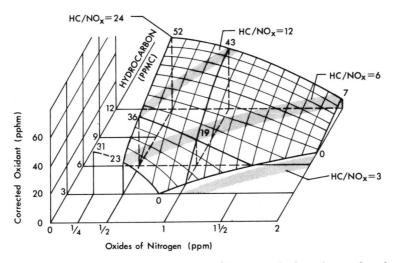

Figure 1.20. Oxidant concentration at equilibrium vs. hydrocarbon and oxides of nitrogen concentration. (Figure from Reference 12.)

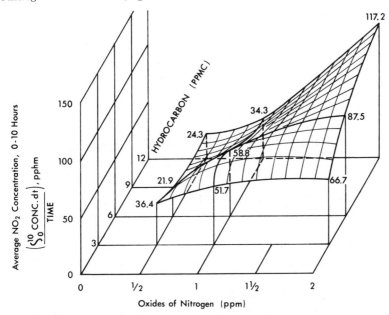

Figure 1.21. Average NO_2 concentration vs. hydrocarbon and oxides of nitrogen concentration. (Figure from Reference 12.)

DISCUSSION

The preceeding data allow us to draw some conclusions regarding smog chamber results.

(1) Reducing hydrocarbon concentration from levels currently found in smog atmospheres will reduce peak as well as long-term smog products, except NO_2 which may increase a little.

(2) Reducing nitric oxide concentration will, in general, increase some smog indicators (such as oxidant concentration, NO_2 formation rate, or hydrocarbon disappearance rate) while decreasing the equilibrium NO_2 level, the latter being beneficial.

(3) Under conditions where NO is reduced virtually to zero (probably less than 0.2 ppm) further reduction will decrease all smog products.

(4) Since over 50% of the atmospheric NO input is nonautomotive and derives from numerous sources as diverse as home heating and electric power generation, there is doubt as to the reality of expecting a reduction of NO to a level low enough to realize a smog benefit.

(5) Extrapolation of controlled smog chamber data to the atmosphere is tenuous.

REACTIVITY

The smog-forming potential or reactivity of a particular hydrocarbon compound can be assessed by various indicators from smog chamber results such as shown in Figure 1.9. These smog indicators include:

- rate of disappearance of the hydrocarbon compound, the criteria of Figure 1.12,
- rate of disappearance of the nitric oxide or formation of nitrogen dioxide, the criteria of Figure 1.11,
- equilibrium yield of nitrogen dioxide, the criteria of Figure 1.17,
- rate of formation of the oxidant products, and
- equilibrium yield of the oxidant products, the criteria of Figure 1.13.

Aerosol formation, plant damage, and eye irritation may also be used as smog indicators. The smog chamber results discussed previously are greatly influenced by the particular hydrocarbon specie used in the experiment.

Jackson[7] has assessed the smog forming potential of hydrocarbon compounds based on the rate of formation of NO_2 (disappearance of NO) under fixed test conditions of ultraviolet radiation with NO = 0.38 ppm, NO_2 = 0.02 ppm and HC = 1 ppm. The reactivity of each hydrocarbon specie is assessed on a relative basis by defining the rate of NO_2 formation (equal and opposite to the rate of NO disappearance) arising from 2,3-dimethyl-2-butene as equal to 100. This can be formalized as:

$$\text{specific or relative reactivity of } HC_x = \frac{\text{NO photo rate of } HC_x \times 100}{\text{NO photo rate of 2,3-dimethyl-2-butene}}$$

Relative reactivity has also been termed specific reactivity. The product of the concentration of each hydrocarbon compound and its relative reactivity is called the reactivity index:

$$\text{reactivity index of } HC_x = (\text{concentration})(\text{relative reactivity of } HC_x)$$

The reactivity index is a measure of the total contribution of a hydrocarbon to the smog-forming potential of the mixture of which it is a part. The total reactivity index for a mixture is:

$$\text{total HC reactivity index} = \sum_{x=1}^{x=i} (\text{reactivity index of } HC_x)$$

The smog-forming ability (reactivity) varies widely for hydrocarbons and is strongly related to the structure of the molecule. Table 1.8 shows six reactivity grouping for various hydrocarbon compounds. Methane has a reactivity of virtually zero, and other saturated hydrocarbons (paraffins and naphthenes) have little smog-forming potential.

However, unsaturated hydrocarbons can be very reactive, depending on the location of the double or triple bond. For example, olefins which have double bonds on terminal carbon atoms fall into Class 3 (moderate reactivity) whereas those which have internal double bonds fall into Classes 4, 5, or 6 (high reactivity). The structure and classification of such hydrocarbon molecules will be discussed in detail in Chapter 2. Olefin compounds are the principal contributor to both exhaust and evaporative emission reactivity.

Table 1.9 shows reactivity ranges for hydrocarbon families and their typical relative contribution to overall reactivity. Table 1.10 shows reactivity for some specific hydrocarbon compounds.

Table 1.8

GM Scale of Hydrocarbon Reactivity Classes
and Class Specific Reactivity

Class	Specific reactivity	Hydrocarbons
I	0	methane ethane propane acetylenes benzene
II	2	mono alkyl benzenes C_4 and higher molecular weight paraffins ortho and para dialkyl benzenes cyclic paraffins
III	5	ethylene meta dialkyl benzenes formaldehyde and higher aldehydes
IV	10	1-olefins (other than ethylene) diolefins tri and tetra alkyl benzenes
V	30	internally bonded olefins
VI	100	internally bonded olefins with substitution at the double bond cyclo olefins

Data from Reference 10.

A reactivity scale similar to that of General Motors but based upon the rate of hydrocarbon loss in a smog chamber has been proposed by McReynolds.[14] Altshuller[13] of the U.S. Department of Health, Education and Welfare has formulated a reactivity scale based on six criteria: equilibrium oxidant, PAN, formaldehyde and aerosol formation, eye irritation and plant damage. The observed effect of each hydrocarbon type was rated between 0 and 10 for each of the six categories (0 = no effect and 10 = maximum effect). The results are tabulated in Table 1.11. The average of the six

Table 1.9

Reactivity Ranges for Hydrocarbon Families and Typical Per Cent Contribution to Overall Reactivity (GM Scale)

Hydrocarbon family	Range in reactivity	Per cent contribution		
		Exhaust	Carburetor evaporative	Fuel tank evaporative
Paraffins	0 ⟶ 2	4.7	15.4	25.5
Olefins	5 ⟶ 100	86.1	83.6	74.4
Naphthenes	2	—	—	—
Aromatics	0 ⟶ 10	9.2	1.0	0.1
Acetylenes	0	0	0	0

Data from Reference 10.

Table 1.10

Reactitvity of Selected Hydrocarbons (GM Scale)

Compound	Reactivity
Propane	0
Toluene	2
Ethylene	5
Propylene	10
1-butene	10
Trans-2-butene	30
2,3,3-trimethyl-1-butene	55
2-methyl-2-butene	100
2,3-dimethyl-2-butene	100

Data from Reference 10

categories is the relative reactivity. The HEW scale rates reactivity between 0 and 8.

Table 1.12 compares the GM and HEW scales, revealing some interesting differences. For example, aldehydes rate relatively more reactive on the HEW scale because of eye irritation and equilibrium oxidant level. Internally substituted olefins rate relatively less reactive on the HEW scale because of the averaging of six responses and inclusion in the broader group of internal olefins. A sample reactivity calculation using the GM scale is included in Table 1.13.

Table 1.11

Comparison of Product Yields and Effects Caused by Various Organics—Basis of HEW Scale

Substance or Sub-Class	Response on 0 to 10 Scale						Averaged Response
	Ozone or Oxidant	Peroxyacyl Nitrate	Formaldehyde	Aerosol	Eye Irritation	Plant Damage	
C_1-C_5 paraffins	0	0	0	0	0	0	0
acetylene	0	0	0	0	0	0	0
benzene	0	0	0	0	0	0	0
C_6 paraffins[a]	0–4	0[b]	0[b]	0	0[b]	0	1
toluene (and other monoalkylbenzenes)	4	ND[c]	2	2	4	0–3	3
ethylene	6	0	6	1–2	5	+[d]	4
l-alkenes[e]	6–10	4–6	7–10	4–8	4–8	6–8	7
diolefins	6–8	0–2	8–10	10	10	0[b]	6
dialkyl and trialkylbenzenes	6–10	5–10	2–4	+[d]	4–8	5–10	6
internally double-bonded olefins[f]	5–10	8–10	4–6	6–10	4–8	10	8
aliphatic aldehydes	5–10	+[d]	+[d]	ND[e]	+[d]	+[d]	—

[a] Averaged over straight-chain and branched-chain paraffins.
[b] Very small yields or effects may occur after long irradiations.
[c] No experimental data available.
[d] Effect noted experimentally, but data insufficient to quantitate.
[e] Includes measurements on propylene through 1-hexene, 2 ethyl-1-butene and 2,4,4-trimethyl-1-pentene.
[f] Includes measurements on straight-chain butenes through heptanes with double-bond in 2 and 3 position, 2-methyl-2-butene, 2,3-dimethyl-2-butene, cyclohexene.
Data from Reference 13.

Table 1.12

Relative Reactivity Scales

General Motors[1]			Health, Education & Welfare[2]	
Compounds	Reactivity	Class	Compounds	Reactivity
CH_4, C_2H_6, C_3H_8	0		CH_4, C_2H_6, C_3H_8, C_4H_{10}, C_5H_{12}	0
22 DMPr		I	benzene	0
Benzene			acetylenes	
Acetylenes		II	C_6 + paraffins	1
Monoalkylbenzenes	2	III	monoalkylbenzenes	3
C_4 + paraffins		IV	ethylene	4
Ethylene	5		aliphatic aldehydes	5–6
Diakylbenzenes				
Aldehydes			diolefins	6
Cyclohexene	10		2 & 3 alkylbenzenes	
3 & 4 Alkylbenzenes		V	1-olefins except ethylene	7
1-Olefins except ethylene			Internally double bonded olefins	
Diolefins			cyclohexene	8
Cyclopentenes	30			
Internal olefins		VI		
Internal olefins with double bond sub.	100			

[1] Scale based on oxidation of NO.
[2] Scale based on product yield and biological properties including eye irritation and plant damage.

Table 1.13

Example of Exhaust Reactivity
Calculation Using GM Scale*

Compounds	Conc. ppm	Mole Fraction	Reactivity Class	Relative or Spec. React.	React. Ind.	Total React.
Paraffins						
Methane	250	.250	I	0	0	
Isopentane	50	.050	II	2	.100	
Hexane	50	.050	II	2	.100	
Octane	50	.050	II	2	.100	
	400	.4				.300
Acetylene	100	.100	I	0	0	0
Aromatics						
Benzene	50	.050	I	0	0	0
Toluene	100	.100	II	2	.200	
1, 3, 5 Trimethyl-benzene	2	.002	IV	10	.020	
1, 2, 4 Trimethyl-benzene	8	.008	IV	10	.080	
Other	40	.040	II, III, IV	6	.240	
	200	.2				.540

Olefins	Conc.	Mole fr.		%	Ave. Spec. React/mole
Ethylene	150	.150	III	5	.750
1-Butene	50	.050	IV	10	.500
2-Methyl-2 butene	10	.010	VI	100	1.000
1-Heptene	20	.020	IV	10	.200
trans-2-Pentene	20	.020	V	30	.600
Other	50	.050	IV, V, VI	40	2.000
	300	.300			5.050

Summary

Family	Conc.	Mole fr.	Total React. Index	%	Ave. Spec. React/mole
Paraffins	400	.4	.3	5.1	.75
Acetylenes	100	.1	.0	0	0
Aromatics	200	.2	.54	9.2	2.70
Olefins	300	.3	5.05	85.7	16.80
	1000	1.0	5.89	100.0	5.89

*Exhaust gas contains 1000 ppm unburned hydrocarbons.

1. Haagen-Smit, A. J. "Chemistry and Physiology of Los Angeles Smog." Ind. Eng. Chem. **44** (6), 1342 (1952).
2. Haagen-Smit. A. J. "The Control of Air Pollution," Sci. Am. **210** (1), 25 (1964).
3. "The Automobile and Air Pollution: Part I, Part II," Report of the Panel on Electrically Powered Vehicles, U.S. Dept. of Commerce, Oct. 1967.
4. Agnew, W. G. "Automotive Air Pollution Research," Proc. Roy. Soc. **307A**, 153 (1968).
5. Babcock, Lyndon R. "A Combined Pollution Index for Measurement of Total Air Pollution," J. APCA **20** (10), 653 (1970).
6. Caplan, John D. "Spotting the Chemical Culprits in Smog Formation," SAE Journal **73** (12), 62 (1965).
7. Jackson, Marvin W. "Effects of some Engine Variables and Control Systems on Composition and Reactivity of Exhaust Hydrocarbons," SAE Preprint 660404, 1966.
8. Korth, M. W., A. H. Rose, and R. C. Stahman. "Effect of Hydrocarbons to Oxides of Nitrogen Ratios on Irradiated Auto Exhaust," presented in the Air Pollution Control Assoc. Annual Meeting, June 9–13 1963.
9. Air Conservation, Pub. No. 80 (Washington, D.C.: Assoc. Adv. Science, 1965).
10. Caplan, John D. "Smog Chemistry Points the Way to Rational Vehicle Emission Control," SAE **PT-12**, 20 (1963–66).
11. Romanovsky, J. C., et al. "Estimation of Smot Effects in the Hydrocarbon-Nitric Oxide System," J. APCA **17** (7), 454 (1967).
12. Korth, M. W. "Effects of Hydrocarbon to Oxides of Nitrogen Ratios on Irradiated Auto Exhaust, Part I," J. APCA **14** (5), 169 (1964).
13. Altshuller, A. P. "An Evaluation of Techniques for the Determination of the Photochemical Reactivity of Organic Emissions," J. APCA **16** (5), 257 (1966).
14. McReynolds, L. A., et al. "Hydrocarbon Emissions and Reactivity as Functions of Fuel and Engine Variables," SAE **PT-12**, 10, (1963–66).
15. Federal Register **21** (61), Part II (1966).
16. Federal Register, **33** (108), Part II (1968).
17. Federal Register, **35** (214) Part II (1970).
18. Federal Register, **36** (128), Part II (1971).

2

ENGINE
FUNDAMENTALS

This chapter will review the fundamental principles of engine operation, the four- and two-stroke cycles, types of fuels and their specifications, carburetion and the effect of fuel and engine parameters on performance. The purpose of this discussion is to draw attention to the major factors that have a great effect on emissions and that affect engine performance, mainly power and economy. In future chapters on exhaust emissions reference will be made to these fundamental concepts

Part I Cycle Analysis

INTRODUCTION

Reciprocating internal combustion engines operate on either the four-stroke or the two-stroke cycle. The four-stroke cycle engine is the most commonly used for automotive purposes especially in road vehicles. The two-stroke engine is sometimes used in small passenger cars, motor cycles, and as outboard marine engines.

In the four-stroke cycle engine as well as the two-stroke cycle engine the following four processes take place during the cycle of operation:

(1) Charging the cylinder with a fresh charge. This charge is composed of a mixture of fuel and air in the gasoline engine and air only in the diesel engine.

(2) Compression of this charge to a temperature suitable for the proper combustion process which usually starts before the maximum compression pressure is reached. In the gasoline engine the combustion process starts by ignition from a spark plug. In the diesel engine auto-ignition occurs when the fuel is injected in the air which is compressed to a temperature high enough to cause self-ignition. The process of combustion results in a substantial increase in the gas temperature and pressure.

(3) Expansion of the high pressure gases.

(4) Discharging the exhaust gases.

39

These processes take place in two piston strokes in the two-cycle engine and in four piston strokes in the four-cycle engine.

THE FOUR-STROKE CYCLE ENGINE

The four strokes of this engine are the intake stroke, the compression stroke, the expansion stroke, and the exhaust stroke. The indicator diagram shown in Figure 2.1 gives the pressure-volume relationship during a complete four-stroke cycle. The pressure in the cylinder during the intake stroke, in naturally aspirated engines, is always lower than the atmospheric pressure. The difference between the two pressures causes the flow of the charge into the cylinder and overcomes the flow restriction in the air filter, carburetor, manifolds, and intake valves. The intake valve is closed after bottom dead center at point 2 in Figures 2.1, 2.2, and 2.3 to improve the volumetric efficiency of the engine. The pressure rise due to compression starts at a slow rate before the closing of I.V. during the piston motion from B.D.C. to T.D.C. on the compression stroke. The effective compression occurs after the closing of the I.V. at point 2. Normally before the end of the compression stroke an electric spark starts the ignition process in the gasoline engine, or the fuel is injected in the diesel engine.

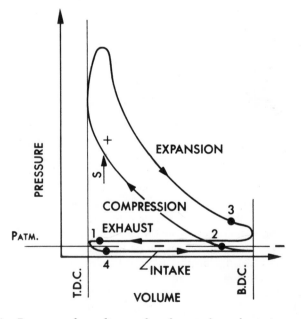

Figure 2.1.   Pressure-volume diagram for a four-stroke cycle engine.

Figure 2.2 shows a conventional representation of the valve timing events. Typical values for the valve events w.r.t. the top and bottom dead centers are:

	a	b	c	d
Automotive S.I.	20	20	60	60
Automotive C.I.				
(Nat. Aspirated)	10	10	40	40

Figure 2.3 shows an ignition delay period elapsing between the spark or fuel injection and the pressure rise due to combustion. The rate of pressure rise due to combustion in the gasoline engine depends mainly upon the flame speed, density of the charge and the design of the combustion chamber when the spark is at MBT. The rate of pressure rise in the diesel engine depends mainly upon the ignition delay, the rate of injection, and the cetane number of the fuel.

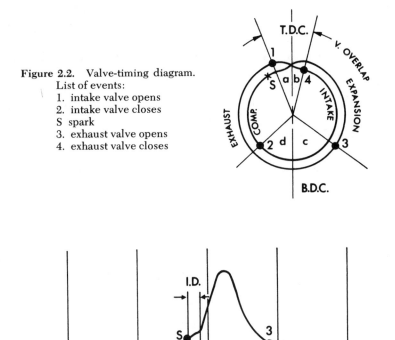

Figure 2.2. Valve-timing diagram.
List of events:
1. intake valve opens
2. intake valve closes
S spark
3. exhaust valve opens
4. exhaust valve closes

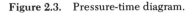

Figure 2.3. Pressure-time diagram.

The maximum pressure reached in the cycle depends mainly upon the charge pressure at the time of inlet valve closing, compression ratio, the fuel-air ratio, engine speed, and the spark or injection timing. The maximum temperature in the cycle depends mainly upon the fuel-air ratio of the mixture, and the spark or injection timing.

The exhaust valve is opened before the end of the expansion stroke at point 3. This allows the high pressure gases in the cylinder to expand in a blow-down process. The exhaust valve is timed so that at the start of the exhaust stroke the valve opening is big enough to reduce a build up of pressure in front of the piston. Any such pressure build-up causes loss in useful work. The exhaust valve starts closing before the end of the exhaust stroke and is completely closed after the T.D.C. at point 4.

The opening of the intake valve starts before the piston reaches T.D.C. on the exhaust stroke so that the area of flow is large enough at the start of the intake stroke. This improves the volumetric efficiency and reduces the loss in useful work, termed the pumping loss.

Figure 2.4 shows the area of flow through the inlet and exhaust valves. The hatched area indicates the net area of flow through the two valves during the overlap period.

The net positive work done by the gases on the piston during the whole cycle is equal to the difference between the positive and negative areas on the P-V diagram of Figure 2.1. The negative

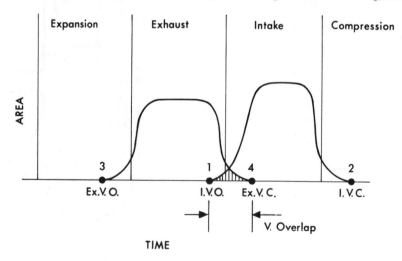

Figure 2.4.   Area of flow through the intake and exhaust valves of a four-stroke cycle engine.

area is known as the pumping losses, and is mainly a function of the throttle valve and/or the choke valve openings in the gasoline engine. This area is very small compared to the whole cycle in the naturally aspirated diesel engine. This area represents positive work for supercharged diesel engines. However, under this condition the work done to drive the supercharger should be accounted for in the calculation of the net work. Change in valve timing can affect the unburned hydrocarbons and nitric oxide emissions.[9]

THE TWO-STROKE CYCLE ENGINE

In the two-stroke cycle engine the processes of charging and discharging the cylinder occur while the piston is approaching B.D.C. before the end of the expansion stroke and after the beginning of the compression stroke. The pressure head required for the flow of the fresh charge into the cylinder is produced in the crankcase, Figures 2.5 and 2.6, or by a blower driven by the crankshaft.

This engine requires two piston strokes or only one revolution

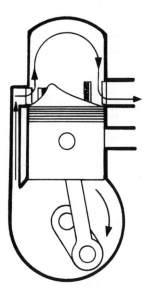

Figure 2.5. Two-cycle half-loop, crankcase scavenged engine.

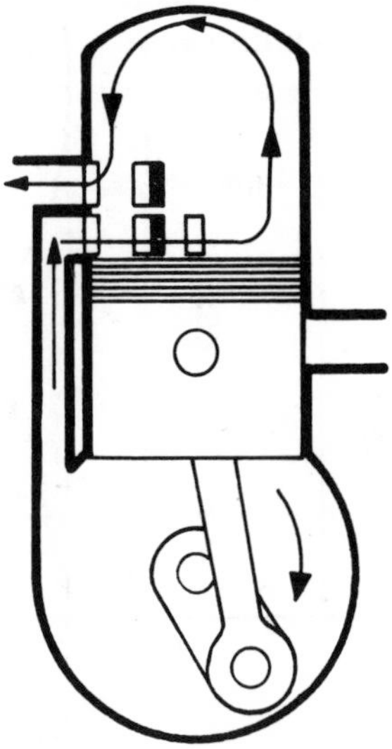

Figure 2.6. Two-cycle, full-loop, crankcase scavenged engine.

for each cycle. In the two-stroke cycle engine shown in Figure 2.7, 2.8 and 2.9, the exhaust ports are opened near the end (at 60 to 85%) of the expansion stroke, permitting the blowdown of the exhaust gases, and reducing the pressure in the cylinder. The charge of air (diesel engine) or the combustible mixture (gasoline engine) flows into and is compressed in the crankcase compartment to a few pounds per sq. in. above the atmospheric pressure. Intake ports are uncovered by the piston soon after the opening of the exhaust, and the compressed charge flows into the cylinder. Part of the fresh charge flows out of the exhaust ports at the end of the scavenging period. In gasoline engines, this results in the loss of fresh fuel in the exhaust and high unburned hydrocarbons emitted with the exhaust gases. Figure 2.8 shows the timing of the port events. Typical values for gasoline engines are a = 80° and b = 60°.

The main advantage of the two-stroke cycle engine, if compared with the four-cycle engine, is that it has twice as many expansion

TWO STROKE CYCLE

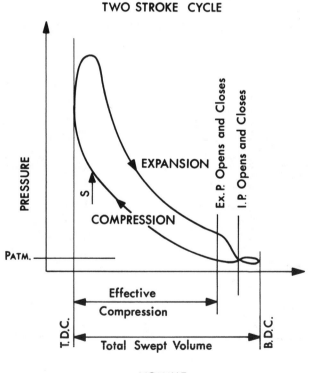

Figure 2.7.   Pressure-volume diagram for a two-stroke cycle crank scavenged engine.

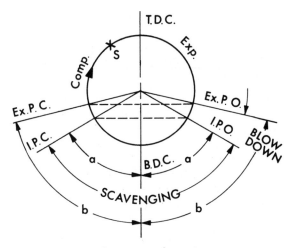

Figure 2.8.   Timing diagram, for a two-cycle engine.

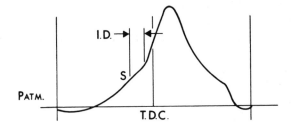

Figure 2.9.   Pressure-time diagram, for a two-cycle engine.

strokes per cylinder per revolution. But, because of the poor scavenging and volumetric efficiencies of these engines the power output per unit piston displacement volume is only about 30% more than the four-stroke cycle engine. Another advantage of the two-cycle engine is that the load on the piston pin is always in one direction except at very high speeds.

The main disadvantages of this engine are the poor scavenging efficiency and the difficulty of lubrication. In some crankcase scavenged engines, lubricating oil is added to the fuel for piston-liner lubrication, which results in additional unburned hydrocarbons in the exhaust. In carburetted engines, poor fuel economy is an additional disadvantage of the two-stroke cycle engine.

Part II   Performance Parameters

These parameters are used to evaluate the performance of internal combustion engines with respect to power and fuel economy.

POWER

Power is defined as the rate of producing mechanical work and is defined as either brake horsepower or indicated horsepower.

   a. Brake horsepower

$$\text{B.H.P.} = \frac{2\pi TN}{33000} = \frac{TN}{5250}$$

where

    B.H.P. = brake horsepower
    T   = torque produced by the engine, $(lb_f)(ft)$
    N   = engine speed, rpm
    The torque is measured by a dynamometer, $T = (F)(r)$

where

    F = force on the dynamometer scale, lb_f
    r = dynamometer arm, ft.

   b. Indicated horsepower

The indicated horsepower is equal to the rate of doing work on the piston and can be calculated from the area of the (P-V) diagram.

    I.H.P. = Wn/33000

where $W = \oint PdV$

    P = gas pressure in lb_f/sq ft
    V = gas volume in ft^3
    n = number of working cycles per minute; N/2 for a four-cycle engine, and N for a two-cycle engine.

The difference between the indicated horsepower and the brake horsepower is a measure of the rate of work performed to overcome the frictional losses, and is known as the friction horsepower.

$$\text{I.H.P.} = \text{B.H.P.} + \text{F.H.P.}$$

The ratio between the B.H.P. and I.H.P. is known as the mechanical efficiency:

$$\eta_m = \text{B.H.P./I.H.P.}$$

MEAN EFFECTIVE PRESSURE

MEP is defined[6] as the theoretical constant pressure which can be imagined exerted during each power stroke of the engine to produce work equal to the engine work. The relationship between the mean effective pressure and the horsepower is

$$\text{H.P.} = (\text{MEP}) (V_d)(N)/\text{Constant}$$

where V_d = displacement volume

or   H.P. = (MEP,psi)(V_d,cu.in.)(n,cycles/min.) / (33000)(12).

The mean effective pressure is known as brake or indicated mean effective pressure if it is calculated from the brake horsepower, or the indicated horsepower respectively.

THERMAL EFFICIENCY

The thermal efficiency, η_{th}, is a measure of the ratio between the useful work done by the engine and the thermal energy input to the engine.

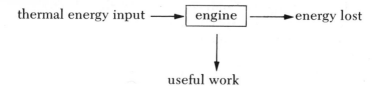

$\eta_{B.Th.}$ = brake thermal efficiency

$$= \frac{(\text{B.H.P.}) \, (2545, \, \text{BTU/H.P.Hr.})}{(\text{Fuel Cons., lb}_m/\text{Hr})(Q_c, \text{BTU/lbm})}$$

where Q_c = heat of combustion.

SPECIFIC FUEL CONSUMPTION

The brake specific fuel consumption, B.S.F.C., is given by
$$\text{B.S.F.C.} = (\text{lb}_m/\text{hr})/\text{B.H.P.}$$
The relationship between the $\eta_{B.Th.}$ and B.S.F.C. is
$$\eta_{B.Th.} = (2545) \, / \, (\text{B.S.F.C.})(Q_c).$$
Other performance parameters are given in Reference 6.

Part III   Fuels

Internal combustion engine fuels are derived from crude petroleum, a mixture of many hydrocarbon components of different molecular structures and weights. Petroleum also contains small fractions of organic compounds such as sulfur and nitrogen. Fuels are termed paraffinic or naphthenic depending on whether the residue left after distillation is mainly paraffin wax or asphalt.

In the refining process the distillate is separated into various fractions according to boiling points. The boiling point generally depends on the number of carbon atoms in the molecule. The lightest fractions are principally butane C_4H_{10}, propane C_3H_8, and ethane C_2H_6. These are driven off at comparatively low temperatures. Next are the gasolines, naphthas, kerosenes, diesel fuels, and lubricating oils. Figure 2.10 shows the distillation curves of the different fuels used in internal combustion engines.

Since the demand for gasoline far exceeds the straight-run gasoline naturally produced from the distillation of the crude petroleum, refinery processes have been developed to crack the larger molecules into smaller molecules or to polymerize small molecules into larger ones having boiling points in the gasoline range. Cracking can be achieved by either a heating process known as thermal cracking or in the presence of a catalyst. In general catalytically cracked hydrocarbons have better antiknock characteristics.

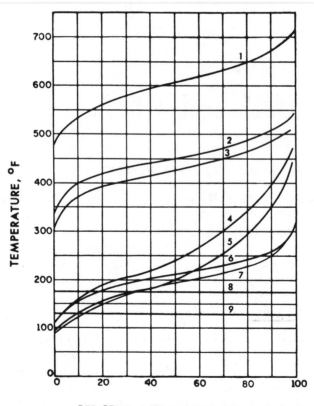

Figure 2.10.   Typical ASTM distillation curves. (Data from Reference 2.)

1. heavy-diesel oil	5. winter gasoline
2. distillate	6. aviation gasoline
3. kerosene	7. low exhaust emission gasoline
4. summer gasoline	8. ethyl alcohol
	9. benzene

TYPES OF HYDROCARBONS

The hydrocarbons in the crude petroleum can be classified into four groups: paraffins (C_nH_{2n+2}), olefins (C_nH_{2n}), naphthenes (C_nH_{2n}), and aromatics (C_nH_{2n-6}).

A. PARAFFINS (ALKANES)

Paraffins which have open straight chain structures are termed normal paraffins, whereas those with a branched chain structure are termed isomers. A prefix "n" refers to the straight chain structure and a prefix "iso" refers to the branched chain structure. The name of each compound in the paraffin group ends with "ane," and the prefix indicates the number of carbon atoms in the molecule.

The following are samples of different paraffins:

```
     H            H  H           H  H  H  H  H  H  H  H
     |            |  |           |  |  |  |  |  |  |  |
  H–C–H      H–C–C–H      H–C– C– C– C– C– C– C–C–H
     |            |  |           |  |  |  |  |  |  |  |
     H            H  H           H  H  H  H  H  H  H  H
  Methane      Ethane                    n-Octane
```

The number of carbon atoms in the molecules is indicated in the name of the compound as follows:

No. of Carbon Atoms	Prefix
1	*meth-*
2	*eth-*
3	*prop-*
4	*but-*
5	*pent-*
6	*hex-*
7	*hept-*
8	*oct-*
9	*non-*
10	*dec-*
16	*hexadec-*

To compare the molecular structure of normal and isomer paraffins, consider n-octane and isooctane (2,4,4-trimethylpentane).

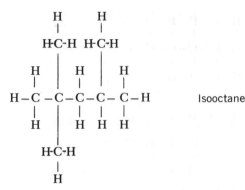

Isooctane

Each of these two fuels has eight carbon atoms connected to each other by a chain-like structure, and the chains are saturated with H atoms. This means that each carbon atom shares one electron with each hydrogen to which it is linked. The length of the chain in the n-octane is eight carbon atoms, while in isooctane it is only five. In general, the shorter the chain, that is, the fewer carbon atoms there are in the chain, the higher the temperature for self-ignition and the better the antiknock quality of the fuel. Being more compact, the molecule of isooctane is more difficult to break up thermally than the straight chain type; thus its ignition temperature (1350°F) is much higher than that of n-octane (880°F). Isooctane is rated 100 on the isooctane scale, n-heptane is rated zero, and n-octane is rated − 17.

The octane isomer designated 2,2,4-trimethylpentane indicates five carbon atoms in the straight chain (pentane) with three methyl (CH_3) groups located respectively at carbon atoms number 2,2, and 4. Typically, paraffins, including cycloparaffins, represent 24% of the unburned hydrocarbons in the exhaust of gasoline engines using commercial fuels.

B. OLEFINS (ALKENES)

The compounds of this family have the open chain structure of the paraffins, but have two bonds between two of the carbon atoms. The position of the double bond is designated by a number indicating the smaller number of carbon atoms at one side of the double bond. The name of each compound in this group has an ending "ene" for one double bond (monoolefins) and "diene" for two double bonds (diolefins). The chemical formula for the diolefins is $C_n H_{2n-2}$.

The olefins and diolefins are unsaturated compounds and have fewer hydrogen atoms than the normal paraffin molecule with the same number of carbon atoms. The olefins are scarce in

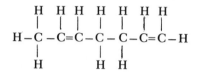

$$H-C-\underset{\underset{H}{|}}{\overset{\overset{H}{|}}{C}}-\underset{\underset{H}{|}}{\overset{\overset{H}{|}}{C}}-\underset{\underset{H}{|}}{\overset{\overset{H}{|}}{C}}-\underset{\underset{H}{|}}{\overset{\overset{H}{|}}{C}}-\overset{\overset{H}{|}}{C}=\overset{\overset{H}{|}}{C}-H$$

1-Heptene (C_7H_{14})

$$H-\underset{\underset{H}{|}}{\overset{\overset{H}{|}}{C}}-C=C-\underset{\underset{H}{|}}{\overset{\overset{H}{|}}{C}}-\underset{\underset{H}{|}}{\overset{\overset{H}{|}}{C}}-C=\overset{\overset{H}{|}}{C}-H$$

1,5-Heptadiene (C_7H_{12})

$$-C-C=C-C-$$

trans-2 Butene

$$-C-C=C-C-$$

cis-2-Butene

straight-run products but are present in considerable quantities in certain highly cracked gasolines. Typically olefins, including cycloolefins, represent 45% of the unburned hydrocarbons in the gasoline engine exhaust.

C. NAPHTHENES OR CYCLOPARAFFINS (CYCLANES)

The naphthenes have a ring structure in which each carbon atom is joined by single bonds to two other carbon atoms. Attached to each of these carbon atoms are two atoms which may be either a hydrogen or carbon atom or both. The name of the compounds in this family is preceded by "cyclo" and has an ending "ane."

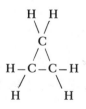

Cyclopropane

Cyclohexane

D. AROMATICS (BENZENE DERIVATIVES)

The aromatics have a six-carbon atom benzene structure to which are attached H or groups of C and H atoms.

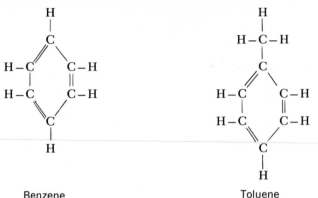

Benzene   Toluene

Aromatic fuels have molecules of compact structure and in general have a high self-ignition point and a high octane number. Aromatic compounds are found in crude petroleum but are predominate in coal distillation products. Aromatics are very susceptible to surface ignition, leading to preignition problems, including rumble. Aromatics represent about 20 % of the unburned hydrocarbons in the gasoline engine exhaust.

E. ACETYLENES

The acetylenes have the same formula as diolefins, C_nH_{2n-2}, and have triple bonds. Their names have a suffix "yne."

$$H-C\equiv C-H \qquad\qquad \text{Acetylene}$$

$$H-\underset{\underset{H}{|}}{\overset{\overset{H}{|}}{C}}-C\equiv C-\underset{\underset{H}{|}}{\overset{\overset{H}{|}}{C}}-H \qquad\qquad \text{Butyne-2}$$

Typically acetylenes represent 10 % of the unburned hydrocarbons in the exhaust of gasoline engines.

F. ALCOHOLS

Alcohols (R-OH) as well as nitrated hydrocarbons are trace constituents in the exhaust gases.

PROPERTIES AND SPECIFICATIONS FOR I.C.E. GASOLINE

In general commercial gasoline is classified as regular or premium. This designation refers to the octane number range. Some gas stations blend top quality gasoline with lower quality to obtain intermediate gasoline blends.

The most important properties for S.I. engine gasolines are volatility and ignition quality. Table 2.1 shows the ASTM specifications for gasolines.

A. VOLATILITY

1. Equilibrium Volatility

The volatility of gasoline is determined by Reid vapor pressure, ASTM distillation data, or the Equilibrium Air Distillation (EAD) data.

a. Reid Vapor Pressure

The Reid vapor pressure is the vapor pressure of gasoline at 100°F determined in a special bomb in presence of a volume of air which occupies four times the volume of liquid fuel.

b. ASTM Distillation Curves

A typical ASTM curve indicates the temperature at which the different percentages of the fuel sample evaporate (in absence of air) under specified test conditions. The characteristic indicating the starting quality of a fuel is generally considered to be represented by the percentage vaporized at a fixed temperature of 158°F. The warm-up characteristic is related to the temperature at which 50% of the fuel is vaporized. Fuel economy is related to the

Table 2.1

Specifications for Gasoline (ASTM D439-60 T)

Type	T, °F, for min per cent evaporated					Max distill residue, per cent	Max Reid vapor pr, psia			Min research method, Oct. No.
	10 per cent			per cent						
	W°	F°	S°	50	90		W°	F°	S°	
A	140	149	158	284	392	2	15.0†	11.5	10†	87 or 96
B	140	149	158	257	356	2	15.0†	11.5	10†	87 or 96
C	167	167	167	284	392	2	15.0†	11.5	10†	

Type A for use under normal conditions
Type B for use where overall volatility greater than that of Type A is desired
Type C for use where a relatively nonvolatile fuel is desired
° Seasons. Winter, fall, and summer.
† For deviations from these specifications, see ASTM Standards, pt. 7, 1961.
Max copper-strip corrosion is No. 1 See Secs. 7-19 and 7-20 for sulfur and gum content.
Table from *Combustion Engine Processes* by L. C. Lichty (New York: McGraw-Hill Book Co., 1967). Used with permission of publisher.

temperature at which 90% of the fuel is vaporized, because of the heavy ends having higher heating values. Figure 2.11 shows the relationship between the different portions of the distillation curve and the engine problems.

The shape and level of the distillation curve affect both the evaporative and exhaust emissions. The effect on the evaporative emissions is discussed later. In gasoline engines hydrocarbon and carbon monoxide emissions are reduced with more volatile fuels because leaner mixtures may be used during warm-up.[8] Curve 7 of Figure 2.10 shows one such high volatility fuel. The major modification is in the heavy end of the fuel.

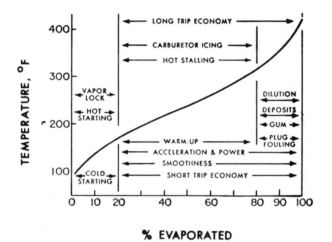

Figure 2.11. Effects of volatility characteristics on engine performance. (Figure from Reference 14.)

c. Equilibrium Air Distillation (EAD)

In the ASTM distillation test the process of evaporation occurs in the presence of fuel vapor only, while in the gasoline engine induction system the fuel is vaporized in the presence of incoming air. In another distillation process, suggested by Brown and Bridgeman, the liquid fuel and air are supplied to a steady-flow open system kept at a controlled temperature. The liquid fuel remaining is collected as it leaves the system. The percentage of fuel vaporized at the system temperature is then calculated. Figure 2.12 shows typical EAD curves. A correlation between the EAD values and the ASTM values is usually given in the form of equations and charts. Used with the ASTM distillation curves,

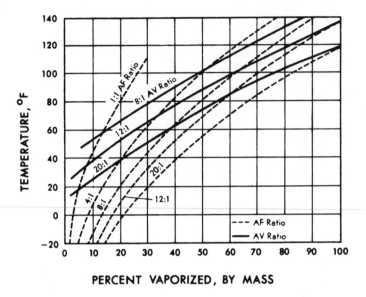

PERCENT VAPORIZED, BY MASS

Figure 2.12.   Air-vapor volatility curves from the EAD test. (Figure from Reference 6.)

these charts can estimate the air-vapor ratio at a given temperature. Unfortunately, however, the air vapor ratio determined in this manner is for conditions of operation in the EAD apparatus, and these conditions may be considerably different from those encountered in the actual engine induction system. For example, EAD results are based upon equilibrium conditions between the air and fuel vapor. In the actual induction system such factors as manifold geometry, wall surface conditions, throttling effects, pressure pulsations, heat transfer and the short time available for mixing lead to deviations from equilibrium.

2. *Effect of Volatility on Engine Performance*

a. *Effect on cold starting*

For ignition of the charge, the fuel-vapor air mixture delivered by the carburetor of a gasoline engine must be within the limits of inflamability—6:1 (lb air/lb fuel) for the rich mixture and 20:1 for the lean mixture. The fastest burning mixture is about 12.5:1. During cold starting the fuel and air temperatures are low resulting in a small percentage of the fuel evaporated. This necessitates the use of a choke valve to reduce the air flow and increase the fuel flow. For example, if only 5% of the liquid fuel were to vaporize, the required fuel-air ratio should be 1:1 in order to provide the leanest combustible mixture.

The effect of volatility on starting time of several gasoline engines is shown in Figures 2.13 and 2.14. It is noted that the starting time is essentially independent of front-end volatility at temperatures above 20°F, but varies considerably at temperatures below 0°F. Figure 2.14 shows that the starting varies to a considerable extent from one engine to another particularly in the low ambient temperature range.

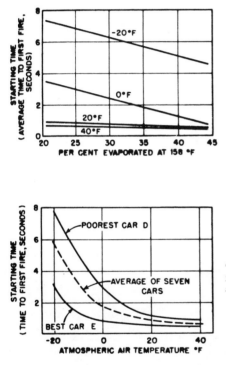

Figure 2.13. Effect of fuel volatility on cold starting performance. (Figure from Reference 3.)

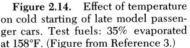

Figure 2.14. Effect of temperature on cold starting of late model passenger cars. Test fuels: 35% evaporated at 158°F. (Figure from Reference 3.)

b. *Effect on warm-up and acceleration*

Warm-up engine performance is judged by how smoothly the car accelerates from a given speed in high gear. Warm-up performance is usually measured by the speed attained after a six-second acceleration from 20 mph. In addition the number of sags or hesitations may be measured. Figure 2.15a shows a definite correlation between the temperature at which 50% of the fuel is vaporized and the warm-up performance. The effect of ambient temperature on warm-up time is shown in Figure 2.15b, for a fuel

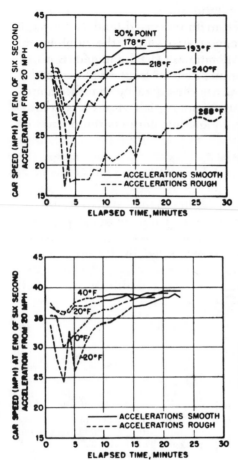

Figure 2.15a. Effect of fuel volatility on performance during the warm-up period. 0°F atmospheric temperature. Test fuels: 35% evaporated at 158°F, 90% evaporated at 312–339°F. (Figure from Reference 3.)

Figure 2.15b. Effect of atmospheric temperature on performance during the warm-up period. Test fuel: 50% Evaporated at 193°F. (Figure from Reference 3.)

having a 193°F, 50% point. This figure indicates difficulties in accelerating performance for 0 and − 20°F ambient temperatures.

The warm-up performance is greatly affected by the rate at which the automatic choke begins to open. Fast-opening chokes improve fuel economy and reduce exhaust emissions, and slow-opening chokes depreciate them but may provide smoother warm-up periods and result in very rich mixtures in cylinders near the carburetor and lean mixtures in cylinders farther away. This causes poor economy and increased unburned hydrocarbons. Rapid manifold heating is a critical design factor for improved fuel distribution. Other design features include a chokeless carburetor with a miniature starting carburetor (Weber).

c. *Effect on carburetor icing*

High fuel volatility may result in an increased tendency toward carburetor icing. This phenomenon arises from the drop in air temperature caused by the evaporation of the lighter fractions of the fuel in and below the venturi. The ice may slide down the throttle plate and restrict the mixture flow past the throttle, thereby causing the engine to run slower and to stall, especially at idle. Figure 2.16 shows that the high violatility fuel caused a drop in the throttle plate temperature from 40°F to 10°F after four stalling cycles. The stalling cycle consists of (1) starting the engine, (2) accelerating to 1500 rpm, (3) maintaining 1500 rpm for 30 seconds, (4) returning to idle, (5) idling for 15 seconds, (6) immediately restarting and returning to item (2) if engine stalls, otherwise returning to item (2) upon completion of idle period. With less volatile fuels the temperature drop is lower and the icing problem reduced. Carburetor icing can be prevented by (a) providing a heat source to the carburetor during warm-up periods, (b) using less volatile fuels, or (c) adding anti-icing additives (isopropyl alcohol or methyl alcohol) to the fuel.

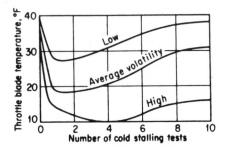

Figure 2.16. Effect of fuel volatility on throttle-blade temperature. Curves represent a six-engine average; 40°F ambient temperature. (Figure from Reference 7.)

d. *Effect on vapor lock*

Vapor lock of the fuel system occurs when fuel vapor forms in a quantity large enough to reduce the liquid-fuel flow to less than that required for engine operation. Vapor formation begins to occur in fuel lines, pumps, etc. when the fuel reaches a temperature at which the vapor pressure of the fuel is equal to the pressure in the system. After a hard run vapor lock is usually detected by the inability of the engine to idle. Figure 2.17 shows the temperature in the different parts of the fuel system of an automobile after shutdown to idle. The idling high temperatures result from the reduced cooling air flow.

The temperature of the ASTM 10% point has been found to be

an approximate indicator of relative tendency to vapor lock. The vapor-forming tendency can also be related to the Reid vapor pressure (RVP) of the fuel. A modification of the vapor/liquid ratio for the Reid vapor-pressure bomb has been proposed[4,5] for a better correlation of the bomb data and engine tendency to produce vapor lock.

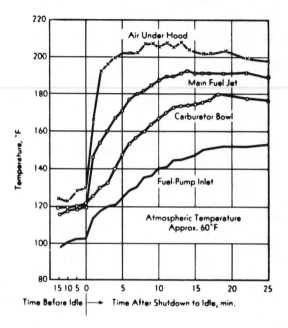

Figure 2.17.   Fuel-system temperatures. (Figure from Reference 6.)

e. *Effect on evaporation loss*

Evaporation losses from the fuel tank and carburetor are directly related to fuel volatility. The carburetor loss is primarily due to a distillation process and therefore is strongly related to the ASTM distillation curve of the fuel in the temperature range near 160°F. The fuel tank loss is caused mainly by an evaporation process and is therefore related to the Reid pressure of the fuel which is measured at 100°F. The Reid pressure and the ASTM distillation curve around 160°F can be varied independently. The evaporation loss is about 3.5 gallons per year from the tank and 2 gallons per year from the carburetor.[5] The loss from tanks one-quarter full was 60% more than from tanks half full.[5]

f. *Effect on crankcase dilution*

Dilution of the crankcase oil with the gasoline is the result of the incomplete evaporation of the heavier ends in the cylinder. This condition is exaggerated during the starting and warm-up periods, and is a minimum under normal operating engine temperature. The tendency of the fuel to cause dilution of the lubricating oil is directly related to the 90% ASTM temperature. Crankcase dilution is severe in winter.

B. Ignition Quality

The most important ignition quality of the S.I. engine fuel is its resistance to autoignition. Autoignition usually occurs in the end gases under high load, low speed conditions, Figure 2.18.

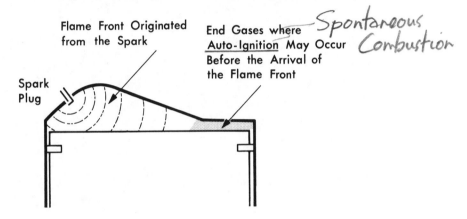

Figure 2.18.   Detonation of end gases in a S.I. engine.

The peaks of the pressure waves associated with detonation can be very high. Figure 2.19 shows the pressure traces for an engine with successive detonations. It can be noticed that the sharp pressure rise caused by detonation occurred in each trace near the maximum cycle pressure. This indicates that detonation is the result of the high rate of combustion of the end gases. Also, the maximum cycle pressure reached increased during the successive detonations. Local gas temperatures with detonation are expected to be much higher than in the nondetonating engine. The effect of these very high temperatures on the formation of nitrogen oxides will be studied in a later chapter.

In addition to the increase in the formation of NO_x compounds, detonation may lead to overheating of spark-plug electrodes or

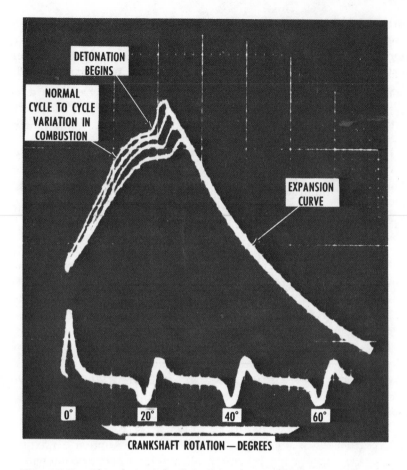

Figure 2.19. This photograph of portions of several consecutive engine pressure-time cycles shows the normal cycle to cycle variation experienced in a typical engine. The distorted portion at the peak pressure is caused by detonation. The multiple oscilloscope pressure traces show that detonation of the end gas occurs in a precise time relationship to increasing combustion pressures. These tests, under mild detonation conditions, were made at 1,000 rpm, 9:1 compression ratio, 99% power spark advance of 14° using 92 octane commercial gasoline. The time axis is calibrated in crankshaft degrees after top-dead-center. (Figure from Reference 16.)

other parts of the combustion chamber, resulting in preignition. Severe detonation or preignition causes loss of power and economy, and rough operation may damage the piston, the cylinder head, or the exhaust valves.

a. *Rating of S.I. engine fuels according to the ignition quality*

The tendency of a fuel to detonate is measured by its *octane* *number.* This is defined as the percentage (by volume) of isooctane* in a mixture of isooctane and n-heptane which will give borderline detonation under the same conditions as the fuel under test. The engine used for rating S.I. engine fuels is the CFR (Cooperative Fuel Research) single cylinder engine, and is run under specified conditions. The octane number of the fuels on the market is about 94 for regular gasoline and 100 for premium gasoline.

For fuels whose detonation characteristics are superior to those of isooctane, the rating can be made in terms of the "Performance Number." The performance number is defined as the ratio of the knock limited I.M.E.P. of the fuel under test to that of isooctane when the inlet air pressure is increased by supercharging.

b. *Effect of operating variables on detonation in engines*

An increase in any of the following variables will increase the tendency of the engine to produce detonation: inlet pressure, inlet temperature, compression ratio, spark advance and coolant temperature. An increase in engine speed, with all the other variables kept constant, will reduce the tendency toward detonation.

The effect of fuel-air ratio on detonation can be shown by plotting the knock limited indicated mean effective pressure versus the relative fuel-air ratio as shown in Figure 2.20. The relative fuel-air ratio is equal to the actual fuel-air ratio divided by the stoichiometric fuel-air ratio.

A significant conclusion to be drawn from Figure 2.20 is that autoignition tendency is maximized near stoichiometric mixture ratios. This conclusion relates to all autoignition phenomena including droplet combustion and engine run-on.

c. *Antiknock additives*

Antiknock additives, particularly organo-metallic compounds, when added to the fuel in very small amounts, decrease the tendency of the fuel-air mixture to autoignite. The most effective antiknock compound known is tetraethyllead (TEL), $(C_2H_5)_4 Pb$, which has a boiling point of 390°F. The effect of adding TEL to one gallon of regular and premium fuels is shown in Figure 2.21a. Tetraethyllead produces nonvolatile combustion products which tend to accumulate on the spark plugs and cause the engine to misfire. Therefore, TEL is always blended with ethylene dibromide and ethylene dichloride so that the lead compounds

---

*2,2,4-trimethylpentane

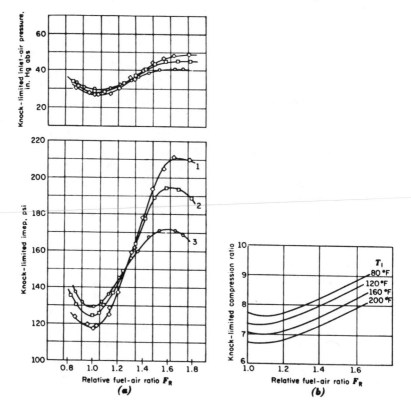

Figure 2.20. Effect of fuel-air ratio on knock-limited inlet pressure, imep, and compression ratio. (a) Aircraft fuels, r = 7, 1800 rpm, $T_c = 212°F$, $T_t = 250°F$ (b) CFR engine, 1200 rpm, isooctane fuel, unsupercharged, $T_c = 211°F$. (Figure from Reference 2.)

formed during combustion are sufficiently volatile and are discharged in the exhaust of the engine as a vapor.

The lead compounds represent the majority of the particulate mass-emissions in the gasoline engine exhaust. The lead compounds retained in the cylinder increase the exhaust emissions and those emitted inhibit the effectiveness of the exhaust treatment devices.

Nonmetallic additives can also increase the octane number of the fuel, without the undesirable effects cited above. Figure 2.21b shows the effect of adding aromatics (benzene) or ethyl-alcohol to n-heptane. However, because of the relatively large quantities required, undesirable exhaust emissions such as polynuclear aromatics and aldehydes may increase.[10,11]

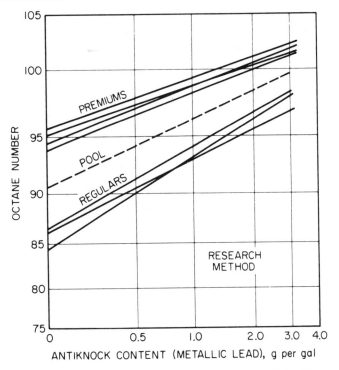

Figure 2.21a. Antiknock content (metallic lead), g per gallon. (Figure from Reference 15.)

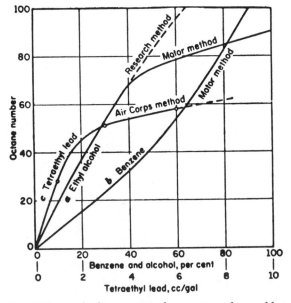

Figure 2.21b. Motor-method octane-number-increase from addition of ethyl alcohol or benzene to normal heptane. (Figure from Reference 2.)

Part IV   Effect of Engine Parameters on Performance

EFFECT OF COMPRESSION RATIO

The compression ratio is defined as:

$$\text{C.R.} = \frac{\text{vol. of cylinder at beginning of compression stroke}}{\text{vol. of cylinder at end of compression stroke}}$$

$$= \frac{V_d + V_c}{V_c}$$

where V_d = volume swept by the piston
       V_c = clearance volume

This is sometimes known as the nominal compression ratio. The actual or effective compression ratio is defined as:

$$\text{effective C.R.} = \frac{\text{vol. at closure of inlet valve or port}}{\text{clearance volume}}$$

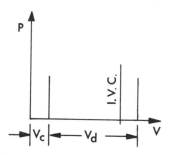

The nominal compression ratios in commercial gasoline engines are between 8:1 and 11:1, while in diesel engines these ratios are between 14:1 and 25:1.

A. EFFECT OF COMPRESSION RATIO ON THERMAL EFFICIENCY AND MEAN EFFECTIVE PRESSURE

The increase in thermal efficiency and mean effective pressure with compression ratio is shown for an experimental C.F.R. single cylinder engine in Figure 2.22. This figure shows that an increase in compression ratio from 4:1 to 10:1 resulted in an increase in brake thermal efficiency from 13.4 % to 23 %. At the low compression ratios this increase rate is high, but it is not as significant at high compression ratios. It is to be noted that the values cited here for the brake thermal efficiency of the single cylinder engine are lower than those of multicylinder engines.

Figure 2.22 also shows that the compression ratio at which audible knock occurs is 6.5:1 for a 60 octane fuel, 8:1 for an 80 octane fuel and 10:1 for a 95 octane fuel. Both the brake thermal efficiency and the B.M.E.P. increase with compression ratio up to the knock limit, after which they drop with any further increase in compression ratio.

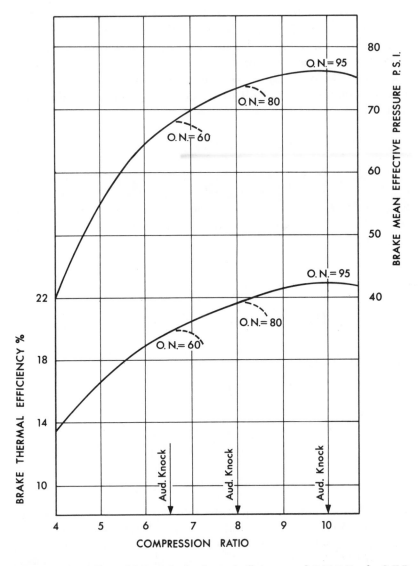

Figure 2.22   Effect of C.R. on brake thermal efficiency and B.M.E.P. of a C.F.R. engine.

B. EFFECT OF COMPRESSION RATIO ON MAXIMUM TEMPERATURE
IN THE CYCLE

The maximum cycle temperature is one of the main factors that contribute to the formation of nitrogen oxides during the combustion process and their emission in the exhaust gases. The formation of nitrogen oxides will be discussed in a following chapter.

The maximum temperature reached in the cycle depends on many parameters in combination with the compression ratio. Some of these factors are the fuel-air ratio, spark timing, ambient air temperature, and cooling losses (cylinder wall temperature, engine speed). When these parameters are constant, an increase in compression ratio will result in an increase in the maximum cycle temperature.

EFFECT OF FUEL-AIR RATIO

The proper amount of air required for the complete combustion of a hydrocarbon fuel can be calculated from a balance of the different atoms in the reactants and products. For example, the combustion of isooctane in air proceeds according to the following equation:

$$C_8H_{18} + 12.5\ O_2 + 12.5 \times 3.76\ N_2 =$$

$$8CO_2 + 9H_2O + 12.5 \times 3.76\ N_2 \tag{2.1}$$

$$(8 \times 12 + 18) + (12.5 \times 32) + (12.5 \times 3.76 \times 28) =$$

| lbs | lbs | lbs |
| C_8H_{18} | O_2 | N_2 |

$$8(12 + 32) + 9(2 + 16) + (12.5 \times 3.76 \times 28)$$

| lbs | lbs | lbs | |
| CO_2 | H_2O | N_2 | (2.2) |

Equation 2.1 shows that one mole of isooctane reacts with 12.5 moles of oxygen. Approximately 47 moles of nitrogen in the air are required for complete combustion. In most of the chemical reactions, nitrogen is assumed to be an inert gas, *i.e.*, it does not take part in the reaction. This assumption is justified in the computa-

tions related to the heat of combustion. But, <u>for exhaust emission computations of nitrogen oxides, the reactions between the nitrogen and oxygen must be taken into consideration.</u>

Equation 2.2 gives the masses of the reactants and products in pounds, from which the stoichiometric mixture ratio can be obtained, as follows:

$$\frac{\text{mass of air}}{\text{mass of fuel}} = 15.05$$

or the stoichiometric fuel-air ratio is equal to 0.0665 lb of fuel per lb of air. The ratio of carbon to hydrogen for commercial gasoline may vary from 6:1 to 6.8:1, compared with a ratio of 5.33:1 for isooctane. The corresponding stoichiometric fuel-air ratio may vary from 14.7:1 to 14.4:1 compared with 15.05:1 for isooctane.[6] "Indolene" gasoline is a specially blended fuel whose properties are carefully controlled. Often used as a standard test fuel, its carbon to hydrogen ratio is about 6.5:1.

A. Effect of Fuel-Air Ratio on Mean Effective Pressure and Thermal Efficiency

The effect of fuel-air ratio on the B.M.E.P. and B.S.F.C. of a six-cylinder automobile engine is shown in Figure 2.23. The data plotted in this figure are for the engine at a constant speed of 1800 rpm, constant throttle opening, and under steady-state conditions.

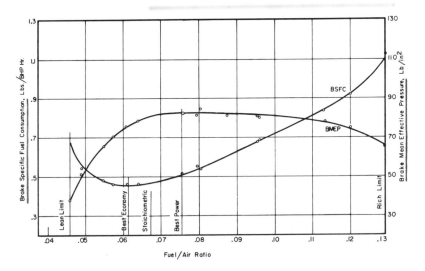

Figure 2.23. Effect of fuel-air ratio on B.M.E.P. and B.S.F.C. of a 6-cyclinder gasoline engine, 1800 rpm, fixed throttle.

The fuel-air ratio was varied by changing the area for fuel flow in the main jet of the carburetor. The tests covered a very wide range of fuel-air ratio, from the lean limit of 0.0465 to the rich limit of 0.130. Outside these two limits the engine misfired. The results of Figure 2.23 show that best economy is at a lean fuel-air ratio of 0.061, and maximum B.M.E.P. is at a rich fuel-air ratio of 0.076.

At very lean fuel-air ratios the increased B.S.F.C. and the drop in B.M.E.P. are mainly caused by the long period of combustion resulting from slow flame speeds at the lean mixtures. For very rich mixtures (richer than maximum power ratio) the losses in B.M.E.P. and efficiency are usually caused by incomplete combustion and slow flame speed. Maximum B.M.E.P. occurs at a rich mixture because of chemical equilibrium.

B. Effect of Fuel-Air Ratio on the Maximum Temperature in the Cycle

Maximum cycle temperatures occur with a slightly rich mixture because of the combined effect of chemical equilibrium and change in number of molecules during the reactions. With the rich fuel-air mixtures the combustion products would include carbon monoxide because of the lack of oxygen available for complete combustion.

3. EFFECT OF IGNITION TIMING

The combustion process requires an appreciable amount of time before completion (1 to 2 milliseconds); thus the ignition timing should be sufficiently advanced in order for combustion to occur before as well as after T.D.C. The combustion process in the gasoline engine can be considered to take place in two stages, the ignition delay period and the pressure-rise period (see Figure 2.24).

A. The Ignition Delay Period

This period is the time required for a mixture of fuel and air to autoignite when subjected to some sufficiently high temperature at some pressure. At the end of this period, preflame reactions occur at such a rate that chemical energy is liberated faster than it is dissipated by heat transfer or other methods. This results in an increase in the temperature of the gases and a corresponding rise in pressure.

The length of the ignition delay period depends upon many factors including the charge pressure, temperature, fuel-air ratio,

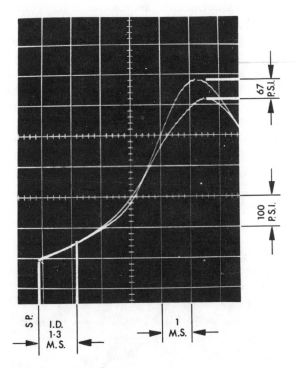

Figure 2.24.   The two stages of combustion in a C.F.R S.I. engine.

and type of fuel (octane number). In general the ignition delay is independent of the engine speed. Thus at higher engine speeds, the ignition delay occupies a larger number of crank angles than at lower speeds.

B. THE PRESSURE-RISE PERIOD

During this period the chemical reactions occur at a very fast rate and the flame front proceeds through the main body of the fuel-air mixture. The length of this period depends upon the gas pressure, temperature, fuel-air ratio, type of fuel, turbulence, etc. Since the turbulence is proportional to the engine speed and the flame speed is proportional to the turbulence, the pressure rise period occupies approximately the same number of crank-angle degrees at different engine speeds.

The great effect of spark timing on the engine performance results because the more heat that is added at T.D.C. the higher will be the mean effective pressure and the thermal efficiency. It is desirable to burn as much of the charge as possible at the highest compression ratio (center charge about T.D.C.). In order to have most of the combustion process occur near top dead center, ignition should start early before T.D.C. The optimum spark timing depends upon many engine parameters, but mainly upon engine speed and manifold pressure.

The effect of spark-timing on the pressure-volume diagram of a C.F.R. engine is shown in Figures 2.26 to 2.29. All these traces are taken with the throttle valve fully opened, at a C.R. of 8:1, and speed of 1000 rpm.

Figure 2.25 is for the engine motored without ignition. Notice that the upper trace is the compression curve and the lower trace is the expansion curve. The heat losses and blowby losses are the main factors that cause the pressures on the expansion to be lower than those during the compression stroke.

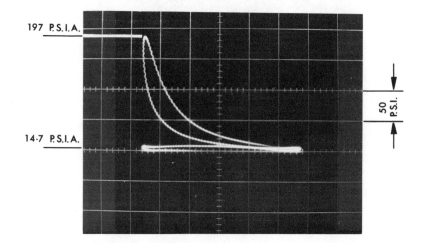

Figure 2.25. Pressure-Volume Trace for a motored C.F.R. engine, at 1000 R.P.M.

Figure 2.26 is for the engine with optimum spark timing at 27.5 degrees before T.D.C. The maximum cycle pressure is 532 psia. When the spark occurs at T.D.C., Figure 2.27, the gas pressure during the early part of the expansion stroke falls below the pressure during the compression stroke, resulting in a negative loop near T.D.C. This has a detrimental effect on the mean effective pressure and thermal efficiency of the engine. After the piston moved approximately 20% of the expansion stroke, the pressure started to rise because of late combustion. In this case the maximum pressure is about equal to that when the engine was mo-

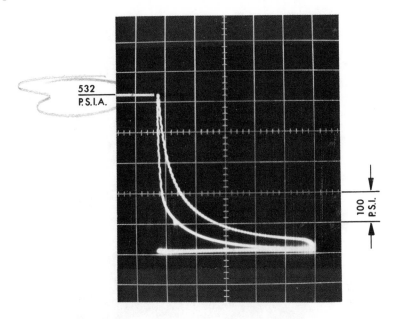

Figure 2.26. Pressure-volume trace for a C.F.R. engine at 1000 rpm and optimum spark timing, 27.5°B.T.D.C.

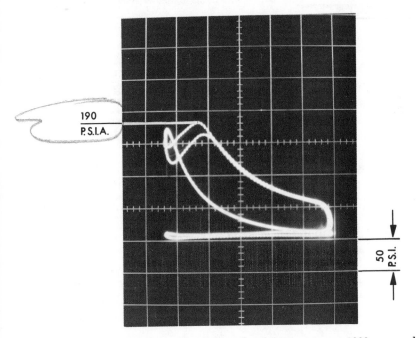

Figure 2.27. Pressure-volume trace for C.F.R. engine at 1000 rpm and spark timing at T.D.C.

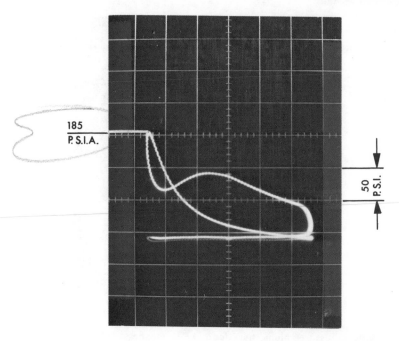

185
P. S.I.A.

50 P.S.I.

Figure 2.28. Pressure-volume trace for a C.F.R. engine at 1000 rpm, and spark timing at 10° after T.D.C.

tored, Figure 2.25. A pressure trace with a very late spark timing, 10 degrees after T.D.C., is shown in Figure 2.28. In this case the area of the negative work loop near T.D.C. is larger than the previous case of Figure 2.27.

A pressure trace for the engine with a very early spark timing, 55 degrees before T.D.C., is shown in Figure 2.29. It should be noticed that the maximum cycle pressure reached a value of 655 psia, much higher than that with optimum timing. Also this early spark timing resulted in a great loss in mean effective pressure and efficiency because of the great losses near T.D.C. as indicated by the negative loop in this region. Under this condition the maximum cycle temperatures are expected to be much higher than in any case discussed previously.

From the above discussion it can be concluded that there is an optimum spark timing, for any combination of engine running conditions, which will result in maximum mean effective pressure and thermal efficiency. Commonly this timing is termed MBT, minimum advance for best torque.

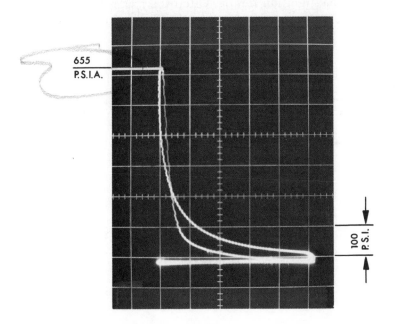

Figure 2.29. Pressure-volume trace for a C.F.R. engine at 1000 rpm, spark timing overadvanced at 55° B.T.D.C., M.B.T. = 27.5° B.T.D.C.

EFFECT OF ENGINE SPEED ON OPTIMUM SPARK TIMING

Increasing engine speed increases the turbulence, the compression temperature and pressure, and has little effect on the length of the ignition delay period. Thus the ignition delay period occupies more crank angle degrees at higher engine speeds, and the spark must be advanced to maintain maximum power. This is achieved by the centrifugal advance device.

EFFECT OF MANIFOLD PRESSURE ON OPTIMUM SPARK TIMING

The power output of the gasoline engine is varied by the throttle valve opening. At part load, throttling reduces the manifold pressure which results in greater dilution of the smaller charge with the residual gases. Under throttled conditions the carburetor is usually designed to provide the maximum economy (or lean) mixture. These diluted lean mixtures require more combustion time than full load, wide open throttle mixtures. Hence economical part-load operation requires more spark advance than optimum full-load ignition timing. Often the part-load advance is achieved by a vacuum advance device. Figure 2.30 shows the spark advance for a typical automobile engine.

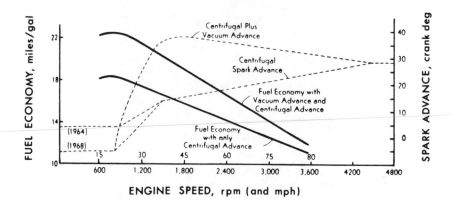

Figure 2.30. Effects of centrifugal and vacuum spark advance on performance. (Figure from Reference 6.)

Part V Carburetion

The carburetor supplies the intake manifold with metered amounts of fuel and air. The quantity and quality of the fuel-air mixture must be appropriate to the different engine operating conditions. Relatively small metering errors may depreciate power and economy noticeably and increase exhaust emissions substantially.

A. *FUEL-AIR REQUIREMENTS OF AUTOMOTIVE GASOLINE ENGINES*

1. STEADY RUNNING MIXTURE REQUIREMENTS

Under steady running condition the engine is warmed up and running without sudden changes in speed and load. Different ratios of fuel and air are required, depending upon the speed and load on the engine, as illustrated in Figure 2.31. Three conditions exist: idling and low load, medium loads or cruise, and high load.

(a) *Idling and Low Load*

During idling and low load the throttle valve is near the closed position, and the engine requires a rich mixture as represented by line AB in Figure 2.31. Under these conditions the pressure in the intake manifold is far below atmospheric, Figure 2.32, while the pressure at the end of the exhaust stroke is always close to atmospheric. When the intake valve opens, a higher pressure exists in

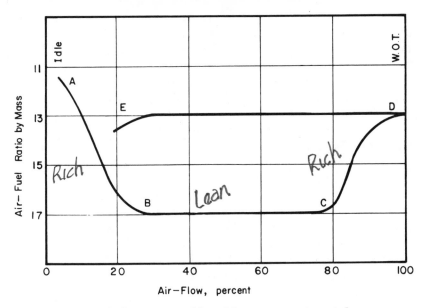

Figure 2.31.   Air-fuel ratio required by a S.I. engine at various air flow rates.

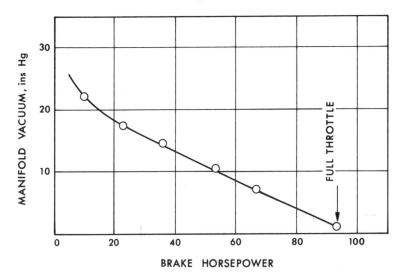

Figure 2.32   Manifold vacuum versus B.H.P. for an automobile engine, 289 CID, 2500 rpm.

the cylinder than in the intake manifold, and the relatively high-pressure exhaust gas expands into the intake manifold. Later, as the piston moves on the intake stroke, the exhaust gases are drawn back into the cylinder along with a portion of the fresh charge, resulting in an overall mixture containing a high percentage of exhaust gases. To ensure proper combustion of the diluted charge a very rich mixture is required. The dilution is maximum under no-load conditions and is gradually reduced with the increase in load or throttle valve opening.

The exhaust gas dilution is greatly increased by the amount of valve overlap. With high overlap and at part throttle, the exhaust gases enter the intake manifold before the exhaust stroke is completed, resulting in additional dilution. Engines with high overlap require an extremely rich mixture at idle and off-idle to obtain relatively smooth operation. For example, a "fast" idling speed is often required in racing cars.

The relative dilution of the fresh charge with the exhaust gases is reduced with opening of the throttle valve as shown in Figure 2.33 for a single-cylinder C.F.R. engine.[12] In Figure 2.33 the residual mass fraction is used to indicate the degree of dilution. The residual mass fraction is defined as the ratio of the mass of the residuals to the mass of the total charge.

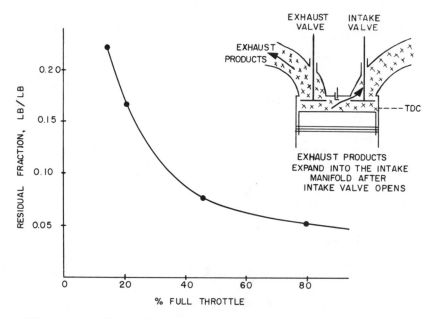

Figure 2.33. Effect of throttle opening on residual fraction. (Data from Reference 12.)

(b) *Medium Loads or Cruise*

Under these load conditions the throttle opening is sufficiently large that the effect of dilution is negligible. Under such conditions a lean mixture is used to provide optimum fuel economy. This is represented in Figure 2.31 by line BC. The air-fuel ratio that gives best economy is determined in a vehicle on the road. Single-cylinder engines can use leaner mixtures than multicylinder engines because in the multicylinder engine the manifold feeds more than one cylinder. Feeding more than one cylinder usually results in uneven distribution of the fuel between the cylinders.

(c) *High Loads*

Under high load conditions when the throttle valve is opened 75 % or greater, a rich mixture is required to give maximum power. This is represented by line CD in Figure 2.31.

2. Transient Mixture Requirements

The principal transient conditions of operation are cold starting, warm up, and acceleration.

(a) *Cold Starting*

When cold, the engine requires the carburetor to provide a very rich mixture so that sufficient fuel-vapor exists to produce a combustible mixture. As discussed under fuel volatility, a fuel-air ratio of 1:1 may be required to produce the combustible mixture. This very rich mixture is obtained by the use of a choke valve.

(b) *Warm Up*

During warm-up a rich fuel-air ratio is required, but the degree of richness must be progressively reduced during the warm-up period. Eventually the engine runs satisfactorily with the normal steady-running fuel-air ratios.

(c) *Acceleration*

During acceleration the throttle valve is suddenly opened and the manifold pressure is increased. Unless some supplementary fuel is added to the mixture, a momentary lean condition will result. This arises from both the inertia of the liquid fuel in the manifold and the decrease in evaporation at the higher manifold pressure. The acceleration pump provides this additional fuel.

B. *ELEMENTS OF A COMPLETE CARBURETOR*

The carburetor is composed of a group of systems which operate individually or simultaneously to supply the engine with the proper fuel-air mixture. Figure 2.34 shows the elements of a simple carburetor. The level of the fuel in the float chamber is kept lower than the open end of the delivery pipe to avoid the spilling of fuel when the engine is not running. The float chamber is vented to the air horn to compensate for the pressure drop in the air cleaner.

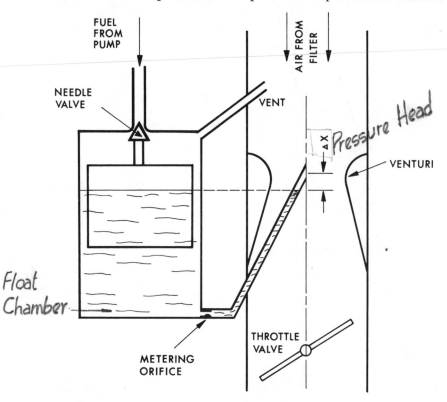

Figure 2.34.   Elements of a simple carburetor.

As the air flows through the venturi, its velocity increases, and pressure drops causing the fuel to flow from the float chamber. In many designs a double or triple venturi (Figure 2.35) is used to obtain relatively high suction on the main jet at relatively low air flow without excessive venturi pressure loss. The fuel is discharged in the smaller venturi. The mixture of fuel and air from the smaller venturi is discharged centrally in the succeeding venturi, leading to better mixing and a more homogeneous mixture.

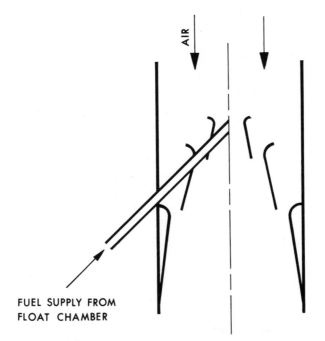

Figure 2.35.   Triple venturi.

The rate of liquid flow through the fuel jet can be given by
Equation 2.3:

$$\dot{m}_f = c_d A \sqrt{2g\rho_f \Delta P} \qquad (2.3)$$

where

$\dot{m}_f =$ fuel flow rate
$c_d =$ coefficient of discharge
$g =$ gravitational acceleration
$\rho_f =$ fuel density
$\Delta P =$ pressure differential between the float chamber
and venturi throat.

Equation 2.3 shows that the fuel flow rate is proportional to the
area of the jet and the square root of the pressure drop, $\sqrt{\Delta P}$. The
pressure drop, ΔP, is a function of the air flow rate through the
venturi. Therefore, the fuel flow rate is directly related to the air
flow rate. This element of the carburetor is termed the main
metering system.

In Figure 2.36 the fuel-air ratio variation provided by the main metering system is shown as a function of air-flow rate (curve AB). At very small air flow rates, the fuel-air ratio is zero at point A. Under these conditions the pressure drop in the venturi is not enough to overcome the head, ΔX, and the viscous and surface tension forces acting on the fuel. On the other hand the mixture becomes too rich with increasing air-flow rate, as shown in curve AB. Curve AB can be raised or lowered by changing the area of the main jet.

The fuel-air ratio required by the engine is shown by curve CD. If the area of the main jet is adjusted for satisfactory idling, (curve A'B'), the mixture is too rich at higher air-flow rates. If it is adjusted for satisfactory cruise or maximum power (curve A"B"), the mixture is too lean for idling. Therefore the metering charac-teristic of the simple carburetor, *i.e.* a main jet alone, is inadequate

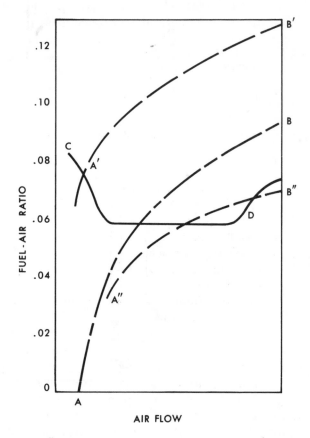

Figure 2.36.   Effect of air flow on the fuel-air ratio from the main jet.

for satisfying all engine requirements. It is apparent that addition-al fuel metering systems must be added to obtain the fuel-air ratios required by the engine.

1. COMPENSATING JETS

The increasing richness of the main jet accompanying the in-crease in air flow is usually compensated for by a restricted air-bleed (Stromberg, Carter RPD, GPD) or an unrestricted air-bleed jet (Zenith).

The unrestricted air-bleed jet is shown in Figure 2.37. It has a large air opening at the top of a fuel well termed the accelerating well. When the engine is not operating, the fuel-level is the same in the accelerating well as in the float chamber. At small throttle valve openings and low engine speeds the fuel flow through the air-bleed jet is controlled by the height of the fuel in the acceler-ating well above the jet. At larger throttle valve openings, the well is emptied and the flow of the fuel is a function of the constant head h. Therefore the mixture delivered by the air-bleed jet be-comes leaner at higher air flows as shown by curve BB, Figure 2.38. The combination of the main jet and the unrestricted air-bleed jet can produce the constant fuel-air ratio required for the cruise region, as shown in Figure 2.38.

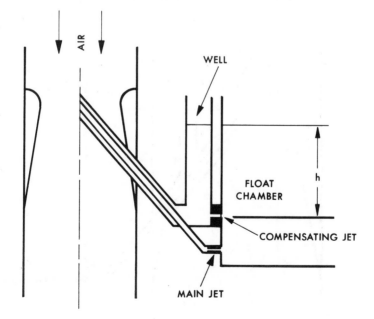

Figure 2.37.   Unrestricted air bleed.

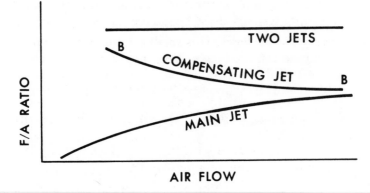

Figure 2.38. Characteristics of the main and compensating jets.

The restricted air-bleed jet is shown in Figure 2.39. It has an orifice (A_b) which meters the air into the fuel jet. Bleeding air into the fuel jet reduces the effective head that causes fuel flow. Because of its construction, more bleed air is mixed with the fuel at higher loads as more holes are exposed to the air at the higher loads.

The restricted air bleed carburetor provides a constant fuel-air ratio through the major range of operation.[1]

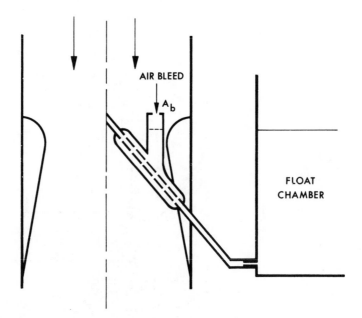

Figure 2.39. Restricted air bleed.

2. THE IDLING SYSTEM

The idling system is added to deliver a small amount of a rich mixture at very low air flows. This small amount of fuel is required so that the engine can produce just enough work to overcome the frictional losses of the engine during idling. Under these conditions the throttle valve is almost closed and no fuel flows through the main jet.

The elements of an idling system are shown in Figure 2.40. The throttle valve is nearly closed and the high vacuum in the inlet manifold acts on the idle discharge port. Fuel flows from the float chamber and is metered by the metering idle jet. The fuel is emulsified with the air from the air bleed. Fuel flow through the idle discharge port can be adjusted by the idle needle.

The off-idle port acts as an air bleed hole when the throttle valve is in the near-closed position. Shortly after the throttle valve starts to open, the off-idle port passes into the vacuum region and the fuel flows from both the idle and off-idle ports. The discharge from the idle system continues to decrease as the throttle valve opening increases.

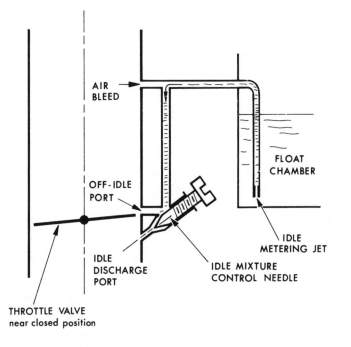

Figure 2.40.   Idling system.

3. High Load Enriching Devices

The rich fuel-air ratio required at high loads can be obtained either by enlarging the fuel orifice or by opening a vacuum or mechanically operated secondary fuel orifice.

4. Accelerating System

During acceleration the throttle valve is suddenly opened, allowing more air to flow into the manifold. Under transient conditions the fuel flow does not increase rapidly in response to the throttle change and a lean mixture can reach the cylinders. To supply the additional necessary fuel an accelerating pump is actuated mechanically by the throttle valve or by a vacuum piston.

5. Choke System

Under cold starting conditions a good part of the fuel delivered by the carburetor is deposited on the cold manifold walls and only the lighter fractions reach the cylinders, forming a combustible mixture. Consequently, the carburetor is required to deliver a very rich mixture for proper engine operation. To achieve this a choke is used. The choke restricts the air flow and causes full manifold vacuum to act across the main orifice thus giving a large flow of fuel.

As the engine warms up, the choke valve is opened either manually by the operator or automatically by a thermostatic control.

C. THE COMPLETE CARBURETOR

The complete carburetor incorporates many or all of the individual elements discussed previously depending on the application. The following discussion of the Rochester Products 2 bbl. carburetor illustrates one example of how the various elements combine to form a complete system.

Main Metering System

Figure 2.41 shows a cross-section of the carburetor through one of the two venturis. Shown are the carburetor venturi into which the delivery tube spills fuel. This carburetor has a single boost venturi. The delivery tube draws fuel from the main well. This is a restricted air bleed carburetor (like that of Figure 2.39) since bleed holes are drilled into the vertical portion of the fuel delivery tube. The main metering orifice meters the fuel from the float

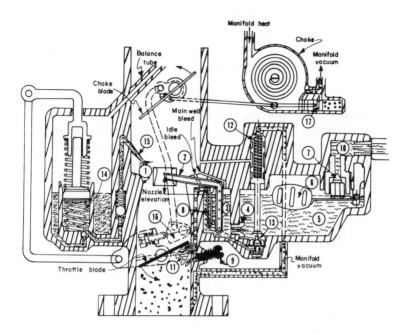

Figure 2.41. Cross sectional view of the Rochester two-barrel carburetor. (Figure redrawn from Reference 13.)

chamber like that of the elementary carburetor of Figure 2.34. Note the elevation of the discharge nozzle above the fuel bowl level. Note also the hinged float and needle valve which maintain fuel level.

IDLE SYSTEM

The idle system of the Rochester 2 bbl. carburetor draws fuel from the main well also. The idle tube has a crimped end which serves as an idle metering jet. Note also the idle system air bleed. As the fuel delivery increases and the main well level drops, the idle system must lift fuel higher also. Thus, with this design in which the idle tube draws from the main well rather than the float bowl itself, the idle fuel delivery will decline more rapidly as the main system delivery increases. The idle mixture control needle and the three off-idle ports, termed transfer holes, are like those of Figure 2.40.

POWER ENRICHMENT SYSTEM

The high load or power enrichment device is a vacuum-controlled piston connected to a plunger. As manifold vacuum drops, the plunger descends, opening a by-pass valve which allows additional fuel to enter the main well parallel to the main metering jet. Because of the construction of this system, the by-pass orifice opens gradually (depending on piston area and spring rate), providing a gradual increase in mixture strength as the throttle is opened fully. (Emission control carburetors may employ an additional main metering system, by-pass jet, and needle valve whose opening, like the idle needle valve, can be adjusted. This provides a means for individually adjusting the main metering system flow to meet emission requirements. Once set the by-pass needle screw adjustment is sealed shut.)

ACCELERATION SYSTEM

The acceleration system of the Rochester 2 bbl. consists of an acceleration pump which is driven by the motion of the throttle linkage. The pump piston is driven through a drive spring and the motion is opposed by a return spring. The pump discharge quantity is equal to the displaced volume of the pump. This may be varied by changing the geometry of the linkage or the area of the piston. The rate of fuel delivery is controlled by the spring rate of the two springs together with the pump discharge nozzle restriction. The presence of the springs causes the flow from the pump to continue after throttle movement has ceased. In addition the ball check valve stops syphoning of the accelerator pump charge at high air flows.

CHOKE SYSTEM

The choke system consists of a butterfly valve connected to a vacuum operated piston and a bi-metallic spring. Upon cranking the engine the choke plate is fully closed, restricting air flow and causing a large pressure differential to exist across the main metering system. This pressure difference causes a large quantity of fuel to be metered to the air stream. Upon starting, manifold vacuum is developed and this vacuum, acting upon the backside of the choke pull piston, immediately pulls the choke to a partially opened position as shown in Figure 2.41. This reduces the fuel delivery from the main system. The trick is to set the proper choke pull angle so that the engine does not stall rich or lean. As the intake manifold, carburetor body, and intake air warm up, it is necessary to open the choke blade gradually to avoid an over-rich vapor-air mixture. This is accomplished with the bi-metal spring.

The manner in which the bi-metal is heated and its torque and coil activity determine the rate at which the choke blade is opened. Rapid opening is desired for low emissions of hydrocarbons and carbon monoxide, but too rapid opening will lead to lean mixture stumble.

D. CARBURETOR TAILORING

The fuel-air ratio provided by a carburetor can be varied by changing the size or location of the various fuel and air bleed orifices. Figures 2.42 and 2.43 show the effect of several such changes on the shape of the delivered air-fuel ratio of the Rochester 2 bbl. In general the effect of such changes in other carburetors will be somewhat different depending on the design of the carburetor.

It can be seen in Figure 2.42 that, in the absence of main well bleeds, the cruise portion of the curve looks like that of Figure 2.36. Varying the main well bleed size tips the cruise portion of

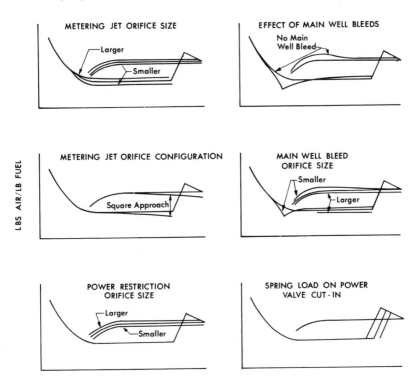

Figure 2.42. Effect of carburetor variations on metering. (Figure from Reference 13.)

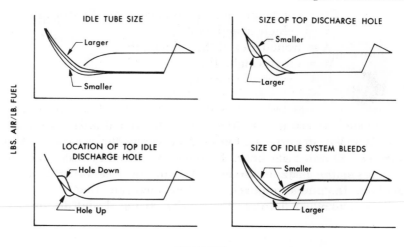

Figure 2.43. Effect of carburetor variations on metering. (Figure from Reference 13.)

the curve. Varying the idle tube size and idle air bleed varies the mixture ratio in the idle and off-idle region. Mixture ratio control in this region is critical for low emissions. Some emission control carburetors have an adjustable needle valve to control the idle air bleed flow and thus more closely control the mixture. The size and location of the idle discharge hole controls the mixture ratio as the throttle is first opened. Obviously care must be exercised to avoid a rich or lean condition just off-idle.

Part VI   Engine-Vehicle Road Performance

The engine-vehicle performance (acceleration) on the road depends on the power needed to overcome the road load requirement, the power available at the engine flywheel, and the transmission efficiency. The road load requirement consists of the following:

(a) rolling resistance
(b) air resistance
(c) (road grade × gross weight).

A typical expression for road horsepower is:

$$\text{road horsepower} = V\ (C_r W + C_a A V^2 + 0.01\ GW)/375 \quad (2.4)$$

where C_r = coefficient of rolling resistance, typically 0.015

C_a = coefficient of air resistance, typically 0.00125
V = vehicle speed, mph
A = frontal area of the vehicle, ft^2
W = gross weight, lbm
G = road grade, per cent

The power needed at the driving wheels of a typical medium-sized American car (4000 lbs, 22 ft^2 frontal area) on a level road is shown in curve aa, Figure 2.44, versus the car speed. At a speed of 40 miles per hour, the power required to overcome the road resistance is 12 horsepower. To run the same car at 80 miles per hour, the power required is 53.5 horsepower.

The power loss between the engine flywheel and the driving

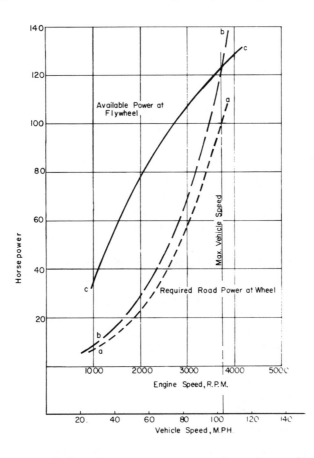

Figure 2.44. Vehicle and engine power curves, for an intermediate size vehicle.

wheels depends mainly upon the type of transmission, manual or automatic, and the drive line efficiency. In general, the losses in manual transmission systems are lower than those of automatic transmissions. Transmission efficiencies range between 95 to 99% for manual and 87 to 93% for automatic.

The required power at the engine flywheel for this vehicle is shown by curve bb in Figure 2.44. An automatic transmission is assumed and the values shown are for top gear operation. An overall power train efficiency of 82.5% was assumed.

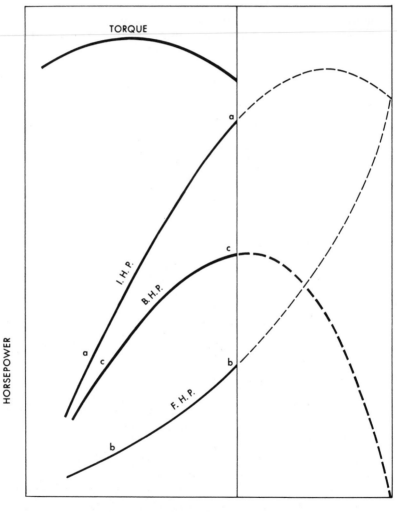

Figure 2.45.   Horsepower and torque for a S.I. engine versus speed.

The brake horsepower available at the flywheel, with the throttle valve fully opened, increases with engine speed as shown in curve cc in Figure 2.44. This brake horsepower curve is a result of the indicated horsepower, curve a, Figure 2.45, and the friction horsepower, curve b, Figure 2.45. The friction horsepower increases at a higher rate with speed. The maximum engine speed, N $_{max}$, is that speed at which the friction horsepower is equal to the indicated horsepower. (Most engines blow up before this speed can be reached.) The torque as a function of speed is shown in top of Figure 2.45.

The power available at the flywheel can be determined from a dynamometer test under full throttle conditions as shown in curve cc, in Figure 2.44. In this figure, at a given speed the difference between the power available and that required is equal to the power available for acceleration at the same speed. The point of intersection of the curves bb and cc is the maximum speed the vehicle can reach, which in this case is 103 miles per hour.

ROAD PERFORMANCE AND FUEL ECONOMY

The fuel economy, expressed in miles per gallon, depends on many factors including the road load requirement, transmission type and efficiency, and engine performance. Figure 2.46 shows

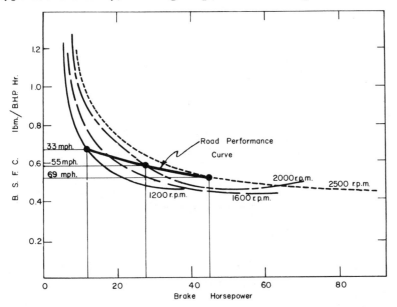

Figure 2.46. Fuel consumption versus B.H.P. at different engine speeds. (Engine of Figure 2.32.)

B.S.F.C. versus horsepower at four speeds: 1200, 1600, 2000, and 2500 rpm. At any speed, these curves show that fuel economy improves at higher power outputs. This is mainly due to lower pumping losses resulting from the increased throttle valve opening, higher mechanical efficiency and lower fuel-air ratio. The change in fuel-air ratio and manifold vacuum with power output at a speed of 1200 rpm is shown in Figure 2.47. Rich fuel-air ratios, were required for B.M.E.P., lower than 20 psi. In this test the power enrichment valve was removed from the carburetor and the fuel-air ratios remained lean at high brake mean effective pressures.

By comparing the performance curves shown in Figure 2.46 it can be noted that at the same brake horsepower, higher engine speed resulted in higher B.S.F.C. However, the brake horsepower required increases with speed. The road performance curve is plotted on the same figure and shows the improved fuel economy in terms of B.S.F.C. But if the miles per gallon versus vehicle speed are plotted, Figure 2.48, it can be concluded that driving at high speed results in loss of fuel economy but gain in time.

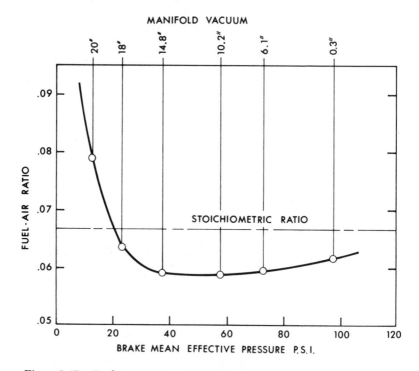

Figure 2.47. Fuel-air ration versus B.M.E.P. for a S.I. Engine at 1200 rpm, with the power enrichment valve removed. (Engine of Figure 2.32.)

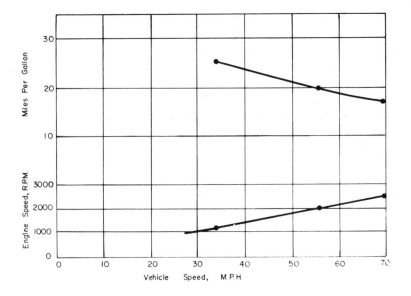

Figure 2.48. Miles per gallon versus vehicle speed, intermediate size vehicle and engine of Figure 2.32.

REFERENCES

1. Lichty, L. C. *Combustion Engine Processes,* (New York: McGraw-Hill Book Co., 1967).
2. Taylor, C. F., and E. S. Taylor. *The Internal Combustion Engine,* 2nd ed. (Scranton, Pa.: International Textbook Company, 1961).
3. Moore, G. T., R. D. Young, and H. A. Toulmin. "Effect of Fuel Volatility on Starting and Warmup of New Automobiles," Trans. SAE **65,** 692 (1957).
4. Caplan, J. D. and C. J. Brody. "Vapor Locking Tendencies of Fuels, A Practical Approach," SAE Trans. **66,** 327 (1958).
5. Holaday, W. M. and D. P. Heath. "Motor Fuel Volatility Trends," SAE Quart. Trans. 3, 429 (1951).
6. Obert, E. F. *Internal Combustion Engines,* 3rd ed., (Scranton, Pa.: International Textbook Co., 1968).
7. Dugan, W. P., and H. A. Toulmin. Carburetor Icing Tendencies of Some Present-Day Engines, SAE Trans. 63, 442 (1955).
8. Progress and Programs in Automotive Emissions Control, General Motors Corporation (1971).
9. Siewert, R. M. "How Individual Value Timing Events Affect Exhaust Emissions," SAE Paper 710609 (June, 1971).
10. Ninomiya, J. S., Golovoy, A., and Labana, S. S. "Effect of Methanol on Exhaust Composition of a Fuel Containing Toluene, n-Heptane and Iso-octane," J. APCA **20,** 314 (1970).

11. Felt, A. E. and Kerley, R. V. "Engines and Effects of Lead-Free Gasoline," SAE Paper 710367, (January, 1971).
12. Daniel W. A. "Why Engine Variables Affect Exhaust Hydrocarbon Emission," SAE **PT-14**, 341 (1967–70).
13. Kehoe, E. A. "Carburetor Fundamentals and Practical Application," Rochester Products Division, General Motors Corporation (1959).
14. "Effect of Automotive Emission Requirements on Gasoline Characteristics," ASTM Special Technical Publication **487**, 105 (1971).
15. O'Neill, Donald. "Switch to Unleaded Fuel Offers Benefits, Poses Problems," Auto. Eng. **78** (8), 17 (1970).
16. General Motors Corp., G.M. Eng. J. (May–June, 1956).

3

COMBUSTION IN
HOMOGENEOUS MIXTURES

Introduction

The undersirable exhaust emissions of a vehicle are formed mainly within the combustion chamber of the engine during or after the combustion process. Chemical reactions, which decrease the concentration of some compounds but may actually increase others, also occur in the exhaust system. Many aspects of the chemistry and physics of exhaust emission formation and the fate of these emissions as they proceed though the engine and exhaust system are not well understood at the present time. The following sections will discuss the fundamental aspects of combustion in the homogeneous mixture of the gasoline engine. Heterogeneous combustion will be discussed in Chapter 8.

The combustion of a hydrocarbon fuel with air may be represented by the simplified chemical reaction below, which has been written for Indolene, a standardized blended fuel often used for emission testing. This fuel has 1.86 atoms of hydrogen for each atom of carbon. An average molecule can be thought of as $7(CH_{1.86})$. The equation for complete combustion of this fuel molecule with a chemically correct amount of air is:

$$C_7 H_{13.02} + 10.255\ O_2 + 38.6\ N_2 \longrightarrow$$

$$7\ CO_2 + 6.51\ H_2O + 38.6\ N_2 \qquad (3.1)$$

It is apparent that the combustion of one molecular weight of fuel (97 lb.) requires 48.855 molecular weights of air (1408 lb) and produces 7 molecular weights of carbon dioxide (308 lb), 6.51 molecular weights of water (117 lb) and 38.5 molecular weights of nitrogen (1080 lb). In addition one pound of this fuel requires about 14.5 lbs of air and produces 3.18 lbs CO_2, 1.21 lbs water, and 11.1 lbs nitrogen when combustion is complete for a chemically correct mixture. The ratio of air to fuel by weight, 14.5/1, is the chemically correct mixture ratio.

Since a molecular weight, or mole as it is often termed, is

related to the number of molecules of the particular compound it is also related to the volume fraction which that compound occupies in a mixture of gases. This follows from Avogadro's hypothesis that equal volumes of different gases at the same temperature and pressure contain equal numbers of molecules. Thus in the above example we can say that since 1 molecule of fuel results in 52.1 molecules of products, then 19,200 parts by volume (molecules) of fuel produces 1,000,000 parts by volume (molecules) of products. If 10 per cent (1920 parts) of the fuel failed to burn, then the products would consist of 900,000 parts of burned products plus the 1920 parts of unburned fuel plus 93,802 parts of unreacted air or a total of 995,722 parts of products. Setting up the proportion

$$\frac{1920}{995,722} = \frac{x}{1,000,000} \tag{3.2}$$

x will be about 1930 parts of unburned fuel per million parts of exhaust.* A formal equation is:

$$\text{ppm by vol.} = \frac{1,000,000f}{M - f[1 + F - M]}$$

where M is the total number of molecules of product resulting from complete combustion of one molecule of fuel, $(1 + F)$ is the total number of reacting molecules (1 molecule of fuel plus air), and f is the fraction of incomplete combustion. This equation is strictly correct for a chemically correct mixture only.

Because f is normally small, and because most commercial fuels and operating air-fuel ratios lead to $(1 + F) \approx M$ with M about 50, one can adopt the following rule of thumb with little error:

0.1%	incomplete combustion		20 ppm	original fuel	
1 %	"	"	200 ppm	"	"
10 %	"	"	2000 ppm	"	"
100 %	"	"	20000 ppm	"	"

The last equality results because the total number of molecules of reactants is also about 50. In fact there is little change in total number of molecules going from reactants to products.

---

*The unburned fuel would be 13,510 ppm carbon since there were seven carbon atoms per molecule in this example.

When less air is available, some CO and H_2 are found in the products, whereas if excessive air is available some O_2 is found in the products. Figure 3.1 shows the products of combustion of an automotive-type engine for a C_8H_{17} fuel. Note that traces of O_2 are found as a product of rich mixtures and traces of CO and H_2 are found as products of lean mixtures. This results from uneven fuel distribution to each cylinder and mixture ratio variation from cycle to cycle within the same cylinder. Neither NO nor unburned hydrocarbons other than methane are reported in Figure 3.1 although they are normally found in the exhaust.

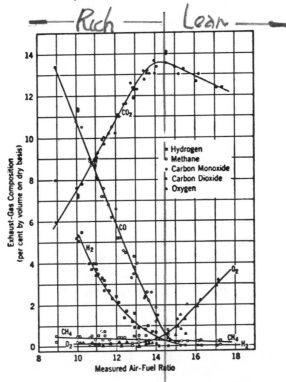

Figure 3.1. Exhaust gas composition versus measured air-fuel ratio, for unsupercharged automotive-type engines, Fuel C_8H_{17}. (Figure from Reference 1.)

Chemical Equilibrium

A more detailed examination of the combustion of the hydrocarbon fuel and air shows that several competing chemical reactions occur simultaneously and that the products of combustion vary depending on the pressure and temperature environment of these products. For example, in the cylinder of an engine running at wide open throttle (WOT), the combustion products exist at temperatures near 4000°F and pressures up to 1000 psi. This same mass of products is expanded to about 2000°F and 70 psi within the cylinder and further expanded to atmospheric pressure and cooled to 1200°F and lower in the exhaust system. Chemical species which exist in significant quantities immediately after combustion may cease to exist in measurable amounts in the exhaust system.

For a given amount of hydrocarbon fuel burned with a given amount of air, the products consist of a fixed mass of these four atoms: H, C, O, and N. If the products are given sufficient time to soak at the prevailing temperature and pressure, an equilibrium situation will be reached. Under such conditions and for the temperature and pressure ranges encountered in gasoline engine operation, ten chemical compounds can be detected. These are O_2, N_2, CO_2, H_2O, CO, H_2, OH, NO, O, and H. Between these ten compounds six independent chemical equations can be written. These are:

$$
\begin{cases}
CO + \tfrac{1}{2}O_2 & \rightleftharpoons & CO_2 & (3.3) \\
H_2 + \tfrac{1}{2}O_2 & \rightleftharpoons & H_2O & (3.4) \\
\tfrac{1}{2}N_2 + \tfrac{1}{2}O_2 & \rightleftharpoons & NO & (3.5) \\
\tfrac{1}{2}H_2 + \tfrac{1}{2}O_2 & \rightleftharpoons & OH & (3.6) \\
\tfrac{1}{2}H_2 & \rightleftharpoons & H & (3.7) \\
\tfrac{1}{2}O_2 & \rightleftharpoons & O & (3.8)
\end{cases}
$$

Four additional equations expressing the conservation of mass of the four basic atomic constituents C, H, O, and N provide the necessary additional equations to solve for the concentrations of the ten compounds.

Graphs A, B and C of Figure 3.2 show the solutions to the ten equations for a fixed collection of mass at various temperature levels and 800 psia. Each graph is for one equivalence ratio, F_r. The equivalence ratio is the ratio of the actual fuel-air ratio to that for a chemically correct mixture. For rich mixtures F_r is greater than one and for lean mixtures F_r is less than one.

Graph A of Figure 3.2 shows that for equilibrium conditions large concentrations of OH, NO, H, O, and even O_2 are present in the products of a fuel-rich mixture when the temperature is sufficiently high. Below 4000°R these constitutents are less than 0.03% by volume. (One per cent by volume equals 10,000 parts per million by volume.) For leaner mixtures the OH, NO, H, and

Rich   Stoichiometric   Lean

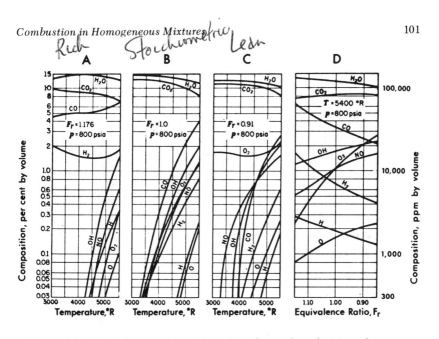

Figure 3.2. Equilibrium composition of products of combustion of octene-air mixtures (Data from Reference 3.)

O remain prevalent at lower temperatures but disappear by the time the temperature has reached that of the exhaust (as seen in Figure 3.1). Graph D of Figure 3.2 shows the effect of equivalence ratio on the ten species at a fixed temperature of 5400°R and pressure of 800 psia.

Because the above results assume that equilibrium is achieved and since this is often not the case, some constituents formed during the high temperature combustion process may persist in nonequilibrium amounts during expansion and exhaust. Such is the case with NO. When this occurs the equilibrium concentration is said to have been frozen at the higher temperature.

Molecular Aspects of Combustion

The preceeding sections describe a grossly simplified combustion process. In fact, the combustion of fuel with air involves enormous numbers of individual collisions between atoms and molecules. Although all the reactions in the combustion of complex hydrocarbons are not known, the simplified treatment presented below provides a basic understanding of the larger problem.

Let us assume that molecules a and b collide and react to form molecule c.

$$a + b \longrightarrow c$$

The rate of formation of c might be written

$$\frac{d(c)}{dt} = k\,(a)(b)$$

where the parenthesis denotes "concentration of " in molecules/in^3 and k is the specific reaction rate constant. The above equation has assumed that the rate of formation of c is proportional to the concentrations of a and b each to the first power. The sum of exponents of a and b (which in this case is 2) is termed the order of the reaction — second order in this case.

The equation for the formation of c from a and b is thus termed second order and bimolecular; k depends on the number of collisions and their relative velocity. It can be estimated from probability theory. The equation for k is of the form

$$k = Z e^{-E_a/\bar{R}T}$$

where Z, the number of collisions/in^3/sec, is proportional to a power of absolute temperature and $e^{-E_a/RT}$ is the fraction of the Z collisions which have a relative kinetic energy sufficient to cause a successful chemical reaction. E_a is termed the activation energy of the reaction, R is the universal gas constant and T is the absolute temperature of the reaction. The collision number, Z, is large, of the order of 10^{14} collisions/in^3 • sec. E_a is of the order of 60,000 cal/gram-mole for many hydrocarbon fuels. From the equation for k, we see that when T is very high the exponent approaches zero and the resulting reaction rate is very high. On the other hand when the activation energy for the fuel is high the number of successful reactions decreases.

In complex combustion processes there are many competing reactions of the form

$$a + b \longrightarrow c$$

and other forms as well. How quickly equilibrium is established depends on how fast the molecular interactions occur. Certain atoms and molecules are very effective in promoting reactions. They are termed chain carriers and include the species O, H, OH, and CHO. Reactions which create chain carriers are termed chain branching whereas reactions in which the carriers are consumed are termed chain breaking or quenching reactions. A reaction which involves chain carriers but neither increases nor decreases the chain carrier population is termed a chain propagation reaction.

Consider the reactions between hydrogen and oxygen. If we

have H_2 and O_2 in a container at an elevated temperature, the following thermal dissociation reactions occur:

$$H_2 \rightleftharpoons 2H \qquad (3.9)$$

$$O_2 \rightleftharpoons 2O \qquad (3.10)$$

The chain carriers thus formed may then react as follows:

$$OH + H_2 \longrightarrow H_2O + H \qquad k_1 \text{ chain propagating} \qquad (3.11)$$

$$H + O_2 \longrightarrow OH + O \qquad k_2 \text{ chain branching} \qquad (3.12)$$

$$O + H_2 \longrightarrow OH + H \qquad k_3 \text{ chain branching} \qquad (3.13)$$

$$OH + H + M \rightarrow H_2O + M \qquad k_4 \text{ chain breaking} \qquad (3.14)$$

The arrow shows the predominate direction of the reactions. Other reactions may occur also. The rate of formation of hydrogen atoms can be written:

$$\frac{d(H)}{dt} =$$
$$k_1 (OH)(H_2) - k_2(H)(O_2) + k_3(O)(H_2) - k_4(OH)(H)(M) \qquad (3.15)$$

Similar equations can be written for O and OH. The compound M in the chain breaking Equation 3.14 may be an element of wall area, combustion chamber deposit, particulate matter in the combustion gas or a large gaseous molecule. Its function is to soak up the excess energy in the collision of the H and OH so that the H_2O molecule does not fly apart. The chain breaking or quenching role of a wall is a major factor causing the hydrocarbon emissions of gasoline engines. With chain carriers destroyed near the wall, the reactions slow down and stop close to the surface of the combustion chamber leaving a layer of partially reacted or unreacted hydrocarbons.

For the reaction between a complex fuel molecule such as propane and air,

```
      H   H   H
      |   |   |
  H - C - C - C - H        Propane molecule
      |   |   |
      H   H   H
```

Lewis and Von Elbe[2] suggest the following reactions:

$$CH_3CH_2CH_3 + O_2 \longrightarrow CH_3CH(OO)CH_3 + H$$
$$\longrightarrow CH_3CHO + CH_3O + H$$
$$CH_3O + C_3H_8 \longrightarrow CH_3OH + C_3H_7$$
$$CH_3O + O_2 \longrightarrow CO + H_2O + OH$$
$$CH_3CHO + O_2 \longrightarrow CH_2O + CHO + OH$$
$$CHO + O_2 \longrightarrow CO + HO_2$$
$$CH_2O + O_2 \longrightarrow CO_2 + H_2O$$
$$HO_2 + C_3H_8 \longrightarrow H_2O_2 + C_3H_7$$
$$H_2O_2 \longrightarrow H_2O + O$$

Additional reactions occur which eventually lead to an equilibrium distribution of products such as indicated in Figure 3.2. If the reactions are interrupted as they are when the flame approaches the combustion chamber wall, many of the above intermediate species will be found in the exhaust.

Flame Propagation

Mixtures of fuel and air that lie within certain limits (flammability limits) will support combustion. The speed at which a flame proceeds through a combustible mixture is termed the flame velocity. For a particular mixture this depends upon the equivalence ratio of the mixture, the mixture temperature and pressure, and the extent of dilution by inert gases. Normally the flame propagates fastest when the mixture ratio is about 10% richer than chemically correct. Data in Figure 3.3 for a propane-air mixture typify hydrocarbon fuels. These data were measured in a bunsen burner-type experiment under laminar flow conditions. In engines where turbulence is high, the effective flame velocity may be several times higher. Figure 3.4 shows the effect of turbulence (Reynolds number greater than 3000) on flame propagation through a premixed mixture in a pipe at constant pressure. The ratio of turbulent to laminar velocity is plotted on the abscissa. It is not unusual for the turbulent flame velocity in gasoline engines to exceed four times the rate predicted from laminar experiments.

Flame Propagation in Engines

Flame propagation in an engine combustion chamber is similar to the constant pressure combustion discussed in the preceeding section but is more complex because it occurs in a confined re-

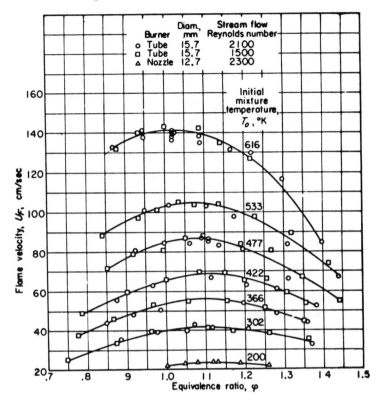

Figure 3.3. Flame velocity as function of equivalence ratio at various initial mixture temperatures for propane-air flames at 1 atmosphere, measured by outer-shadow-edge total-area burner method. (Figure from Reference 5.)

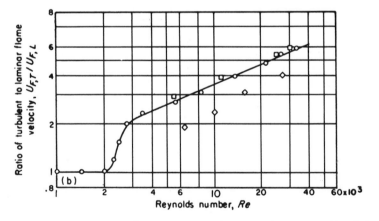

Figure 3.4. Town-gas-air flames. Constant density and viscosity. (Symbols indicate points of constant fuel-air ratio unspecified by reference.) (Figure from Reference 5.)

gion. Figure 3.5 shows flame propagation in a highly simplified rectangular combustion chamber. Piston motion is ignored. The spark plug is assumed to be located at the left end of the chamber and the flame front is presumed to proceed as a plane wave perpendicular to the long axis of the chamber. Let us assume that the gas in the chamber is divided by imaginary boundaries into four equal mass elements labeled 1 through 4 in Figure 3.5. The heavy dot represents an element of gas.

First assume that all the gas in the first region (element 1) is inflamed at constant volume. The pressure in element 1 is now much higher than that in elements 2, 3, and 4. Next let element 1 expand and thereby compress 2, 3, and 4 until pressure equilibrium is achieved (center figure). Next assume that all the gas in the second region is inflamed at constant volume. Its pressure then exceeds that in elements 1, 3 and 4. If pressure equilibrium is now allowed, element 2 expands and compresses elements 1, 3 and 4 further. The progressive combustion process continues until all the boxes are inflamed. At the end of the combustion process the chamber looks about the same as in the left hand figure, that is the imaginery boundaries are nearly uniformly spaced. As the number of divisions assumed increases, the real combustion process is approached.

The following conclusions can be reached about progressive burning:

(a) Each element of gas is ignited at a different pressure and temperature. Before passage of the flame those furthest from the spark are compressed the most.

(b) Each burned element is further compressed by the combustion of the later burning elements. The first element to burn, that at the spark, is compressed the most after combustion. This creates a temperature stratification within the combustion chamber with the hottest gas near the spark plug.

(c) A small element of gas first travels away from the spark, then

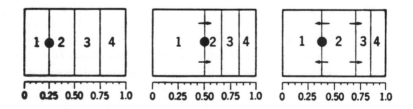

Figure 3.5.   Progressive combustion in S.I. engines.

backward toward the spark, and nearly resumes its initial position.

(d) Each element of combustion chamber surface area is swept by the flame under different conditions of gas pressure and temperature.

(e) The apparent progress of the flame through the mixture is strongly influenced by the expansion of the burned gas behind the flame front. Figure 3.6 shows this effect. For example, when 10% of the mass is burned, the flame occupies nearly 30% of the combustion chamber volume.

The relationship between volume inflamed and mass burned in engine combustion chambers is shown in Figure 3.6. The curve was calculated from flame photographs of engine combustion by subtracting the piston motion effect on volume. It is important to recognize that what the eye sees in viewing engine combustion is largely the expansion phenomena not the basic chemical reaction propagation rate.

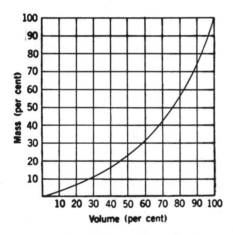

Figure 3.6. Relation between mass and volume of burned charge. (Figure from Reference 6.)

Figure 3.7 shows calculated combustion chamber gas temperature distribution as a function of the mass fraction burned measured from the spark plug. Constant volume combustion was assumed. The lower curve shows the temperature of the unburned gas ahead of the flame front. The center curve is the temperature of the gas behind the flame front, just after combustion. The upper curve is the temperature at the end of combustion. The instantaneous temperature distribution throughout the charge at various times during the combustion process is shown by the dotted lines. This calculation shows that theoretically an 800°F gradient in temperature existed in the combustion chamber after

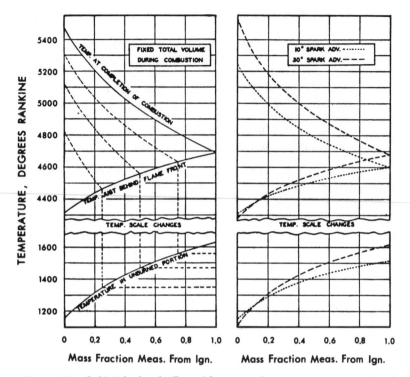

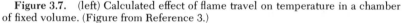

Figure 3.7. (left) Calculated effect of flame travel on temperature in a chamber of fixed volume. (Figure from Reference 3.)

Figure 3.8. (right) Calculated effect of flame travel on temperature in a chamber of variable volume. Calculations were made for 30° and 10° spark advance, assuming flame travel occupied 40° of crank revolution. (Figure from Reference 3.)

combustion was completed. The spark plug is the hottest region of the chamber. Because of heat transfer and diffusion the actual gradient is considerably smaller, about 400°F for operating conditions equivalent to Figure 3.7. The fact that preignition usually occurs in the spark plug region is explained by the high gas temperature there that results from progressive burning. Figure 3.8 shows the additional calculated effect of piston motion on combustion temperatures for two spark timings assuming combustion occupied 40 crank angle degrees. The retarded timing of 10° reduces both unburned and burned gas temperature.

The effect of spark retard on pressure is similar to that on the temperature. Retarding the spark is an effective way of reducing gas temperature and pressure, thereby reducing knock or preignition tendency. Figure 3.9 shows the calculated absolute pressure versus mass fraction burned.

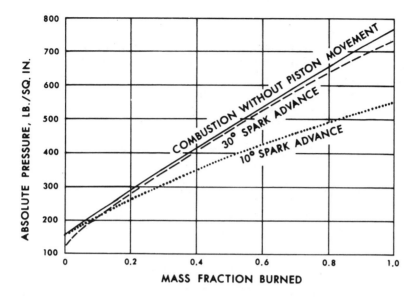

Figure 3.9. Change of pressure with progress of combustion for three conditions of firing. (Figure from Reference 3.)

Effect of Design Variables

The pressure development in an engine combustion chamber is the result of both piston motion and combustion. Using engine pressure-time records, Withrow and Rassweiler[11] calculated the pressure rise caused by combustion only by subtracting the piston motion contribution to total pressure rise. They then plotted the per cent pressure rise caused by combustion and the per cent mass burned as a function of crank angle. Their result is shown in Figure 3.10. Ideally the combustion process should be centered about top dead center to optimize the efficiency of the engine. Typically the combustion process including ignition delay occupies about 50 crank angle degrees. In general the relationship between pressure development and crank angle depends upon the shape of the combustion chamber, the location of the spark plug within the combustion chamber volume, and the ignition timing.

Figure 3.11 shows two different combustion chamber shapes which were tested on the same engine. The measured pressure-crank angle relationships are shown also. Each test was run with best power spark timing for that particular combustion chamber. Figure 3.12 shows that the compact chamber, design B, burned the charge faster. Combustion is initiated later for optimum efficiency, and is completed sooner in this chamber. The peak pressure is higher.

Figures 3.13 and 3.14 show similar data for two additional different combustion chambers. Again identical tests were run on a single engine using each chamber. The differences between the combustion characteristics of each chamber can be understood better by a plot of flame front area versus flame travel. Such a plot,

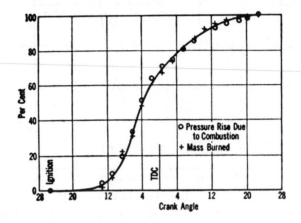

Figure 3.10. Relationship between pressure rise of combustion and mass burned at constant volume. (Figure from Reference 11.)

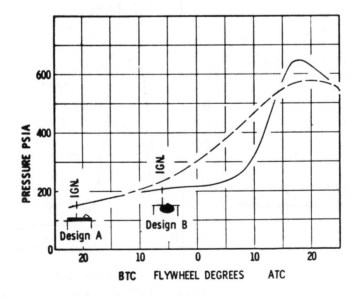

Figure 3.11. Effect of chamber design upon the combustion portion of the pressure time trace. 1000 rpm, 9:1 compression ratio. (Figure from Reference 8.)

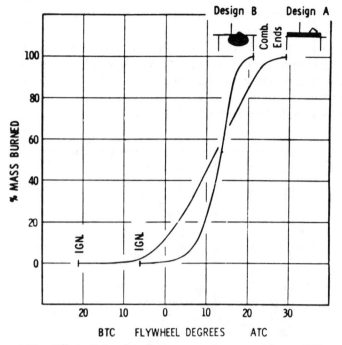

Figure 3.12. Effect of chamber design upon the rate of burn. 1000 rpm, 9:1 compression ratio. (Figure from Reference 8.)

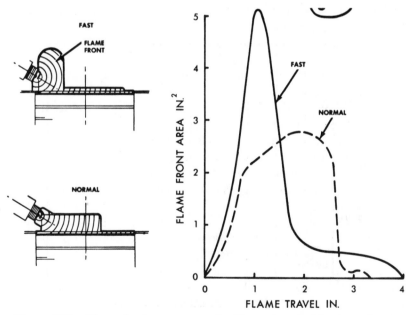

Figure 3.13. Flame front area curves for fast and normal-burn combustion chambers. The maximum flame front area will predict the pressure rate. (Figure from Reference 9.)

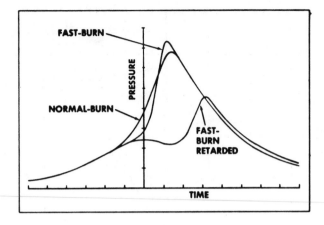

Figure 3.14. Pressure-time cards of fast and normal-burn combustion. Fast-burn with retarded spark timing is also shown. (Figure from Reference 9.)

shown in Figure 3.13, assumes that the flame spreads spherically from the spark plug, and the spherical flame front is truncated by the combustion chamber walls. Note that the fast burn chamber has nearly twice the maximum flame front area for combustion reactions to occur. From the previous discussion of the relationship between mass fraction burned and pressure, it should be anticipated that in a chamber which has twice the maximum flame front area the rate of pressure rise should be double also, if all other variables are held constant. This conclusion has been verified experimentally by Andon.[9,10]

Combustion chamber shape relative to the spark plug is an important variable that design engineers use to control the progress of combustion and the rate of pressure development. It is good practice to limit the maximum rate of pressure rise (which occurs near best torque) to 30–35 psi/deg in order to avoid an engine noise problem termed 'roughness.'

Combustion rate can be used to control the octane requirement of the engine. Fast burning chambers have a relatively low octane requirement since the time available for knock reactions is short. Figure 3.15 shows octane requirements for the chambers of Figure 3.11 and 3.12 with and without combustion chamber deposits. The fast burn chamber with a 0.040″ quench thickness had an octane requirement ten numbers lower than the slow burn chamber. Note that a 0.040″ quench thickness was much more effective than a 0.100″ quench thickness in suppressing combustion reactions. Crevices of unburned mixture in the combustion chamber can be a major source of hydrocarbon exhaust emissions.

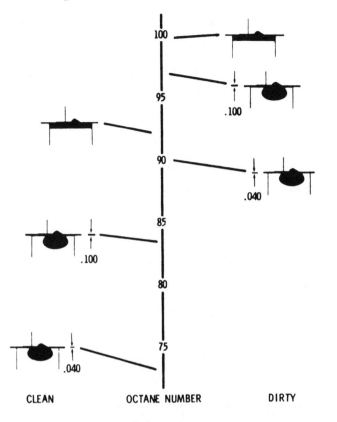

Figure 3.15. Effect of combustion chamber deposits upon 99% power octane requirements. 9:1 compression ratio. (Figure from Reference 8.)

Effect of Operating Variables

Figure 3.16 shows the effect of engine speed on the duration of combustion. The spark timing was adjusted for each test so that 10% of the flame travel would occur at TDC. In going from 500 to 1000 rpm the combustion duration changed from 57 crank degrees to 67 degrees. Thus, the number of crank angle degrees occupied by the combustion process did not change significantly, especially if the ignition delay is disregarded. Thus, doubling the engine speed nearly doubled the flame propagation rate. This is a basic characteristic of gasoline engine combustion. Increasing speed increases mixture swirl and turbulence which increases the combustion rate. This proportionality between engine speed and combustion rate in gasoline engines makes high speed engine operation possible.

Figure 3.17 shows similar data for the effect of air-fuel ratio

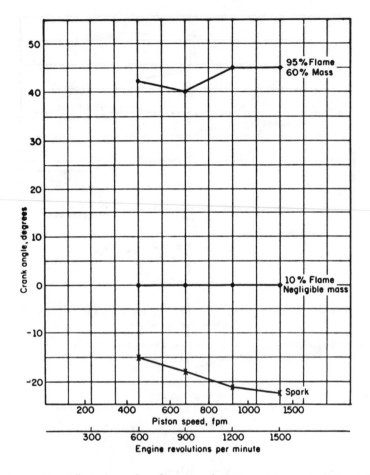

Figure 3.16.   Effect of speed on flame travel; CFR engine, $p_i = 14.0$, $T_i = 510°R$, point of 10% travel taken as zero. (Figure from Reference 7.)

on flame propagation. Maximum combustion rate occurred at 10–20% richer than stoichiometric ($F_r = 1.1–1.2$). This result is in good agreement with the steady burner results of Figure 3.3. Leaner operation than $F_r = 0.7$ or richer than $F_r = 1.5$ resulted in misfire.

The other major operating variable which affects flame propagation rate is the dilution of the charge by residual exhaust gas. High dilution from light load operation or dilution resulting from high back pressure will decrease flame speed. Table 3.1 shows this effect.

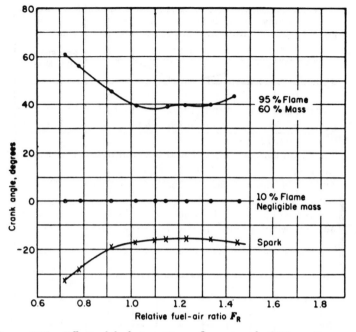

Figure 3.17. Effect of fuel-air ratio on flame travel; CFR engine, $p_i = 14.0$, $T_i = 510°R$, point of 10% travel taken as zero. (Figure from Reference 7.)

Table 3.1

Effect of Exhaust Dilution of Flame Speed

$\dfrac{P_{exhaust}}{P_{intake}}$	Crank Angle for Flame Travel		
	10–95%	10–50%	50–95%
0.6	37	19	18
2.0	48	27	21
% change	30%	42%	17%

Data from Reference 7.

REFERENCES

1. Obert, E. F. *Internal Combustion Engines Analyses* and *Practice,* 2nd ed. (Scranton, Pa.: International Textbook Co., 1950), p. 316.
2. Lewis B., and von Elbe, G. *Combustion, Flames and Explosions of Gases* (New York: Academic Press, 1961) Chapter IV.
3. Hottel, H. C., and Eberhardt, J. E. "A Mollier Diagram for the Internal Combustion Engine," *2nd symposium on Combustion,* 1937, reprint (Pittsburgh, Pa.: The Combustion Institute, 1965) p. 235.

4. Friedman, R., and Johnson, W.   "The Wall Quenching of Laminar Propane Flames as a Function of Pressure, Temperature, and Air-Fuel Ratio," J. Appl. Phy. **21** (8), 791 (1950).

5. "Basic Considerations in the Combustion of Hydrocarbon Fuels With Air," NASA Report **1300** (1959) p 135.

6. Obert, E. F.   *op. cit.*, p 451.

7. Taylor, C. F., and Taylor, E. S.   *The Internal Combustion Engine*, 2nd ed. (Scranton, Pa.: International Textbook Co., 1962) p. 95–97.

8. Caris, D. F., et. al.   "Mechanical Octanes for Higher Efficiency," SAE Trans. **64,** 76 (1956).

9. Andon, J., and Marks, C.   "Engine Roughness – The Key to Lower Octane Requirement," SAE Trans. **72,** 636 (1964).

10. Andon, J.   "Fundamentals of Combustion Chamber Design," Auto. Ind. (May, 1963).

11. Rassweiler, G. M., and L. Withrow.   "Motion Pictures of Engine Flames Correlated with Pressure Cards," SAE Trans. **42(5)** 185 (1938).

4

EMISSION FORMATION IN HOMOGENEOUS MIXTURES AND GASOLINE ENGINES

Part I   Unburned Hydrocarbons

Hydrocarbon exhaust emissions may arise from three sources — wall quenching, incomplete combustion of the charge, and exhaust scavenging as in a two-cycle engine. In an automotive-type four-cycle engine, wall quenching is the predominate source of exhaust hydrocarbons under most operating conditions.

WALL QUENCHING

Wall quenching is a combustion phenomena which arises when a flame tries to propagate in the vicinity of a wall. Normally the effect of the wall is a slowing down or stopping of the reaction. In general, wall quenching results both from the chain breaking reactions discussed in Chapter 3 and from the cooling of the layer of charge adjacent to the wall by the cool wall. As a result the flame will not propagate completely to the wall surface.

The wall quenching phenomena was first observed when it was noted that a flame was incapable of propagating through a premixed mixture confined between two plates or within a tube if the plate spacing or tube diameter was too small. Friedman and Johnson[1] measured the critical slit width which prevented the flame from propagating into the enclosed space, as shown in Figure 4.1. Figures 4.2 and 4.3 show data obtained by Friedman and Johnson[1] on the effect of mixture temperature, pressure, and propane-air equivalence ratio on the minimum slit width through which a flame will propagate. The effect of temperature is more clearly shown in Figure 4.4. For rich and stoichiometric mixtures at atmospheric pressure their results showed:

$$d_{slit} \alpha T^{-0.5} \tag{4.1}$$

For lean mixtures the exponent increases. The effect of pressure is

117

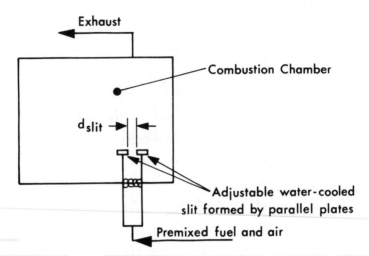

Figure 4.1. A method of measuring critical slit widths. (Figure from Reference 1.)

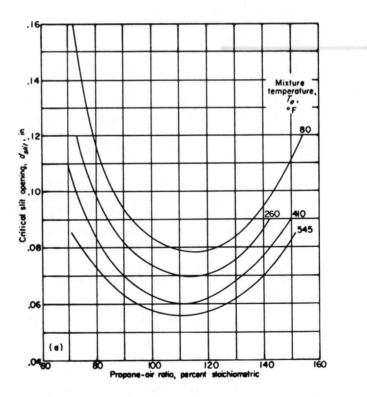

Figure 4.2. Effect of equivalence ratio on quenching distance of propane air flame at P = 29.02 in Hg. (Figure from Reference 1.)

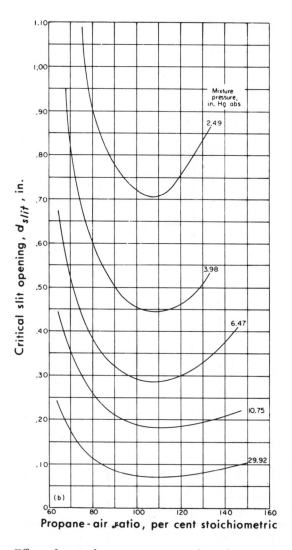

Figure 4.3. Effect of equivalence ratio on quenching distance of propane air flame at T = 75°F. (Figure from Reference 1.)

more clearly shown in Figure 4.5. The pressure dependence is approximately

$$d_{slit} \propto P^{-0.9} \tag{4.2}$$

To summarize, 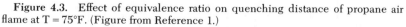 this data suggests that quench distance is almost inversely proportional to combustion chamber pressure and to the square root of the absolute temperature.

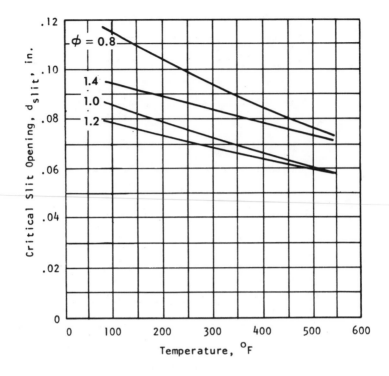

Figure 4.4.   Effect of temperature on quenching distance. (Data from Reference 1.)

Daniel[2] was the first to study wall quenching in an engine. He took photographs of the combustion process through a quartz L-head CFR engine. The pictures showed that as the flame passed through the chamber a dark region of unreacted mixture was left adjacent to the wall. The thickness of this region varied from 0.002 to 0.015 inches depending on engine operating conditions. One of Daniel's photographs is shown in Figure 4.6. The quench distances measured by Daniel (0.002 – 0.015″) were smaller than these found by Freidman and Johnson (0.06 – 0.14″). Differences in pressure between the two experiments explain the variance. Moreover, Friedman and Johnson measured a double wall quench distance whereas Daniel's data were for a single wall. Daniel then calculated the approximate hydrocarbon emissions for his engine based on the quench distance that he observed. The result was in good agreement with measured engine emission data. As a result of this work, there is little doubt that wall quenching is a principal source of exhaust hydrocarbon emission.

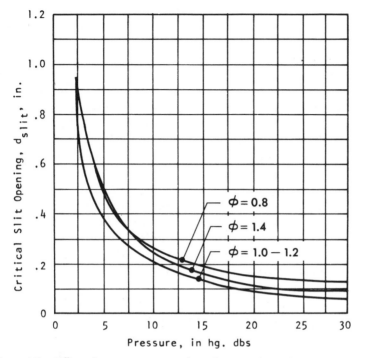

Figure 4.5.   Effect of pressure on quenching distance. (Data from Reference 1.)

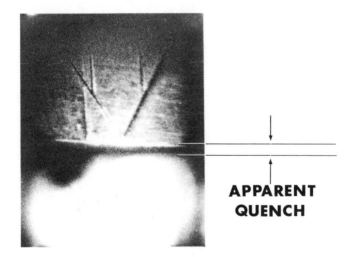

Figure 4.6.   The photo shows "thin layer" of unreacted hydrocarbons where flame front encounters quenching action near combustion chamber wall. The layer thickness ranges from two- to ten-thousandths of an inch. (Figure from Reference 3.)

As discussed earlier, many hydrocarbon types are likely to be found in the region near the wall. Gad El-Mawla,[4] using a steady porous burner technique, measured the concentration of quenched hydrocarbons at various distances from the surface of the porous plate. Figure 4.7 shows an example of his findings for a propane-air flame. The principal unburned hydrocarbon compounds are shown. The quench distance as measured by concentration is about 0.04 inches, whereas the visible dark region was about 0.005 inches. The actual flame thickness is 0.04 inches, beyond which hydrocarbons disappear and combustion is complete. The true quench distance is apparently much greater than the visible distance measured by Daniel. However, note the large concentration of unburned pure propane left adjacent to the wall. Referring to Figure 4.7, the propane concentration is 10^5 higher than the concentration of the other hydrocarbons. Thus in terms of mass, it is reasonable to say that most of the unburned hydrocarbons are in the dark region between the luminous zone and the wall.

The propagation of a flame toward a wall and the subsequent quenching may be viewed in the highly simplified manner shown

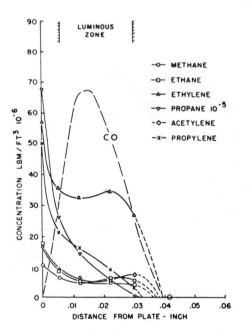

Figure 4.7. Typical hydrocarbon concentration profiles. (Figure from Reference 4.)

in Figure 4.8. Curve 1 shows the temperature profile through the flame front as it propagates toward but is still far from the wall. Unburned mixture, initially at T_u, is heated in the preheat zone primarily by conduction from the burned gases behind the flame front. Diffusion of active centers (O, H, OH, etc.) into the preheat zone also occurs. At some temperature, T_i, appreciable reaction begins with the result that the internal heat generation at this point exceeds the heat losses by conduction and radiation and the reaction becomes self-sustaining. Continued reaction occurs until all the mixture is consumed. The temperature of the products rises to T_b, the burned gas temperature. The distance λ is termed the flame front thickness.

Curve 2 shows the flame closer to the wall. The leading edge of the preheat zone is just touching the wall surface. For simplicity the wall temperature has been assumed constant and equal to the unburned mixture temperature.

Curve 3 shows the temperature profile at a still later time. The heat transfer to the wall from the gas coupled with the chain breaking reactions at the wall do not permit the gas temperature or concentration of active centers near the wall surface to increase to a sufficiently high level (such as T_i) where appreciable reaction

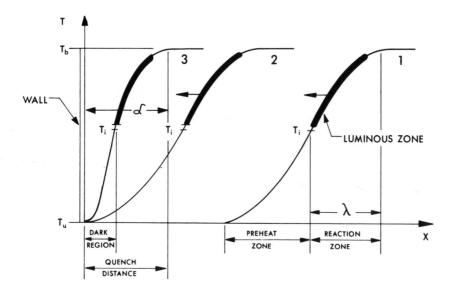

Figure 4.8. A flame propagating toward a wall. The arrow indicates direction of propagation. T_b – burned mixture temperature, T_u = unburned mixture temperature, T_1 = ignition temperature.

can occur. Thus for gas closer to the wall than T$_i$, virtually no reaction can occur. This distance is probably 0.005 inches in Figure 4.7, and it contains the bulk of the unburned hydrocarbons. Further away, increasing degrees of reaction do occur. Further yet the wall effect is not a significant factor. This is the outer limit of the quench region which is about 0.04 inches in Figure 4.7.

The quench distance is influenced by several variables other than mixture temperature, pressure, and equivalence ratio. Wall surface material including combustion deposits has an effect. (In an engine, combustion deposits on the wall may act as a sponge to soak up raw fuel during the intake and compression strokes. This fuel may be vaporized and expanded into the exhaust during the later part of the expansion stroke and the exhaust process. This phenomenon is distinct from wall quenching.) Wall temperature affects quench distance also. Figure 4.9 shows that the quench distance at the stoichiometric fuel-air mixture was 50% greater

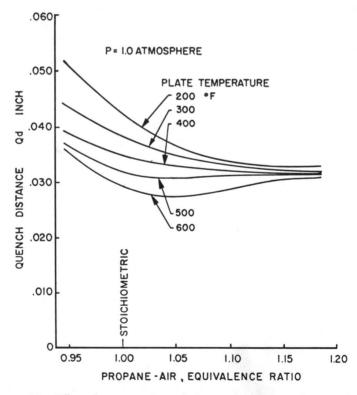

Figure 4.9. Effect of mixture ratio and plate temperature on the quench distance at a chamber pressure of 1.0 atm. (Figure from Reference 4.)

when the wall temperature was 200°F than when it was 600°F. If one assumes that the density of the unburned boundary layer depends primarily upon wall surface temperature, then in terms of mass of hydrocarbons an increase in wall temperature has a twofold advantage in reducing hydrocarbon emissions.

Moreover the quenching phenomenon precludes flame propagation into small crevices. One would not expect the mixture to burn within regions such as the space between the top piston ring and piston top, the region around the spark plug ceramic, or a crevice left by an imperfectly fitted head gasket. Mixtures in crevices narrower than 0.040 to 0.050 inches probably do not burn at all.

The above evidence plus that of other research has demonstrated that wall quenching is the principal source of unburned hydrocarbons in the exhaust of spark ignition engines under most normal operating conditions. Of course, if the mixture ratio becomes excessively rich or lean or if exhaust dilution becomes high, then incomplete flame propagation or even complete misfire may result and hydrocarbon emission becomes extremely high.

INCOMPLETE COMBUSTION

Under engine operating conditions where mixtures are extremely rich or lean, or where exhaust gas dilution is excessive, incomplete flame propagation may occur in some cycles. Occasionally, a complete misfire may occur. Normally, the carburetor does provide a mixture in the burnable range. Thus incomplete flame propagation usually results from high exhaust gas dilution arising from high vacuum operation such as idle or deceleration. However, during transient engine operation, especially warm-up and deceleration, it is possible that mixtures which are too rich or too lean to burn completely find their way to the cylinder. When incomplete flame propagation occurs, the hydrocarbon emissions from that cycle are very high.

Factors which promote incomplete flame propagation and misfire include:

(a) poor condition of the ignition system, including spark plugs
(b) low charge temperature
(c) poor charge homogeneity
(d) too rich or too lean gaseous air-fuel ratio in the cylinder at ignition and after
(e) large exhaust residual quantity

(f) lack of combustibles in residual as determined by previous cycle

(g) poor distribution of residual within cylinder.

Carburetion and mixture preparation, evaporation and mixing in the intake manifold, atomization at the intake valve and swirl and turbulence in the combustion chamber are some factors which influence the gaseous mixture ratio and degree of charge homogeneity including residual mixing. The engine and intake system temperature resulting from prior operation of the engine affect charge temperature and can also affect fuel distribution. Valve overlap, engine speed, spark timing, compression ratio, intake and exhaust system pulsations affect the amount, composition and distribution of the exhaust residual. Fuel volatility is a critical factor.

The effect of air-fuel ratio and exhaust residual on incomplete combustion and hydrocarbon emission was studied by Wentworth and Daniel.[5] They used flame photographs to measure the degree of incomplete flame propagation. While their results apply strictly to the CFR engine used in the study, they are applicable to all gasoline engines. In their work an effort was made to obtain good fuel-air preparation in order to minimize the effect of this variable on the test results.

Plotted in Figure 4.10 are the regions of complete flame propagation, partial flame propagation and the misfire limit as a function of air-fuel ratio and intake manifold vacuum. At a vacuum of 18

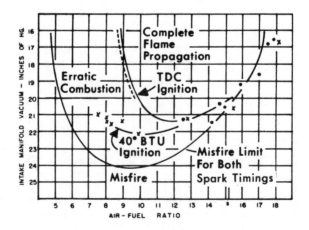

Figure 4.10. Regions of misfire and complete and incomplete flame propagation at various air-fuel ratios and manifold vacuums. Engine conditions at which residual fractions were determined: speed, 500 rpm; fuel, isooctane; compression ratio, 6.7; spark timing, tdc and 40 btc. (Data from Reference 5.)

inches (idle), the flame photographs showed that complete burning occurred from rich mixtures of 9:1, to lean mixtures near 17:1 with TDC ignition. The dashed curve indicates that a flame was visible in the exhaust for these rich mixtures. For mixtures richer than 9:1, erratic incomplete burning was observed. The richer the mixtures, the more incomplete the combustion. Finally, near 5:1, misfire occurred. Misfire was defined as one complete misfire every 50 cycles. Advancing the spark to 40° BTC helped to broaden the complete combustion region on the rich side. For lean mixtures the onset of incomplete flame propagation was coincidental with that of misfire. At higher vacuums (higher exhaust residual dilution) the combustible region is decreased. With TDC ignition, 21.5 inches of vacuum was the limit for complete flame propagation whereas 22 inches was the limit with 40° BTC ignition. For vacuums higher than 24 inches, misfire always occurred.

Figure 4.11 shows the unburned hydrocarbons (per cent of the incoming fuel) as a function of manifold vacuum for an air-fuel ratio of about 11:1. From 16 to 21 inches a slight increase is noted. Over 21 inches, a marked increase in hydrocarbon emission occurred as a result of incomplete combustion caused by the increased charge dilution.

Figure 4.12 shows the effect of air-fuel ratio on unburned hydrocarbons at vacuums of about 16 and 20 inches of mercury. Leaner than 16 or 17 to 1 and richer than 9.5 or 9 to 1, a sharp increase in hydrocarbon emissions occurred due to misfiring. At a mixture

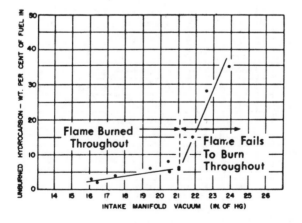

Figure 4.11. Weight per cent hydrocarbons in exhaust gas as a function of manifold vacuum. Engine conditions: speed, 500 rpm; fuel, isooctane; mixture ratio, 11:1; compression ratio, 6.7; spark timing, tdc. (Figure from Reference 5.)

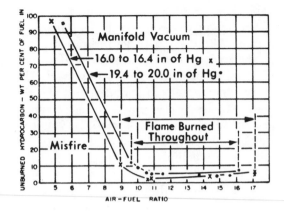

Figure 4.12. Weight per cent hydrocarbons as function of air-fuel ratio. Engine conditions: speed, 500 rpm; fuel, isooctane; compression ratio, 6.7; spark timing tdc. (Figure from Reference 5.)

ratio near 5:1, virtually all the fuel went through the engine unburned.

The effect of exhaust gas dilution per se is shown in Figure 4.13. Regions of complete and incomplete flame propagation are shown as functions of air-fuel ratio and residual weight fraction. The residual was varied by changing the intake manifold pressure. It was measured using a sampling valve in the exhaust valve corner of the chamber, the place where incomplete combustion usually occurred in the engine. When the exhaust residual exceeded 34% of the charge weight, complete flame propagation did not occur. Also shown in Figure 4.13 are the limits of inflammability measured at low pressures in a steady tube burner using gasoline air mixtures.

The engine operating point at which residual becomes too high for combustion depends upon compression ratio, valve overlap, engine speed, and exhaust back pressure. In general, it will be different for each engine. High vacuum (up to 26″ Hg) and exhaust gas dilution during deceleration is more of a problem in manual transmission vehicles because the vehicle can motor the engine at high speeds during decelerations. Devices which either crack the throttle (vacuum limiters) or shut off the fuel during deceleration are effective in reducing those hydrocarbon emissions resulting from this excessive dilution of the charge.

SCAVENGING

In two-cycle gasoline engines a third source of hydrocarbon emission results from scavenging the cylinder with a fuel-air mix-

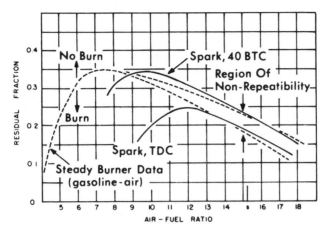

Figure 4.13. Comparison of exhaust-gas dilution in exhaust-valve corner with limiting exhaust-gas dilution in tube. Engine conditions: speed, 500 rpm; fuel, isooctane; compression ratio, 6.7 (Figure from Reference 5.)

ture, part of which blows through the cylinder directly into the exhaust and escapes the combustion process completely. Hydrocarbon emissions from this type of engine may be several times larger than those from naturally aspirated four-stroke engines. Supercharged four-stroke gasoline engines may have some hydrocarbon emission from this source also.

Concluding Remarks

Wall quenching is the principal source of unburned hydrocarbons in the exhaust of four-stroke gasoline engines under most normal operating conditions. Because each element of wall is intercepted by the flame at a different pressure and temperature as the combustion process sweeps across the chamber, in general we would expect the mass of unburned hydrocarbons to be different in amount and composition at each point of the combustion chamber. Moreover, depending on whether an element of wall area is intercepted early in the cycle, right after ignition, or late in the cycle, the quenched gases have a greater or lesser time to diffuse into the bulk of hot products of combustion and undergo some degree of after-reaction there. During the exhaust blowdown process and exhaust stroke, the amount of unburned hydrocarbons leaving the chamber depends upon the location of the exhaust valve.

The emission of unburned hydrocarbons from the cylinder is strongly related to the manner in which the exhaust gas exits.

Figure 4.14 shows the mass flow rate versus crank angle for a particular engine run at virtually wide open throttle. Nearly 50 per cent of the mass leaves the cylinder during the initial 20 per cent of the exhaust process. (The proportion leaving the cylinder during blowdown will be smaller for part load operation.) As a result the initial mass of exhaust will be relatively low in unburned hydrocarbons because it consists mainly of products of combustion from the center of the chamber. As the movement of the piston completes the exhaust process, the gases near the wall which are rich in unburned hydrocarbons finally leave. Daniel[6] has measured the concentration of hydrocarbons in the exhaust port of a CFR engine as a function of crank angle by means of a sampling valve. His result is shown in Figure 4.15. Immediately after the exhaust valve opened, the concentration in the port dropped to about 100 ppm. This occurs because the gas in the center of the chamber is exhausted first and has a relatively low unburned hydrocarbon concentration. Near the end of the stroke, as the layer of gas rich in hydrocarbons is swept into the exhaust, the concentration increased to 1200 ppm. Just before the valve closed

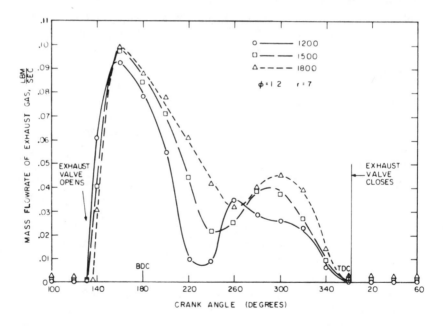

Figure 4.14. Mass flowrate of exhaust gas versus crank angle for an equivalence ratio of $\phi = 1.2$ and engine speeds 1200, 1500, and 1800 rpm. (Figure from Reference 7.)

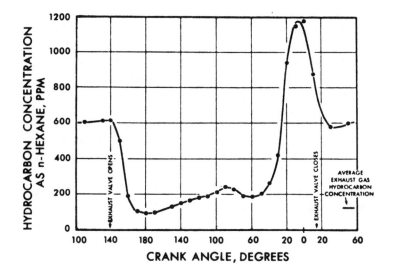

Figure 4.15. Variation in hydrocarbon concentration with crank angle measured 2 in. downstream of exhaust valve. (Figure from Reference 6.)

the concentration in the port dropped and remained about 600 ppm throughout the rest of the cycle during which the gas was stagnant. The drop from 1200 to 600 ppm just before exhaust valve closing was thought to be a result of back flow into the cylinder which diluted the gas in the port with low HC concentration exhaust.

In this experiment, the average unburned hydrocarbon concentration measured in a mixing tank downstream was 130 ppm, only slightly higher than the minimum value attained at blowdown. Again this demonstrates that most of the mass leaves the chamber during blowdown. These concentration variations were verified by Tabaczynski.[7] Tabaczynski calculated the hydrocarbon mass flow rate from his exhaust mass flow rate and concentration data. His result is shown in Figure 4.16. The first peak reflects high mass flow at low concentration. The second peak reflects lower mass flow at higher hydrocarbon concentration.

In an extension of his own work, Daniel[6] determined that at WOT, 34 per cent of the unburned hydrocarbons remained in the cylinder to be burned in the next cycle. The per cent recycle may be even higher at lighter loads. Consequently, recycle is also an important factor affecting how much of the fuel that escapes combustion actually gets into the exhaust.

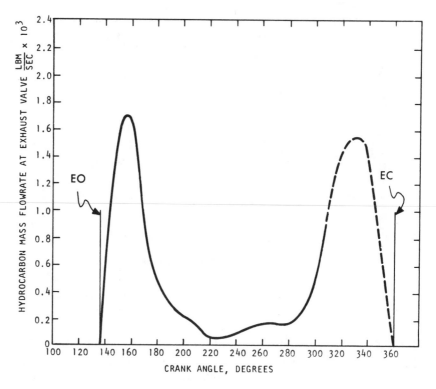

Figure 4.16. Calculated variation of hydrocarbon mass flowrate with crank angle at the exhaust valve. (Figure from Reference 7.)

Part II   Carbon Monoxide

Carbon monoxide is an intermediate product of combustion of hydrocarbon fuels. Figure 3.1 showed that when the mixture is richer than chemically correct, substantial amounts of CO appear in the exhaust. The slope of the CO curve is nearly 3 per cent CO per one air-fuel ratio. Thus a change of only 1/3 air-fuel ratio leads to a change of 1% in exhaust CO. As mentioned earlier, the reason that the CO concentration does not drop to zero when the mixture is chemically correct and leaner arises from a combination of cycle to cycle and cylinder to cylinder fuel maldistribution and slow CO reaction kinetics. Better carburetion and fuel distribution are a key to low CO emission.

Figure 4.17 demonstrates the possible distribution improvement afforded by better carburetion. An experimental atomizing liquid carburetor system was able to virtually eliminate cylinder

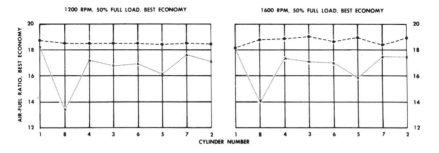

Figure 4.17. Cylinder to cylinder air-fuel ratios for a V-8 engine. Two carburetor systems were used at each speed. The dotted line was an experimental carburetion system which provided almost perfect fuel distribution. The engine was run at the best economy air-fuel ratio with MBT spark for each test. (Figure from Reference 8.)

to cylinder mixture differences which existed with the production carburetor on a V-8 engine. The two curves at each speed were measured at best economy engine operation which was noticeably leaner for the experimental system. In this test some CO exhaust emissions were present (primarily from cylinder number 8) with the standard carburetor in spite of the fact that the average engine mixture ratio was between 16 and 17 to 1. Thus better carburetion can reduce CO emission two ways: first, by making it uniformly low in each cylinder, and second, by allowing leaner overall engine operation.

Part III   Oxides of Nitrogen

Nitric oxide (NO) is formed within the combustion chamber at the peak combustion temperature and persists during expansion and exhaust in nonequilibrium amounts. Upon exposure to additional oxygen in the atmosphere, nitrogen dioxide (NO_2) and other oxides of nitrogen may be formed.

NITROGEN OXIDE COMPOUNDS

The following is a list of some of the different nitrogen oxides and their properties.[9]

NO: nitric oxide, colorless gas, stable, (product of combustion at high temperature), NO from the engine exhaust may react with oxygen to form nitrogen dioxide.

N_2O_4: nitrogen tetroxide, ($N_2O_4 \rightleftharpoons 2NO_2$), colorless.

NO_2:   nitrogen dioxide, dark brown, stable at 320°F, at temperatures between 68°F and 320°F mixtures of NO_2 and N_2O_4 appear.

N_2O: nitrous oxide (laughing gas), colorless, relatively stable, always present in the atmosphere at concentrations of about 0.5 ppm.

N_2O_3:   nitrogen trioxide (nitrous anhydride), colorless gas, with water forms nitrous acid, HNO_2.

N_2O_5:   nitrogen pentoxide (nitric anhydride), colorless, unstable, with water forms nitric acid, HNO_3.

NO_x: engineering terminology for an unknown mixture of nitrogen oxides (usually, NO and NO_2).

It should be noted that all the above compounds, except NO_2, are colorless. Nitrogen peroxides such as NO_3, N_2O_6, N_3O_4, and N_2O_7 are unstable compounds and decompose spontaneously at ambient conditions to nitrogen dioxide, NO_2, and oxygen.[9] A study of the equilibrium formation of the different nitrogen oxides showed that nitric oxide is the only compound having appreciable importance with respect to engine combustion.[10]

GENERAL MECHANISMS OF FORMATION

The nitric oxide formation during the combustion process is the result of a group of elementary reactions involving the nitrogen and oxygen molecules. Mechanisms for nitric oxide formations, proposed in References 11, 12, 13, and 14, are discussed below.

1. Simple reaction between O_2 and N_2:
$$N_2 + O_2 \rightleftharpoons 2NO \qquad (4.3)$$

This mechanism, used by Eyzat and Guibet,[11] predicts nitric oxide concentrations much lower than those measured in internal combustion engines. According to this mechanism the formation process is too slow for NO to reach equilibrium at the peak temperatures and pressures in the cylinders.

2. Zeldovich chain reaction mechanism:
$$O_2 \rightleftharpoons 2O \qquad (4.4)$$

$$O + N_2 \rightleftharpoons NO + N \qquad (4.5)$$

$$N + O_2 \rightleftharpoons NO + O \qquad (4.6)$$

The chain reactions are initiated in Equation 4.5 by the atomic oxygen which is formed in Equation 4.4 from the dissociation of oxygen molecules at the high temperatures reached in the combustion process. In Equation 4.5 the oxygen atom reacts with a nitrogen molecule and produces nitric oxide and a nitrogen atom. In Equation 4.6 the nitrogen atom reacts with the oxygen molecule and forms nitric oxide and atomic oxygen.

According to this mechanism the nitrogen atoms do not start the chain reaction because their equilibrium concentration during the combustion process is relatively low compared to that of atomic oxygen. The change in the equilibrium concentration of O with fuel-air ratio and temperature at a pressure of 800 psia is given in Chapter 3, Figure 3.2. This figure shows that the equilibrium concentrations of both the oxygen atoms and nitric oxide molecules increase with temperature and with leaning the mixture.

If chemical equilibrium prevails during the engine cycle, one would expect that the NO concentration would drop during the expansion stroke because of the decrease in the gas temperature. Measurements by Newhall and Starkman[15] showed that no decomposition of the NO, formed at the maximum cycle temperature, occurred during the expansion stroke.

3. Lavoie, Heywood, and Keck[13] extended the Zeldovich mechanism by adding the reaction between N and OH radical and other reactions:

$$N + OH \rightleftharpoons NO + H \qquad (4.7)$$
$$H + N_2O \rightleftharpoons N_2 + OH \qquad (4.8)$$
$$O + N_2O \rightleftharpoons N_2 + O_2 \qquad (4.9)$$
$$O + N_2O \rightleftharpoons NO + NO \qquad (4.10)$$

Their analysis showed that under the reciprocating engine conditions the NO removal process, Equation 4.10, is very slow and thus the NO concentration remains nearly constant during expansion. Figure 4.18 shows the results of computations made for the NO mass fractions in the burned gas, based on equilibrium conditions, and rate controlled conditions as given in Equations 4.4 to 4.10. These computations were made for two gas elements which burn at different times in the cycle. The first element is taken to be the start of combustion at $\Theta_b = -30$ crank angle degrees. The second element is taken at $\Theta_b = 10$ degrees after top center where about 1/3 of the charge has been burned. The dashed lines of Figure 4.18 show the calculated equilibrium concentrations and the solid lines show the calculated rate controlled results for the two cases. Their experimental results, obtained in a

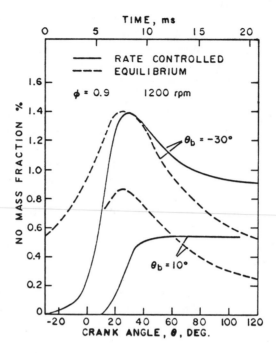

Figure 4.18. Nitric oxide mass fractions as a function of time in the burnt gas for two elements which burn at different times. $\theta_b = -30°$ is the first part of the charge to burn; at $\theta_b = 10°$, one third of the charge is burnt. Equivalence ratio is 0.9, engine speed is 1200 rpm, residual fraction is 0.05. (Figure from Reference 13.)

CFR engine by using spectroscopic techniques, are shown in Figure 4.19. The NO concentration was measured in different locations in the combustion chamber. Window W_2 is nearer to the spark plug than window W_3. Note that the NO concentrations at W_2 are much higher than those at W_3. The dashed lines in Figure 4.19 show the rate controlled concentrations computed using the above equations.

NO FORMATION IN FLAMES

Newhall and Shahed[16] used spectroscopic techniques to record directly the time rate of formation of nitric oxide in the immediate vicinity of a flame front propagating through a high pressure combustion vessel. The combustible mixture used was hydrogen in air. Figure 4.20 shows the measured concentration of NO plotted as a function of time for three fuel-air ratios chemically correct or leaner. Time zero is the point at which the flame passes through

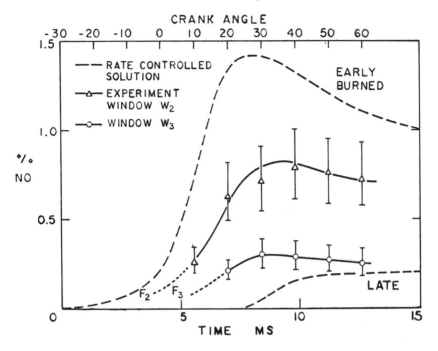

Figure 4.19. Experimental NO concentrations observed at two windows. W_2 is closer to the spark than W_3. Dotted curves are computer solutions for the kinetic NO behavior for early and late burned gas $\phi = 0.9$. (Figure from Reference 13.)

the optical path. This figure shows that the NO formation occurs predominantly in the post flame combustion products.

Figure 4.21 is for nitric oxide concentrations in a 20% fuel-rich mixture. This figure shows that the NO formation occurs at a higher rate than for $\phi \leq 1$. This has been attributed to increased flame velocity and subsequent increase in the rate of pressure and temperature rise in the burned gas. (Note that the chemical equilibrium concentrations are reached more quickly with the rich mixture.) However, the final NO concentrations are lower than those for $\phi \leq 1$.

The solid lines in Figures 4.20 and 4.21 are for the concentrations computed by using the Zeldovich mechanism, Equations 4.4, 4.5, and 4.6.

Bowman[21] noted discrepancies between NO formation rates observed early in the reaction of an H_2-O_2-N_2 flame and those calculated by using Equations 4.4 and 4.5. He concluded that this discrepancy was caused by an oxygen atom concentration overshoot in the reaction zone.

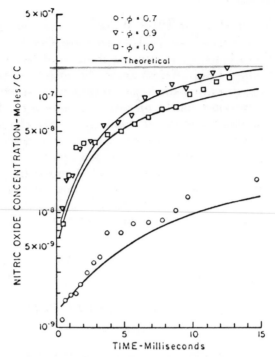

Figure 4.20. Experimental nitric oxide formation rates for fuel-lean and chemically correct mixtures. Recorded pressure levels are 240 psia, 325 psia, and 340 psia for 0.7, 0.9, and 1.0 equivalence ratios, respectively. (Figure from Reference 16.)

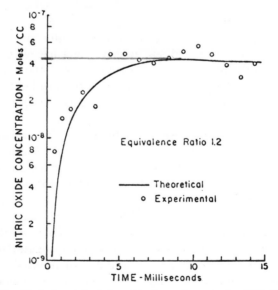

Figure 4.21. Experimental nitric oxide formation rate for 20% fuel-rich mixture. (Figure from Reference 16.)

Fenimore[17] studied the effect of different fuels on the NO formation rate in flames. The fuels used were CO, hydrogen, and various hydrocarbons. By measuring the rate of NO formation in the primary zone of the different flames he postulated that the NO formation in hydrocarbon-air flames results from an attack of carbon, or hydrocarbon radicals, on nitrogen molecules. Thus Fenimore suggests that the nitrogen atoms initiate the chain reactions. This differs from the Zeldovich mechanism, which proposed that the chain reactions are initiated by oxygen atoms.

In conclusion, researchers agree that NO concentrations formed in the engine combustion process are rate limited and once formed are not significantly reduced during expansion. A general agreement on the detailed mechanism of NO formation has not been reached.

Part IV Aldehydes

CHEMICAL FORMULAE OF SELECTED ALDEHYDES

formaldehyde	$HCHO$
acetaldehyde	CH_3CHO
propaldehyde	C_2H_5CHO
acrolein	C_2H_3CHO
butyraldehyde	C_3H_7CHO

Aldehydes are among the undesirable automotive S.I. and C.I. engine emissions. They consist mainly of formaldehyde and acrolein. Formaldehyde, at certain concentrations, is considered to be the cause of the odor and irritant property of diesel exhaust.[18]

Aldehydes are the product of partial oxidation of hydrocarbons and are formed in part during the low temperature preflame reactions within the combustion chamber. They are formed in the exhaust system especially if air is injected. In the preflame zone the temperature rise due to combustion is small and leads to partial oxidation of the fuel. Any chilling in the preflame zone, such as that produced by a cool wall, results in the formation of aldehydes which remain in the chamber to be exhausted.

Withrow and Rassweiler,[19] using a spectroscopic method, found that when the gasoline engine was knocking the gases immediately ahead of the flame front contained formaldehyde. This was always observed when the engine was knocking or was in a condition of incipient knock. When there was no knock, formaldehydes were not observed. This may be taken as strong evidence that formaldehydes are formed because of oxidation that leads to auto-ignition.

Sturgis[20] measured the concentration of aldehydes and the other partial oxidation products in the exhaust of a motored CFR engine. Heptane was used and the mixture was lean (50 % stoichiometric). The compression ratio was adjusted just below that which would produce autoignition. The results, shown in Figure 4.22, indicate a very high concentration of aldehydes before autoignition.

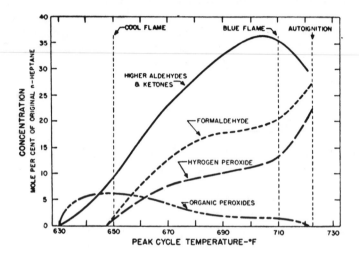

Figure 4.22.   Concentration of aldehydes in a motored engine. Fuel: heptane, F/A = 0.033. (Figure from Reference 20.)

REFERENCES

1. Friedman, R., and W. Johnson   "The Wall Quenching of Laminar Propane Flames as a Function of Pressure, Temperature, and Air-Fuel Rates," J. Appl. Phy. **21** (8), 791 (1950).
2. Daniel, W. A.   "Flame Quenching at the Walls of an International Combustion Engine," 6th Symposium on Combustion, (New York: Reinhold, 1957), p 886.
3. Daniel, W. A.   Personal Communication.
4. Gad El-Mawla, A., and W. Mirsky,   "A Study of Hydrocarbon Concentration and Temperature Profiles through a Steady-State Flame Adjacent to a Wall," Ph.D. Thesis, University of Michigan, 1965.
5. Wentworth, J. T., and W. A. Daniel.   "Flame Photographs of Light-Load Combustion Point the Way to Reduction of Hydrocarbons in Exhaust Gas," SAE P-T-6, 121 (1964).

6. Daniel, W. A., and J. T. Wentworth. "Exhaust Gas Hydrocarbons — Geneses and Exodus," SAE **PT-6**, 192 (1964).

7. Tabaczynski, R. J., et. al. "Time-Resolved Measurements of Hydrocarbon Mass Flow Rate in the Exhaust of a Spark-Ignition Engine," SAE Paper 720112, 1972.

8. Patterson, D. J. "Cylinder Pressure Variation — A Fundamental Combustion Problem," SAE Trans. **75**, 621 (1967).

9. Sneed, M. C., and K. C. Brasted. *Comprehensive Inorganic Chemistry*, vol. V, (New York: Van Nostrand, 1956).

10. Wimmer, D. B., and L. A. McReynolds. "Nitrogen Oxides and Engine Combustion," SAE Paper **380E** (1961).

11. Eyzat, P., and J. C. Guibet. "A New Look at Nitrogen Oxides Formation in Internal Combustion Engines," SAE Paper 680124 (1968).

12. Zeldovich, Ya. B., P. Ya. Sadovnikov, and D. A. Frank-Kamenetskii. "Oxidation of Nitrogen in Combustion," Academy of Sciences, USSR, Moscow-Leningrad (1947).

13. Lavoie, G. A., J. B. Heywood, and J. C. Keck. "Experimental and Theoretical Study of Nitric Oxide Formation in Internal Combustion Engines," Combust. Sci. Technol. **1**, 313 (1970).

14. Heywood, J. B., J. A. Fay, and L. H. Linden. "Jet Aircraft Air Pollutant Production and Dispersion," AIAA Paper **70-115**, New York (1970).

15. Starkman, E. S., and H. K. Newhall. "District Spectroscopic Determination of Nitric Oxide in Reciprocating Engine Cylinders," *SAE* **PT-14**, 214 (1967–70).

16. Newhall, H. K., and S. M. Shahed. "Kinetics of Nitric Oxide Formation in High Pressure Flames," *13th Symposium (International) on Combustion*, Salt Lake City (August, 1970).

17. Fenimore, C. P. "Formation of Nitric Oxide in Premixed Hydrocarbon Flames," 13th Symposium (International) on Combustion, Salt Lake City (August, 1970).

18. Davis, R. F., and M. A. Elliott. Am. Soc. Mech. Eng. **70**, 745 (1948).

19. Withrow, L., and G. M. Rassweiler. Industrial Eng. Chem. **24**, 528 (1932), **25**, 923 (1933) and **26**, 1256 (1934).

20. Sturgis, M. M. "Knock and Antiknock Action," SAE Trans. **63**, 253 (1955).

21. Bowman, C. T. "Investigation of Nitric Oxide Formation Kinetics in Combustion Processes, the Hydrogen-Oxygen-Nitrogen Reaction," Combustion Institute, Eastern Section Meeting, Atlanta, Ga. (Fall, 1970).

5

EFFECT OF DESIGN AND OPERATING VARIABLES ON GASOLINE ENGINE EXHAUST EMISSIONS

Introduction

The exhaust emission of hydrocarbons, aldehydes, carbon monoxide, and nitric oxide can be minimized by the control of several interrelated engine design and operating parameters. Fuel preparation, distribution and composition are also factors. In addition, chemical reactions in the exhaust which may be enhanced by air injection can be optimized to further reduce tailpipe emissions. Often it has been impossible to completely isolate the effect of a single design variable or operating parameter. The following sections discuss the effects on emissions of factors which the engine engineer has under his control when designing and tailoring for minimum exhaust emission. These factors include:

- air-fuel ratio
- load or power level
- speed
- spark timing
- exhaust back pressure
- valve overlap
- intake manifold pressure
- combustion chamber deposit build up
- surface temperature
- surface to volume ratio
- combustion chamber design
- stroke to bore ratio
- displacement per cylinder
- compression ratio.

In the following discussion, the hydrocarbon and carbon monoxide emissions are treated together because once formed they both can be reduced by a chemical oxidation process in either the cylinder or exhaust system. On the other hand nitric oxide, once formed, must be reduced by a chemical reduction process. In the first case for HC and CO reduction, excess O $_2$ is required whereas in the second case for NO reduction a deficiency of O $_2$ is desirable.

Effect on Unburned Hydrocarbons and Carbon Monoxide

Hagen and Holiday[1] have studied the effect of several engine design and operating variables on hydrocarbon and CO emission in a dynamometer engine test. Nondispersive infrared analyzers were used to measure both quantities.

Air-Fuel Ratio

Figure 5.1 shows the effect of air-fuel ratio on exhaust hydrocarbon emission from a 352 CID V-8 engine. Emission is shown on both a concentration and mass basis. The mass emission data of Figure 5.1b reflect the additional engine volume flow required for constant load operation with lean mixtures. Data points on Figure 5.1 are for light (road load), medium and heavy load operation. In every case hydrocarbon emissions decrease as the mixture is leaned. As indicated on the figure, the tolerance of the production carburetor for the vehicle would have provided mixtures between 15 and 16.5 to 1. Leaner operation in the vehicle is precluded

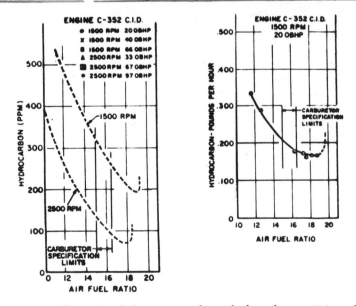

Figure 5.1. Effect of air-fuel ratio on exhaust hydrocarbon emissions, MBT spark. (Figure from Reference 1.)

because of surge and poor driveability. Surge may be defined as the unsteady forward progression of a vehicle resulting from lean carburetion. The dynamometer tests show that the hydrocarbon emission continues to decrease at least to 17:1. When operation leaner than 17 or 18:1 is attempted, emissions increase because of incomplete flame propagation. This increase is suggested in Figure 5.1 by the dotted lines.

Additional hydrocarbon emission data on a mass basis are shown in Figure 5.2. These data indicate the sharp increase in hydrocarbon emission above 18:1 air-fuel ratio. Leaner than 17 or 18:1 (depending on the engine design and operating point), conventional engines begin to misfire as discussed in Chapter 3. Figures 4.10, 4.11, and 4.12 indicate the onset of misfire with lean mixtures and high vacuums. Figure 5.2 also indicates the vehicle fuel economy as a function of air-fuel ratio.

It is not uncommon for the minimum emission air-fuel ratio to occur at a richer air-fuel ratio than the best economy point. This arises from cycle to cycle and cylinder to cylinder variations in mixture ratio resulting from poor carburetion and fuel distribution. The dashed line added to Figure 5.2 suggests the possible effect of poor carburetion. The minimum emissions are greater and occur at a richer mixture.

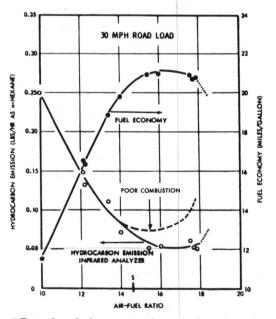

Figure 5.2. Effect of air-fuel ratio on exhaust hydrocarbon emission and fuel economy in car at 30 mph road load. (Figure from Reference 2.)

The basic factors contributing to the shape of Figure 5.1a are the effect of mixture ratio on quench layer thickness, the effect of mixture ratio on fuel concentration within that quenched layer, the effect of mixture ratio on availability of excess oxygen in the exhaust to complete the combustion and finally the effect of mixture ratio on exhaust system temperature. When the temperature is sufficiently high (over 1200°F) and oxygen present, appreciable exhaust after-reaction does occur.

Figure 5.3 suggests the interrelationships of the above factors in a qualitative way. At a given air-fuel ratio the mass of unburned hydrocarbons produced in the chamber is equal to the product of the thickness of the unburned layer, curve 1, and the concentration of fuel in that layer, curve 2. The result is curve 5. Because of the shapes of curves 1 and 2, the minimum value of curve 5 is at a leaner mixture than the minimum for curve 1 (which is at 5–10% rich as the data of Freedman and Johnson in Chapter 4 show).

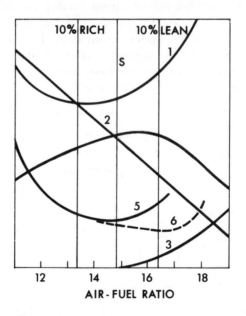

Curve 1 – Quench thickness
Curve 2 – Fuel concentration in quenched layer
Curve 3 – O $_2$ concentration in exhaust
Curve 4 – Temperature of exhaust
Curve 5 – HC emissions leaving combustion chamber
Curve 6 – HC emissions after exhaust reactions

Figure 5.3. Basic factors affecting engine hydrocarbon exhaust emissions. Curve 5 represents the mass of unburned hydrocarbons in the combustion chamber prior to exhaust after reaction. It is the product of Curve 1 and Curve 2. Curve 6 shows the additional HC reduction afforded by exhaust after reaction.

The hydrocarbon emissions measured in the exhaust may be lowered further at the leaner mixtures by after-reactions in the exhaust system. Significant after-reaction does occur in the presence of sufficient O_2 when the average exhaust temperature exceeds 1200°F. Curve 3 shows the O_2 content of the exhaust and curve 4 its temperature as functions of air-fuel ratio.

Curve 6 reflects the additional effect of the exhaust after-reaction. The minimum hydrocarbon is shown to be lower and occurring in leaner mixtures, nearer to the best economy engine operating point. Curve 6 is in qualitative agreement with Figure 5.2. After-reaction does not continue to lower emissions as the mixture becomes even leaner because the exhaust temperature becomes too low to achieve a significant reaction rate.

The importance of a lean air-fuel ratio for carbon monoxide reduction was discussed in connection with Figure 3.1. The gain in emission reduction afforded by the possibility of operating all vehicles at the lean driveability limit (16.5:1 for the carburetion limits of Figure 5.1) suggests the importance of minimum carburetor tolerances and good manufacturing control in addition to uniform fuel distribution. Also it may be noted that variations in the carbon to hydrogen ratio of the fuel lead to variations in the equivalence ratio delivered by the carburetor.

Power Output

Figure 5.4 shows that hydrocarbon concentration does not change as load is increased while speed and mixture ratio are held

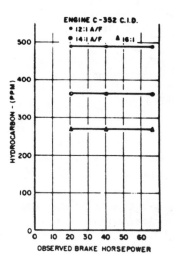

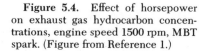

Figure 5.4. Effect of horsepower on exhaust gas hydrocarbon concentrations, engine speed 1500 rpm, MBT spark. (Figure from Reference 1.)

constant and spark is adjusted to MBT. We can view this result as arising from effects of several factors, some of which tend to reduce hydrocarbons while others tend to increase them. Apparently the opposing effects just counterbalance each other.

A factor tending to increase HC concentration as load is increased is reduced residence time within the exhaust system. The residence time of the exhaust gas in the very hot section of the exhaust system is an important factor affecting the amount of exhaust after-reaction. Residence time may be defined as:

$$t_{min} = \frac{\text{volume of hot exhaust system, ft}^3}{\text{volume flow of exhaust gas, ft}^3/\text{min}}$$

If the load is doubled, volume flow is approximately doubled and residence time reduced by 50%. The net effect is the same as if exhaust system volume were reduced by 50% at a given exhaust volume flow. Exhaust volume (residence time effects) will be discussed in more detail in Chapter 7.

Factors tending to reduce HC emission concentration include decreased quench thickness and increased exhaust temperature as load is increased. Friedman and Johnson's data, discussed in Chapter 4, show that quench layer thickness decreases inversely as pressure increases. Mean cylinder pressure increases linearly with load. Thus Friedman's data predict that hydrocarbon concentration will decrease approximately linearly with load increase. (The extrapolation of Friedman and Johnson's data to engine operating pressures may not be possible. Perhaps quench layer thickness in the engine and unburned hydrocarbons are not reduced as much as their low pressure burner data suggest.) In addition higher exhaust gas temperatures as load is increased will tend to increase exhaust after-reaction.

Experimental data from many engines which show no effect of load on HC emission concentrations suggest that the decrease in residence time reduces exhaust reaction enough to offset any advantage of reduced quench layer thickness and increased average exhaust temperature.

Figure 5.5 shows an almost linear increase in hydrocarbon mass emissions as load is increased. A light car with a small frontal area and low power train loss has the advantage on a mass emission basis.

At a fixed air-fuel ratio there is no effect of power output on carbon monoxide emission concentration. However, as in the case with the hydrocarbon emissions, the mass emission of CO will increase directly with increasing power output and air consumption. Again, the small, light, efficient car has the advantage.

Engine Speed

Figure 5.6 shows the effect of engine speed on hydrocarbon concentration at 1500 and 2500 RPM. Emission concentration is markedly reduced at higher engine speeds. Primarily the increase in engine speed improves the combustion process within the cylinder by increasing turbulent mixing and eddy diffusion. This promotes after-oxidation of the quenched layer. In addition, increased exhaust port turbulence at higher speeds promotes exhaust system oxidation reactions through better mixing. Speed has no effect on CO concentration because oxidation of CO in the exhaust is kinetically limited rather than mixing limited at the normal exhaust temperatures. As a result of these findings one would expect mass emission of hydrocarbons to decrease as speed is increased. This is the case. However, the decrease will be less than that predicted by the concentration change because of the increased volume flow required to overcome higher engine friction at higher speed. In a vehicle, the selection of an optimum N/V ratio must be a compromise between performance, economy, and emissions. Recently the trend has been to low N/V ratios for economy and minimized engine noise.

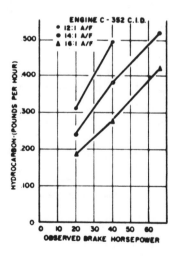

Figure 5.5. Effect of horsepower on exhaust gas hydrocarbon mass emissions, engine speed 1500 rpm. (Figure from Reference 1.)

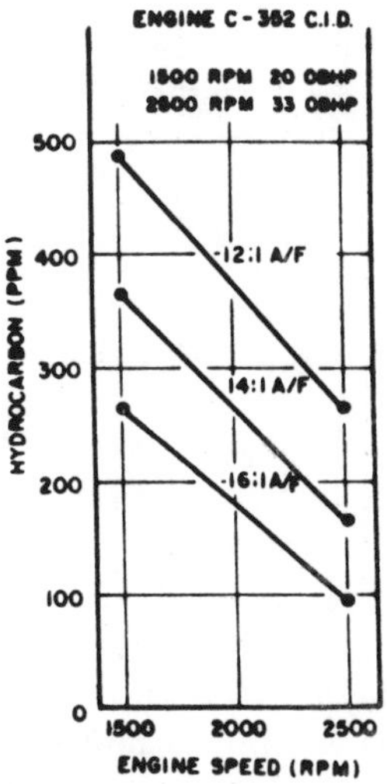

Figure 5.6. Effect of engine speed on exhaust gas hydrocarbon concentrations at 12:1, 14:1, and 16:1 air-fuel ratios. (Figure from Reference 1.)

Spark Timing

Figure 5.7 shows the effect of spark timing on hydrocarbon concentration at a constant power of 13 BHP and 1500 RPM. A retard of 10° from the manufacturers recommended setting of 30°BTC reduced hydrocarbon emission by 10 ppm but increased fuel consumption nearly 10%. The 100 ppm change for 10° retard suggests the importance of precise spark timing and minimum distributor tolerance.

The distributor production tolerance of 5° indicate in Figure 5.7 could result in a 50 ppm difference in emissions from one vehicle to another. Figure 5.7 shows that the more the timing is retarded, the lower are the emissions. Figure 5.8, which shows the data on a mass basis, demonstrates that because of the increased volume flow required to produce the 13 BHP with a retarded spark, the mass emission actually reached a minimum at 5°BTC timing and increased with additional retard. The effect of spark retard on HC emission reduction arises primarily from an increase in exhaust temperature, which promotes CO and HC oxidation, and a decrease in surface to volume ratio during combustion, which lowers

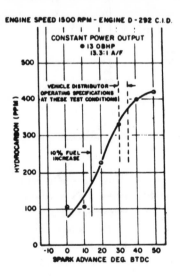

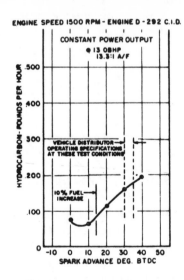

Figure 5.7. Comparison of effect of spark advance on exhaust gas hydrocarbon concentrations, constant load. Engine speed 1500 rpm – Engine D–292 C.I.D. (Figure from Reference 1.)

Figure 5.8. Comparison of effect of spark advance on exhaust gas hydrocarbon emissions, constant load. Engine speed 1500 rpm – Engine D–292 C.I.D. (Figure from Reference 1.)

emitted HC. Surface to volume ratio will be discussed later in this chapter.

In a vehicle the emission reduction achieved by spark retard must be compromised by fuel economy loss considerations. Figure 5.9 shows the effect of spark retard at 30 MPH on fuel economy. A 10° retard from MBT (30°) resulted in a decrease from 21 to 19.3 MPG, nearly 10%.

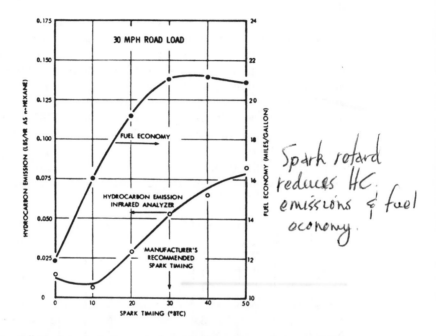

Spark retard reduces HC emissions & fuel economy.

Figure 5.9. Effect of spark timing on exhaust hydrocarbon emission and fuel economy in car at 30 mph road load. (Figure from Reference 2.)

Spark retard has little effect on CO concentration except at very retarded timing where the lack of time to complete CO oxidation leads to increased CO emissions. Because of the increased air flow required to maintain the power level constant, the mass of CO emitted from the cylinder tends to increase. The increase is offset to some extent by higher exhaust temperatures resulting in improved CO cleanup in the exhaust system. Figures 5.10 and 5.11 show the CO emissions for the 292 CID engine on both a concentration and mass emission basis.

It is a common occurrence in vehicle tests that as a result of retarded timing the throttle must be opened and the carburetor operated at a point where the power enrichment valve is open. Where this happens CO increases markedly.

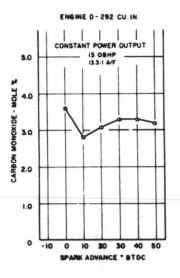

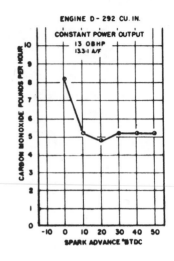

Figure 5.10. Comparison of effect of spark advance on exhaust gas carbon monoxide con-centrations for fixed throttle versus constant load at 1500 rpm. Engine D−292 CID. (Figure from Reference 1.)

Figure 5.11. Comparison of effect of spark advance on exhaust gas carbon monoxide emissions for fixed throttle versus constant load at 1500 rpm. Engine D−292 CID. (Figure from Reference 1.)

Exhaust Back Pressure

Increasing exhaust back pressure increases the amount of residual exhaust gas left in the cylinder at the end of the cycle. If this increase in residual does not increase the percentage dilution of the fresh charge to a level where the combustion process is adversely affected, the HC emission concentration will be lowered. The reduction arises from leaving the tail end of the exhaust, which is rich in unburned HC, in the cylinder. This tail is subsequently burned in the next cycle.

Figure 5.12 shows the HC benefit of increased exhaust back pressure for several medium and high load operating points. Because exhaust dilution was low, an increase in dilution did not lead to poor combustion, at least within the range of the experiment; thus HC concentration was reduced. No doubt if back pressure were increased more and more, eventually HC emission would rise sharply.

On the other hand increasing dilution at idle increased HC emission concentration. At idle, dilution is already quite high

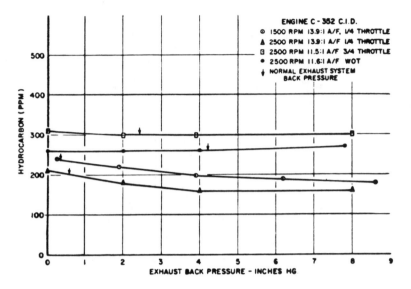

Figure 5.12. Effect of exhaust back pressure on exhaust gas hydrocarbon concentrations. (Figure from Reference 1.)

naturally and combustion marginal. The engine cannot tolerate much more exhaust dilution.

Valve Overlap

Increasing valve overlap has an effect similar to increasing the back pressure. The charge is further diluted with residual gases. Figure 5.13 shows the effect of valve overlap on idle HC concentration. Note that a very slight 2° overlap provided minimum emission. Thus a slight amount of residual increase could be tolerated and reburning a little of the rich exhaust tail did lower the average HC emission value. However a further increase in residual led to incomplete combustion and a HC emission increase.

Another interesting result shown in Figure 5.13 is the deterioration in combustion with lean mixtures as residual is increased (increased overlap). If the mixture ratio must be richened to provide stable idle and off-idle performance, then the HC advantage will be lost and CO will be increased. Similar results have been reported in Reference 5. In general minimum HC emissions are obtained with moderate or low back pressures and minimum overlap. Peak power is reduced when overlap is low; however economy may be increased if leaner stable operation can be achieved.

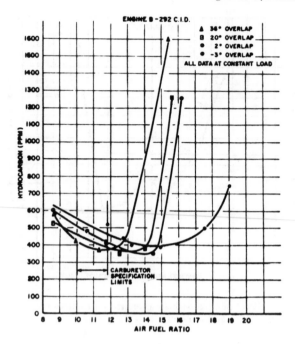

Figure 5.13.   Effect of air-fuel ratio on exhaust gas hydrocarbon concentrations at idle for valve overlap settings of 36 deg, 20 deg (standard), 2 and -3 deg. (Figure from Reference 1.)

There is no effect of overlap on carbon monoxide concentration at a constant mixture ratio. However any increase in mixture strength required to achieve acceptably smooth idle and off-idle performance as a result of increased charge dilution will increase CO concentration directly. Any increase in throttle opening to overcome the increased charge dilution will increase the mass emission of HC and CO.

Intake Manifold Pressure

As indicated previously, at a fixed mixture ratio and speed with best power timing, there is no effect of engine horsepower on hydrocarbon or carbon monoxide emission on a concentration basis. However, because carburetor and distributor settings are variable in the vehicle, there is a change in emission concentration as the throttle is varied at a constant speed.

Figure 5.14 shows the mixture ratio delivered by the automatic carburetor on the 352 CID engine used in Hagen's tests as a

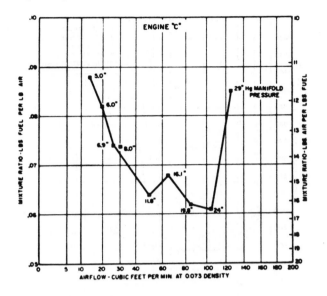

Figure 5.14. Mixture air-fuel ratios supplied by production carburetor at 1500 rpm for various throttle settings. (Figure from Reference 1.)

function of air flow. At selected points, the intake manifold absolute pressure is indicated in inches of mercury. The left most point represents a closed throttle deceleration (25″ vac), the 11.8″ point-road load (18″ vac), the 19.8″ point-in traffic accelerating maneuver (10″ vac) and the 29″ point-WOT acceleration. Car speed is about 40 MPH depending on the N/V ratio of the vehicle. Obviously the throttle setting influences the mixture ratio greatly. Figure 5.15 shows the spark advance provided by the automatic distributor at this constant speed. The maximum vacuum advance was about 20° and was employed when the vacuum exceeded 14″ Hg.

Figure 5.16 shows the hydrocarbon emission concentration measured during this test with automatic carburetor and distributor. Figure 5.17 shows the mass emissions which reflect the effect of increased air flow at the higher loads. Data for two additional engines are shown in this figure also. The air flow to the engine at each manifold pressure can be read from Figure 5.14.

The hydrocarbon concentrations shown on Figure 5.16 are influenced by the several factors discussed in connection with Figure 5.3. Between 9 and 24 inches manifold pressure the fuel-air ratio was lean which minimized HC and CO emissions. Above 24 inches, the carburetor power valve was actuated and the mixture was richened. The rise in hydrocarbon concentration at full load was limited by enhanced exhaust cleanup arising from higher exhaust temperatures. At light loads and low manifold pressures, additional hydrocarbon emissions resulted from the increased wall

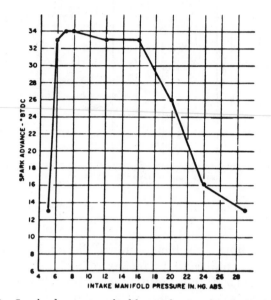

Figure 5.15. Spark advance supplied by production distributor at 1500 rpm for various throttle settings. (Figure from Reference 1.)

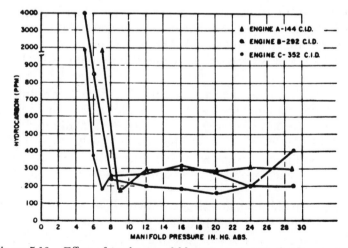

Figure 5.16. Effect of intake manifold pressure (engine load) on exhaust gas hydrocarbon concentrations at 1500 rpm with typical production carburetor and distributor operation. (Figure from Reference 1.)

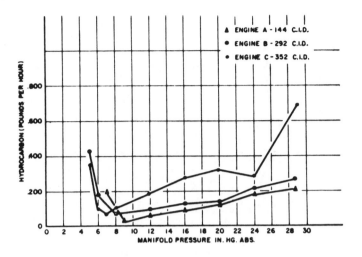

Figure 5.17. Effect of intake manifold pressure (engine load) on exhaust gas hydrocarbon emissions at 1500 rpm with typical production carburetor and distributor operation. (Figure from Reference 1.)

quenching accompanying the rich mixtures delivered by the carburetor and incomplete flame propagation at manifold pressures below 6 inches Hg. In a vehicle, additional enrichment of the mixture at high vacuums resulted from flash vaporization of the liquid fuel on the wall of the intake manifold when the throttle was suddenly closed. Dashpots or other throttle cracking devices are often used to limit intake manifold vacuum during deceleration on American cars. Fuel shut-off devices on the idle system are an alternate solution used on some foreign cars to minimize emissions at high vacuum operating points.

Figure 5.18 shows the carbon monoxide emission concentration for the above tests. The enrichment at light and heavy loads evidences itself in the higher CO levels at these points. Mass emission of CO is particularly high near WOT because of the rich mixture needed for maximum power. One must keep in mind that CO is an intermediate compound in HC oxidation. In this test relatively good HC oxidation in the exhaust at WOT produced some CO which was not completely oxidized.

Combustion Chamber Deposit Buildup

It is well known that in a normal engine the major source of combustion chamber deposits is the TEL [tetraethyl lead— $Pb(C_2H_5)$] fuel additive used to suppress combustion knock. Typically 3 cc TEL per gallon is added. The deposits act to in-

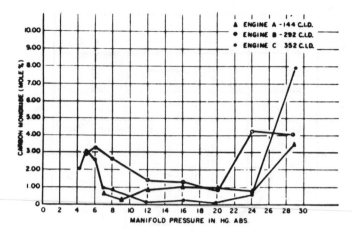

Figure 5.18. Effect of intake manifold pressure (engine load) on exhaust gas carbon monoxide concentrations at 1500 rpm with typical production carburetor and distributor operation. (Figure from Reference 1.)

crease the surface area of the chamber because of their irregular porous surface. As a result the mass of quenched hydrocarbons increases. Deposits also act as a sponge to trap raw fuel which remains unburned and adds to the exhaust hydrocarbons. Deposit buildup also increases compression ratio which in turn increases hydrocarbon emissions.

Figure 5.19 demonstrates the decrease in hydrocarbon emissions when combustion chamber deposits are removed. The numbers are composites for Federal driving cycle tests. Removing the deposits reduced hydrocarbon emission about 40 ppm, a 15% reduction. Changes of 40 to 50 ppm are typical. The effect of deposit removal depends of course on the extent of deposit buildup. Some engines build up deposits more than others.

Tests by Gagliardi[7] have demonstrated that HC emissions increase to the same level even with reduced TEL levels as low as 0.5 cc/gallon. At low TEL levels it takes longer (more miles) to develop stabilized deposits. Gagliardi found that stabilized deposits were formed at 3000–4000 miles with 3 cc/gallon and at 18,000 miles with 0.5 cc/gallon. Emission levels increased to the same value at the stabilized condition. Because of the increase in hydrocarbon emissions caused by TEL addition, the adverse effect on the life of catalytic exhaust converters and environmental lead levels as an adverse health factor, it is generally agreed that lead levels in fuel should be gradually reduced over the years.

Additional fuel additives may be helpful in reducing deposit

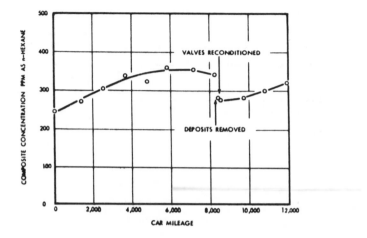

Figure 5.19. Effect of combustion chamber deposit accumulation on exhaust hydrocarbon concentration from car in suburban driving service. (Figure from Reference 2.)

buildup. Ethylene dibromide is commonly added to motor fuel to reduce the deposits arising from TEL addition. Other fuel additives have been discovered which reduce hydrocarbon emissions because they modify the deposit structure. Lubricant additives which leave some ash upon combustion contribute to combustion chamber deposits also. Such deposits arise either from lubricant seeping through the intake valve guide and being inducted into the chamber with the fresh charge, or from lubricant being left as a film on the combustion chamber wall from the motion of the piston. Thus modifications to both fuels and lubricants can indirectly reduce hydrocarbon emissions through deposit modification.

There is no effect of deposit buildup on CO emission.[7]

Surface Temperature

Combustion chamber surface temperature affects the unburned hydrocarbon emissions by changing the thickness of the combustion chamber quench layer and the degree of after-reaction. The effect of temperature on quench thickness has been discussed in Chapter 4 for flat plates with propane-air mixtures at atmospheric pressure. Wentworth[4] studied the effect of such changes on hydrocarbon emissions from an engine. He found a decrease in hydrocarbon emission of 0.35 to 0.58 ppm hexane per one degree Fahrenheit rise in combustion chamber surface temperature. In one test an increase of 100°F decreased hydrocarbon emissions about 33 per cent.

In addition to changing quench distance and after-reaction, changing engine temperature affects fuel evaporation and distribution, combustion temperature, and exhaust system temperature and therefore exhaust reaction. An increase in surface temperature by engine modification is expected to have adverse effects on engine octane requirement, volumetric efficiency, and lubrication.

Surface to Volume Ratio

Because hydrocarbon emissions arise primarily from quenching at the combustion chamber wall surface, it is desirable to minimize the surface area of the chamber. Let us view the combustion process as occurring completely at TDC. This assumption is best for MBT timing. After the flame passes through the mixture, a thin layer of unburned hydrocarbons is left adjacent to the combustion chamber surface. The volume of this layer is $A_c d$ where A_c is the combustion chamber surface area (including crevices) and d the quench layer thickness. This volume is perhaps 1 to 2% of the total volume of the combustion chamber. If we mix this quenched volume with the rest of the contents of the chamber, the concentration of unburned hydrocarbons on a volume basis is

$$HC_{conc.} = \frac{A_c d}{V_c} \propto \frac{A_c}{V_c}$$

where V_c is the combustion chamber volume at TDC. Such a mixing process occurs in the exhaust system.

It is apparent that if A_c is increased by wrinkling the combustion chamber surface and V_c is unchanged, the concentration of unburned hydrocarbons will increase. Conversely if V_c is decreased while A_c is held constant, HC concentration is increased also. This is the case when the cylinder head is milled to increase the compression ratio.

The ratio of surface area to volume of the combustion chamber (s/v) is useful for interpreting the effects of many design and operating variables on hydrocarbon emission concentration. Lowering the s/v ratio reduces hydrocarbon emission concentration. CO concentration is not affected by s/v ratio changes.

Scheffler[3] has studied the effect of several engine factors on s/v ratio. Figure 5.20 demonstrates the correlation between s/v ratio

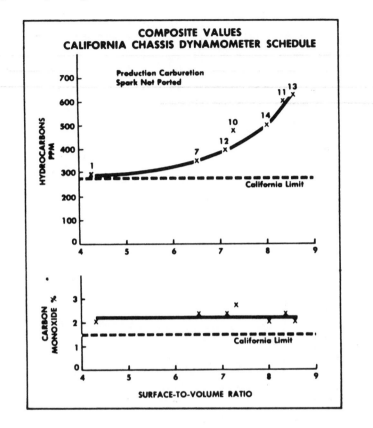

Figure 5.20. Composite exhaust hydrocarbon concentration, measured, corrected, and weighted according to the California Schedule, increased with increasing s/v ratio. Carburetors were tailored to give equal, mid-range air-fuel ratios resulting in equal carbon monoxide concentration. Numbers are for car identification. (Figure from Reference 3.)

and hydrocarbon emission concentration. Composite HC emission values are shown for several pre-emission production test cars. Additional correlation is shown in Figure 5.21 for cars modified for low emissions. These data demonstrate the fact that s/v ratio is strongly linked to hydrocarbon emission.

Combustion Chamber Design

Perhaps one of the most important factors the emission engineer has under his control is the combustion chamber design. For a given clearance volume, reducing surface area is an important way of reducing hydrocarbon emissions. Figure 5.22 shows how cham-

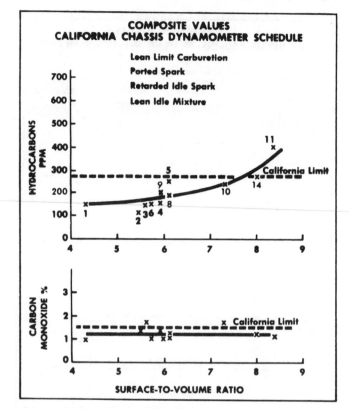

Figure 5.21. Lean air-fuel ratios, plus a ported spark providing no vacuum advance at idle, plus a further 10° retard at idle (returning to the normal curve at 1600 rpm), and plus a lean idle setting reduced the level of emissions. Composite exhaust hydrocarbon concentration again increased with increasing s/v ratio. (Figure from Reference 3.)

ber shape influences s/v ratio. The calculations were made for a V-8 engine of 350 CID with a 4-inch bore. Clearance volume was the same for each chamber shape. The double hemisphere provided the lowest s/v ratio. In the past, chambers have been designed to control combustion rate to 30–35 psi/deg and to suppress knock. Today s/v effect on emissions is a third factor.

Stroke to Bore Ratio

Another design factor is stroke/bore ratio. Engines with small bores and long strokes have lower s/v ratios. This is demonstrated in Figure 5.23. Two cylinders of equal displacement are shown. One has a s/b of 0.813, the other 1.105. Increasing the stroke and

COMBUSTION CHAMBER INFLUENCE ON SURFACE/VOLUME
4" BORE, 350 CU. IN. V-8, 9:1 COMP. RATIO

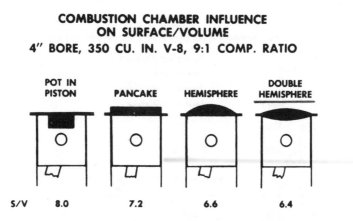

	POT IN PISTON	PANCAKE	HEMISPHERE	DOUBLE HEMISPHERE
S/V	8.0	7.2	6.6	6.4

Figure 5.22. The s/v ratio is influenced by chamber design. Poorer (higher) s/v ratios can result in surface area is not considered in the design. However, most conventional chamber designs have s/v ratios close to the pancake design, and larger reductions in s/v ratio are not possible. (Figure from Reference 3.)

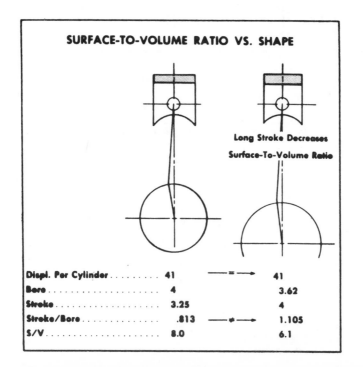

SURFACE-TO-VOLUME RATIO VS. SHAPE

Long Stroke Decreases
Surface-To-Volume Ratio

Displ. Per Cylinder	41	⟶ = ⟶	41
Bore	4		3.62
Stroke	3.25		4
Stroke/Bore	.813	⟶ ≠ ⟶	1.105
S/V	8.0		6.1

Figure 5.23. An increased stroke and decreased bore provides a combustion chamber that is taller and has a smaller diameter. This long stroke chamber more closely approaches the minimum area spherical chamber. A large reduction in s/v ratio is the result. (Figure from Reference 3.)

decreasing the bore lowered s/v from 8.0 to 6.1. This should provide a good emission reduction as seen in Figures 5.20 and 5.21. Unfortunately this modification is opposed to modern engine design practice which favors short strokes for reduced friction, increased power and economy and lower engine silhouette. Long stroke engines tend to be large, heavy and more costly, and they have poor fuel economy and reduced peak power.

Displacement per Cylinder

Figure 5.24 is a sketch of two cylinders of different displacement, each having the same compression ratio and s/b ratio. The larger cylinder has the smaller s/v ratio. The result suggests that for a given displacement engine hydrocarbon emission can be reduced by decreasing the number of cylinders but increasing the displacement per cylinder. On the other hand, for a given number of cylinders, increasing engine displacement reduces s/v ratio and hydrocarbon emission concentration. Mass emission may increase because of increased engine friction.

Compression Ratio

Scheffler summarized the effect of four design factors in Figure

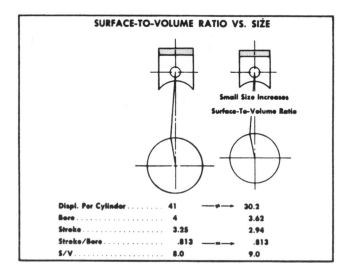

Figure 5.24. Reducing the size of the combustion chamber decreases both the surface area and the volume. The surface decreases as a square function while the volume decreases as a cubic function. The result with smaller size chambers is a larger relative area, a larger s/v ratio. (Figure from Reference 3.)

5.25. The engine used for a baseline had 300 CID, compression ratio of 9, 8 cylinders and s/b of 1. For each curve, 3 of the 4 variables were held constant. This figure shows the important effect of compression ratio. A large reduction in s/v ratio can be effected by decreasing the compression ratio. This increases the clearance volume greatly with little increase in surface area. However, reducing compression ratio results in lower thermal efficiency and reduced engine power.

A compression ratio decrease reduces hydrocarbon emissions a second way. With reduced compression ratio, thermal efficiency is lowered and as a result exhaust gas temperature is increased. This improves exhaust system after-reaction and lowers the hydrocarbon emissions even more. On the other hand as engine efficiency is lowered, mass flow is increased for a given horsepower level. This tends to increase mass emissions.

Surface to volume ratio may also be used to explain at least in part the effect of spark retard and combustion rate on hydrocarbon

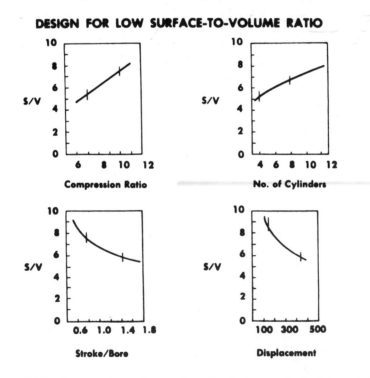

DESIGN FOR LOW SURFACE-TO-VOLUME RATIO

Figure 5.25. Compression ratio, number of cylinders, and displacement all show the size effect. As the individual combustion chamber gets smaller, the s/v ratio gets larger. As the stroke/bore ratio gets larger (longer stroke engines) the s/v ratio gets smaller. Vertical lines on each curve mark the boundaries of present production practice. (Figure from Reference 3.)

emission. If the spark is retarded, the combustion process is delayed until the piston is well down the cylinder. The s/v ratio at this point in the cycle is considerably lower than at TDC. The more retarded the spark, the lower the s/v ratio when combustion occurs. Similarly, any design or fuel change (such as leaning the mixture) which slows down the combustion process will lower the average s/v during the combustion process.

Summary for Hydrocarbon Emissions Analysis*

The study of the effect of any variable on hydrocarbon emission should be made in four steps (see following page):

1. HC formation in the combustion chamber
2. HC after-oxidation in combustion chamber
3. HC leaving combustion chamber
4. HC after-oxidation in the exhaust system

Effect on Nitric Oxide

The concentration of NO in the exhaust gases depends upon the difference between the rate of its formation at the highest temperature in the cycle and the rate of its decomposition as the temperature decreases during the expansion stroke. A study of the decomposition rate of NO indicates that the amount decomposed is negligible because of the short time available during the expansion stroke.

Effect of Equivalence Ratio

The equivalence ratio affects both the gas temperature and the available oxygen during combustion. Theoretically an increase in the equivalence ratio from 1 to 1.1 results in an increase in the maximum cycle temperature of 100°F while oxygen concentration is decreased 50%. Figure 5.26 shows that at an equivalence ratio of 1.1, NO in the exhaust is low. Figure 5.26 also shows that the maximum NO concentration occurs at an equivalence ratio of 0.8. The maximum cycle temperature with this lean mixture is lower than with a richer mixture, but the available oxygen concentration is much higher.

Figure 5.26 also shows the NO concentrations computed at the

---

*For additional discussions of the effect of engine variables on hydrocarbon emissions see Reference 6.

＊

HC in Exh. Pipe   =   HC Produced in Chamber   —   HC Oxidized in Chamber After-Reactions   —   HC not Exhausted   —   HC Eliminated in After-Reaction

HC Produced in Chamber

Depends on:
1. Wall quenching
   a. s/v (effective)
      i. sparking timing
      ii. mix ratio
      iii. comp. ratio
      iv. engine design
      v. deposits
   b. quench thickness
      i. mix ratio
      ii. $T_{reactants}$
      iii. $P_{reactants}$
      iv. T_{wall}
      v. wall material
      vi. turbulence
2. Incomplete comb.
   a. dilution
   b. mixture ratio
3. Scavenging

HC Oxidized in Chamber After-Reactions

1. Quench layer mixing
   a. engine speed
   b. chamber and induction system design
2. O_2 Conc. in c.c.
   a. mix ratio
   b. air inj.
3. Wall temperature

HC not Exhausted

1. Load
2. Exh. pr.
3. Overlap area
4. Turbulence
5. Chamber design
6. Compression ratio

HC Eliminated in After-Reaction

1. O_2 Conc. in exh.
   a. mix ratio
   b. air inj.
2. Exh. temp.
   a. spark timing
   b. mix ratio
   c. insulation
3. Residence time
   a. vol. of exh. system
   b. exh. vol. flow

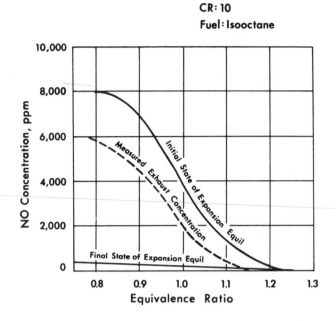

Figure 5.26. Variation of equilibrium concentration of NO with equivalence ratio as compared with exhaust concentrations. (Figure from Reference 10.)

start and the end of the expansion stroke for different equivalence ratios. The results of these computations indicate that the NO concentration in the exhaust gases is nearer to the computed concentrations at the start of expansion, showing that the NO decomposition during the expansion stroke is negligible.

Figure 5.27 shows the effect of air-fuel ratio on NO concentration in a V-8 engine. The three curves represent different loads and thus different peak combustion temperatures. With very rich mixtures, low peak combustion temperature and low oxygen concentration lead to low NO. For mixtures leaner than 15.5:1, additional increases in NO from increased oxygen concentration are more than offset by the lower combustion temperature and lower formation rates in the lean mixture. Thus NO concentration is low for very lean as well as very rich mixtures.

Effect of Spark Timing

The effect of spark timing on the maximum temperatures and pressures reached in the cycle has been discussed in Chapters 2 and 3. The results of Figure 5.28 show that increasing the spark

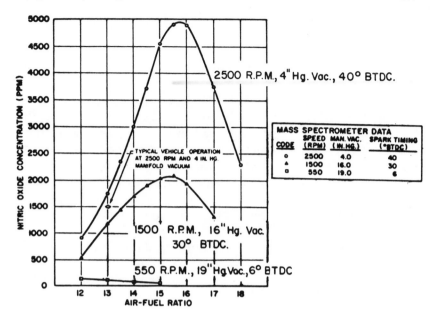

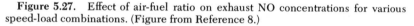

Figure 5.27. Effect of air-fuel ratio on exhaust NO concentrations for various speed-load combinations. (Figure from Reference 8.)

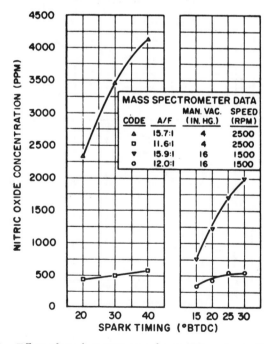

Figure 5.28. Effect of spark timing on exhaust NO concentrations for various speed-load combinations. (Figure from Reference 8.)

advance at any load and speed results in an increase in the NO concentration.

Effect of Intake Manifold Vacuum

An increase in manifold vacuum decreases load and temperature, and increases the mass of residual gases. As a result, the ignition delay is increased and the flame speed is reduced. Both these factors result in an increase in the time of combustion. If the spark timing is held constant as in Figure 5.29, the increase in manifold vacuum would cause a greater part of the combustion process to occur during the expansion stroke. This would result in a reduction in the maximum cycle temperature and a corresponding decrease in NO concentration in the exhaust.

Normally the spark timing is not kept constant as in Figure 5.28. The normal spark advance at high manifold vacuums changes the shape of the curves. NO would be increased somewhat over the levels shown in Figure 5.27.

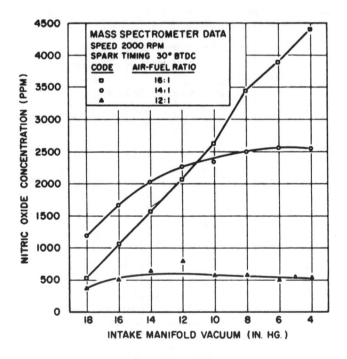

Figure 5.29.   Effect of intake manifold vacuum on exhaust NO concentrations for various air-fuel ratios. (Figure from Reference 8.)

Effect of Engine Speed

An increase in engine speed has little effect on ignition delay, results in an increase in flame speed due to turbulence, and reduces heat losses per cycle, which tends to raise compression and combustion temperature and pressure. If spark timing is held constant, as in Figure 5.30, a greater portion of this combustion

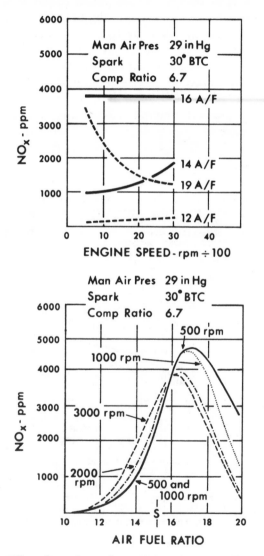

Figure 5.30. Effect of speed on exhaust NO concentration (Figures from Reference 9.)

tends to occur during expansion where temperatures and pressures are relatively low. This is most pronounced for the slowest burning mixture ratio, 19:1. For richer mixtures which burn faster, the effect of reduced heat losses at higher speeds predominates. Thus the results in Figure 5.30 reflect two opposing influences—an increase in the rate of NO formation due to reduced heat losses opposed by a reduction in the rate of NO formation due to late burning. For rich mixtures where combustion and NO formation are rapid, the former effect predominates. For lean mixtures where combustion and NO formation are slow, the latter effect predominates.

Effect of Coolant Temperature

An increase in coolant temperature results in a reduction in the heat lost to the cylinder walls and an increase in the maximum gas temperature. This results in an increase in NO concentration, as shown in Figure 5.31.

The difference between the results of the duplicate runs of Figure 5.31 is due to the deposit build up in the cylinder.[8] An increase in deposit thickness causes an increase in compression ratio, reduction in the heat losses to the coolant, and an increase in NO concentration.

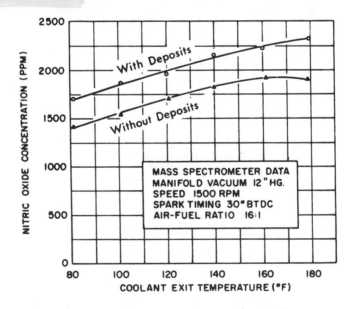

Figure 5.31. Effect of coolant temperature on exhaust NO concentration, for duplicate runs with and without deposits. (Figure from Reference 8.)

Effect of Humidity

The reduction in NO formation caused by an increase in mixture humidity is mainly due to the drop in the maximum flame temperature. Moore[14] found that each 1% (by weight) of water vapor reduced a hydrogen-air and ethylene-air flame temperature by approximately 36°F. This reduced the initial rate of nitric oxide production by about 25%.

The effect of an increase in inlet air humidity on reducing nitric oxide emissions was measured in an engine under steady conditions.[12] The humidity effect on indicated mean effective pressure, nitric oxide and unburned hydrocarbon emissions is shown in Figure 5.32.

The increase in absolute humidity from 20 grains per lb dry air to 160 grains per lb had a negligible effect on the HC and the

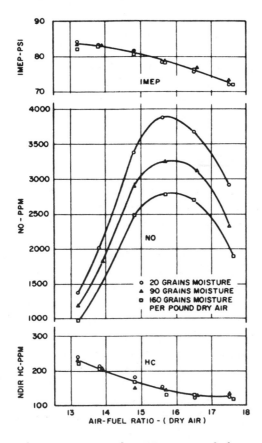

Figure 5.32. Exhaust emissions and IMEP versus air-fuel ratio at 1600 rpm, 11 in. Hg. intake vacuum. (Figure from Reference 12.)

IMEP. However it greatly reduced the nitric oxide emission. The decrease in NO concentration in the exhaust was between 2 and 9 ppm per grain increase in absolute humidity.

Effect of Exhaust Gas Recirculation

Addition of exhaust gases to the inlet charge increases dilution. This reduces both the flame speed and maximum temperature reached in the cycle. Increasing dilution decreases NO_x emission.[17] According to the Zeldovich mechanism discussed in Chapter 4, the chain reactions that result in nitric oxide formation are initiated by an oxygen atom. The oxygen atoms are produced from the dissociation of oxygen molecules at the maximum cycle temperature. The reduction in nitric oxide emission afforded by exhaust gas recirculation has been correlated with the increase in heat capacity of the charge.[15,16]

The effect of exhaust gas recirculation on the NO emissions in a car under steady state operation, at 30 mph and at different throttle valve openings, has been given by Reference 13 and is shown in Figure 7.10. A 5% recycle reduced the maximum NO concentration from 2330 ppm to 1400 ppm. A 10% recycle reduced the NO concentration to 480 ppm.

Effect on Aldehydes

Normally most aldehydes found at the tailpipe probably result from low temperature combustion reactions in the combustion chamber which were quenched part way through the oxidation process. Wall quenching or quenching by excessive exhaust dilution are possible ways that these oxygenated hydrocarbon molecules can arise. During expansion, blowdown and exhaust, additional low temperature combustion reactions may occur, especially with air injection. These may increase or decrease total aldehyde emission. Little published data exists on aldehyde emission from engines. This is partly because of the difficulty in making such measurements in quantity because complex wet chemical techniques must be used. Aldehydes are undesirable exhaust constituents and should be studied further. They are powerful eye and respiratory irritants, particularly the unsaturated aliphatic compounds.[1] Aldehydes fall into reactivity class III on the GM scale. Their specific reactivity is 5.

Effect of Equivalence Ratio

Figure 5.33 shows dynamometer data from a V-8 engine for the effect of air-fuel ratio on both aldehyde and hydrocarbon emission. Aldehydes were measured by the DNPH method[11] and are reported as ppm formaldehyde. Hydrocarbons were measured by a flame ionization detector and are reported as ppm hexane. The engine was run at 1200 rpm, 50% full load, MBT spark. Minimum aldehyde emissions occurred between 11 and 13:1 air-fuel ratio.

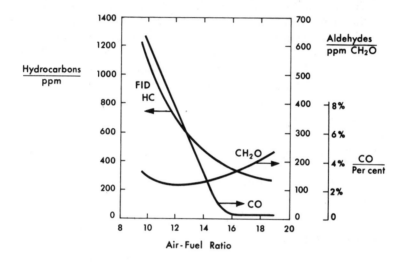

Figure 5.33. Effect of air-fuel ratio on aldehydes, CO and hydrocarbon emissions. CID, V-8, 1200 rpm, 30 HP, MBT spark.

Figure 5.34 shows hot cycle aldehyde emissions for several vehicles reported by Oberdorfer. Comparative NDIR hydrocarbon readings are indicated also. These data show that for mixtures leaner than 15 or 16:1, total aldehyde emission as ppm formaldehyde exceeded NDIR hydrocarbon emissions as ppm hexane. We might assume that the FID hydrocarbon values would be about twice the NDIR reading.

Figure 5.35 shows additional dynamometer data from the V-8 engine for the effect of spark timing on both aldehyde and hydrocarbon emission. The engine was run at 1200 rpm, 50% full load, and 17:1 air-fuel ratio. Indolene was the test fuel. Retarding the spark reduced both aldehyde and HC emission. At 34° spark advance, which was close to MBT, aldehydes are about 1/3 of the FID hydrocarbon reading.

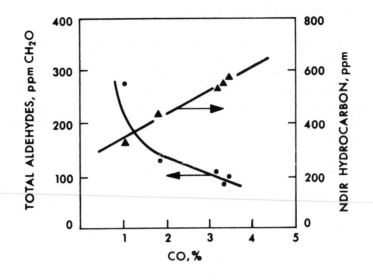

Figure 5.34. Aldehyde and hydrocarbon versus CO various cars, Federal cycle (hot). (Figure from Reference 11.)

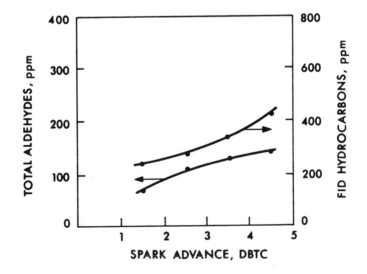

Figure 5.35. Aldehyde and hydrocarbon versus spark timing, 350 CID, V-8, 17:1 A/F, 1200 rpm, 30 HP.

Aldehyde Emission Composition

Table 5.1 shows a gas chromatographic breakdown of the aldehydes from one vehicle test. Formaldehyde is the principal component and is 70 mole % of the total aldehydes. The remaining 30% is approximately equally divided between acetaldehyde, acrolein, and benzaldehyde. Note that the lowest molecular weight compounds of each family constitute the major portion of each type.

Summary: Effect of Design and Operation Variables

The effect of the many design and operating variables on hydrocarbon, CO, and NO emissions is summarized in Table 5.2. Intake mass volume flow is indicated also. The major direction or change is indicated by an arrow. If the change is relatively small a horizontal line is drawn. Obviously, the conclusions one draws about a change often depend on the starting point from which the change is made. The table assumes the starting point is a vehicle which has no special exhaust emission control, such as a 1967 production car.

Table 5.1

Analysis of Individual Aldehydes and Ketones
California Standard Cycle (Hot)

Aldehyde or Ketone	Mole %
Formaldehyde	70.2
Acetaldehyde	7.2
Propionaldehyde and acetone	0.4
n-Butyraldehyde	0.4
iso-Butyraldehyde	Trace
n-Valeraldehyde	0.4
iso-Valeraldehyde	Trace
2-Ethylbutyraldehyde	Trace
Acrolein	9.8
Crotonaldehyde	0.4
Methacrolein	Trace
Benzaldehyde	8.5
Other C_7 + Aldehydes as C_7	2.5

Data from Reference 11.

Table 5.2

Effect of Design and Operating Variables on Exhaust Emissions and Engine Air Flow

Variable increased	HC conc.	CO conc.	NO conc.	CH$_2$O conc.	Intake mass flow constant load
Air-fuel ratio	∪	↘	∧	⌣	↑
Load	—	—	↑		↑
Speed	↓	—	↑ ↓		↑
Spark retard	↓	—	↓	↓	↑
Exhaust back pressure	↓	—	↓		↑
Valve overlap	↓	—	↓		↑
Intake manifold pressure	—	—	↑		↑
Combustion chamber deposits	↑	—	↑		—
Surface to volume ratio*	↑	—	—		—
Combustion chamber area	↑	—	—		—
Stroke to bore ratio	↓	—	—		↑
Displ. per cylinder	↓	—	—		—
Compression ratio	↑	—	↑		↓
Air injection	↓	↓	—↑	↑ ↓	↑
Fuel injection	↓	↓	↑		—
Coolant temperature	—↓	—↓	↑		—

*Engine changes which decrease surface to volume ratio reduce heat loss to the coolant. As a result NO concentration may increase.

REFERENCES

1. Hagen, D. F., and G. W. Holiday. "The Effects of Engine Operating and Design Variables on Exhaust Emissions," SAE **TP-6**, 206 (1964).
2. Jackson, M. W., et al. "Influence of Air-Fuel Ratio, Spark Timing, and Combustion Chamber Deposits on Exhaust Hydrocarbon Emissions," SAE **TP-6**, 175 (1964).
3. Sheffler, C. E. "Combustion Chamber Surface Area, A Key to Exhaust Hydrocarbons," SAE **PT-12**, 60 (1963–66).
4. Wentworth, J. T. "Effect of Combustion Chamber Surface Temperature on Exhaust Hydrocarbon Concentration," SAE Preprint No. 710587 (1971).
5. Siewert, R. M. "How Individual Valve Timing Events Affect Exhaust Emissions," SAE Preprint No. 701609 (1971).
6. Daniel, W. A. "Why Engine Variables Affect Exhaust Hydrocarbon Emission," SAE **PT-14**, 341 (1967–70).

7. Gagliardi, J. C., and F. E. Ghannam. "Effects of TEL Concentration on Exhaust Emissions in Customer Type Vehicle Operation," SAE **PT-14**, 416 (1967–70).

8. Huls, T. A., and H. A. Nickol. "Influence of Engine Variables on Exhaust Oxides of Nitrogen Concentrations from a Multicylinder Engine," SAE **PT-14**, 256 (1967–70).

9. Nebel, G. J., and M. W. Jackson. "Some Factors Affecting the Concentration of Oxides of Nitrogen in Exhaust Gases from Spark Ignition Engines," J.APCA, **8** (3), 213 (1958).

10. Obert, E. F. *Internal Combustion Engines*, 3rd ed. (Scranton, Pa.: Int'l Textbook Co., 1968) p 204.

11. Oberdorfer, P. E. "The Determination of Aldehydes in Automobile Exhaust Gas," SAE **PT-14** 33 (1967–70).

12. Robison, J. A. "Humidity Effects on Engine Nitric Oxide Emissions at Steady-State Conditions," SAE Preprint No. 700467 (1970).

13. Benson, J. D. "Reduction of Nitrogen Oxides in Automobile Exhaust," SAE Preprint No. 690019 (1969).

14. Moore, J. "The Effects of Atmospheric Moisture on Nitric Oxide Production," paper presented in fall meeting, Combustion Institute, Eastern Section, Atlanta, Georgia, 1970.

15. Ohigashi, S., H. Kuroda, Y. Nakajima, T. Hayashi, and K. Sugihara. "A New Method of Predicting Nitrogen Oxides Reduction on Exhaust Gas Recirculation," SAE Preprint 710010 (1971).

16. Quadar, A. A. "Why Intake Charge Dilution Decreases Nitric Oxide Emission from Spark Ignition Engines," SAE Preprint 710009 (1971).

17. Benson, J. D., and R. F. Stebar. "Effects of Charge Dilution on Nitric Oxide Emissions from a Single-Cylinder Engine," SAE Preprint 710008 (1971).

6

HYDROCARBON EVAPORATIVE EMISSIONS

The hydrocarbon evaporative emissions from a vehicle arise from two sources: distillation of the fuel in the carburetor float bowl and evaporation of fuel in the gas tank. Vehicle evaporative emissions in grams per day can be significant. Prior to nationwide control in 1971 evaporative emissions per car per day exceeded exhaust hydrocarbon emissions. Reduction of evaporative losses leads to a significant reduction in overall hydrocarbon emission from vehicles.

Carburetor Distillation Losses

Carburetor hydrocarbon vapor losses, typically 10 to 30 grams per test, arise from distillation of the fuel in the float bowl. Reference to the distillation curve, Figure 2.10, shows, for example, that whenever carburetor fuel temperature rises to 160°F, approximately 25–30% by volume of the fuel will be boiled off.

During most engine operation the vapors generated are vented internally into the intake system. During hot soak, vapors continue to be generated and are vented into the carburetor air horn. Many of these vapors find their way to the atmosphere through the air cleaner snout.

Carburetor fuel temperature often reaches 130°F during warm weather engine operation and may rise up to 180° during a hot soak. During the soak a significant fraction of the fuel in the bowl will be boiled off and a large fraction of this loss finds its way to the atmosphere. Figure 2.17 illustrates the rise in fuel system temperatures following shut down after a hard run.

The basic factors governing the mass of fuel distilled from a carburetor during a hot soak period are:

- maximum fuel bowl temperature,
- amount of fuel in the bowl,
- amount of after fill, and
- distillation curve of the fuel.

EXAMPLE 1

Let us study the interplay of the above factors through a hypothetical example. Suppose a passenger car has a carburetor with a float bowl normally containing 72 cc of fuel, the peak bowl temperature of which is 160°F during the soak period following operation. A petcock in the fuel line is closed to prevent after-fill. Jackson,[1] in studying such a car, found that carburetor distillation loss would be about 12.5 grams for a fuel whose ASTM distillation curve showed 25% distilled at 160°F. A replot of Jackson's results is shown in Figure 6.1.

Case A

Suppose that a less volatile fuel was used which has 20% distilled at 160°F. What would the carburetor distillation loss be?
Answer: 9.75 grams from Figure 6.1, a 22% reduction.

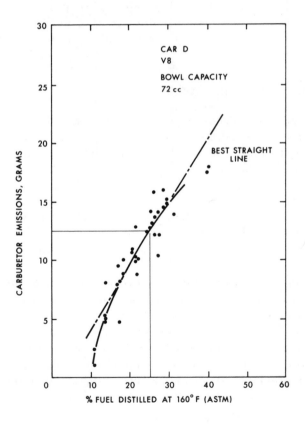

Figure 6.1.   Effect of volatility on carburetor emission. (Redrawn from Reference 1.)

Case B

Suppose the original bowl volume was increased to contain 144 cc of the original fuel. What are the carburetor distillation losses? Answer: approximately twice as much or 25 grams. The effect of bowl volume is suggested in Figure 6.2. It is linear.

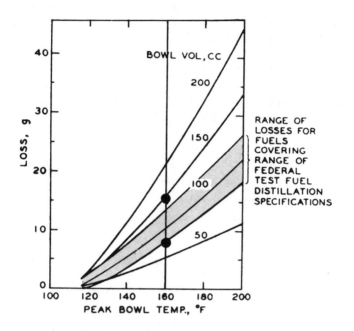

Figure 6.2. Carburetor loss versus peak bowl temperature in 1 hr. hot soak with federal test fuel. (Figure from Reference 10.)

Case C

By placing an insulated spacer between the carburetor and intake manifold, peak bowl temperature is reduced to 140°F. What is the carburetor distillation loss? Answer: Figure 6.3 shows the effect of changing peak bowl temperature for one carburetor. For the fuel in question (25% distilled at 160°F), the reduction is in the ratio of 5.5 to 12 gms. Figure 6.3 cannot be applied directly since the bowl volume was 100 cc. The new distillation loss is $12.5 \times 5.5/12 = 5.75$ grams, a 56% reduction.

Case D

Suppose that during the distillation process, the ·carburetor

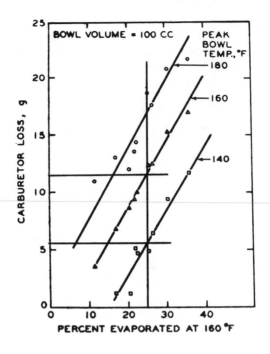

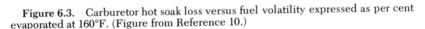

Figure 6.3. Carburetor hot soak loss versus fuel volatility expressed as per cent evaporated at 160°F. (Figure from Reference 10.)

needle valve opens as the liquid level falls in the bowl, and an additional 10 cc of fuel enters the bowl. This after-fill fuel is also exposed to the 160° peak bowl temperature. What are the carburetor distillation losses?

Answer: The effect of after-fill is similar to an increase in bowl volume. The distillation loss would increase from 12.5 to 82/72 × 12.5 = 14.2 grams, a 14% increase.

The above example was intended to illustrate the basic factors which influence carburetor evaporative emissions. Results from any specific vehicle are expected to differ somewhat.

Loss Distribution

Of the fuel distilled from the carburetor, a large fraction is emitted to the atmosphere while smaller fractions are lodged in various portions of the engine system. For one test Martens[2] has measured the distribution of losses as follows:

Carburetor bowl loss		10.4 g
emitted to atmos. via air cleaner	6.8 g	
emitted to atmos. via carburetor leaks	1.3 g	
air cleaner accumulation	0.9 g	
°induction and exhaust system accumulation	0.5 g	
crankcase accumulation	0.7 g	
	10.2 g	10.4 g

In the above listing, only about 75% of the carburetor losses went directly into the atmosphere. However, Martens found that most of the vapors trapped in the induction and exhaust systems were expelled to the atmosphere upon vehicle start up. This illustrates the problem which arises in assuming loss to the atmosphere is equal to either the total carburetor bowl loss or only the vapors trapped at the snout of the air cleaner.

Loss Composition

Unlike exhaust emissions, carburetor and fuel tank evaporative emissions have a composition similar to the light ends of the test fuel itself. Jackson[1] has correlated the reactivity of the carburetor loss with per cent C_4 and C_5 paraffins in the fuel. Figure 6.4 shows the mole per cent C_4 and C_5 olefins in the carburetor distillate versus the mole per cent in the fuel itself. Only the best straight line through his data is shown. Figure 6.5 shows the evaporative emission reactivity versus $C_4 + C_5$ olefins in the fuel. The GM reactivity scale discussed in Chapter 1 was used.

EXAMPLE 2

Let us modify the fuel in the set up of Example 1, so that all the C_4 and C_5 olefins are replaced by C_4 and C_5 paraffins. Thus the per cent distilled at 160°F would still be 25%. What is the reactivity reduction of the distilled emissions if the original fuel contained 5 mole % total of C_4 and C_5 olefins?
Answer: The number of grams distilled would still be 12.5. Figure 6.5 shows that the reactivity of the carburetor emissions was 5 per 100 grams of distillate, whereas with zero olefins it would be about 3, a 40% reduction in smog-forming potential.

°Exhaust system accumulation results from accumulation in a cylinder in which both intake and exhaust valves are open (valve overlap).

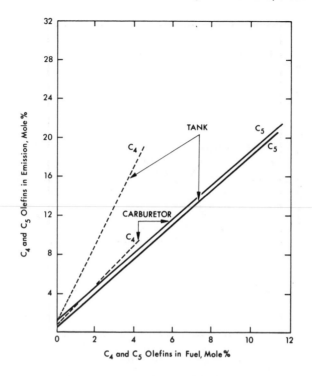

Figure 6.4. Effect of fuel composition on composition of evaporative emissions—C_4 and C_5 olefins. Unlike exhaust emissions, the composition of the evaporative emission is strongly related to the light end composition of the fuel. (Redrawn from Reference 1.)

Fuel Tank Evaporation Losses

The hydrocarbon vapor losses from a fuel tank, typically 50 grams per test, arise primarily from an evaporation process. Because tank temperature changes slowly, the evaporation process is nearly an equilibrium one. Thus the methods of equilibrium thermodynamics may be brought to bear on the problem. At night the tank cools and both liquid and vapor contract, thereby allowing ambient air to be inhaled into the vapor space of the tank. During the day, especially during and after severe hot vehicle operation, tank temperatures rise, perhaps to 120°F or more depending on circumstances.

Figure 6.6 shows the tank liquid and vapor temperature for two complete FTP cycle tests and two 1-hour hot soaks. In the test, the tank temperature reached 110°F in an ambient of 85°F. As a result of such increases in tank temperature, the liquid and vapor in-

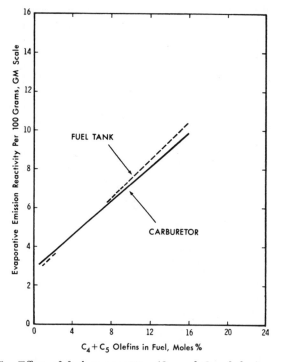

Figure 6.5. Effect of fuel composition (C_4 and C_5 olefins) on reactivity of evaporative emissions. Reactivity based on GM scale. (Redrawn from Reference 1.)

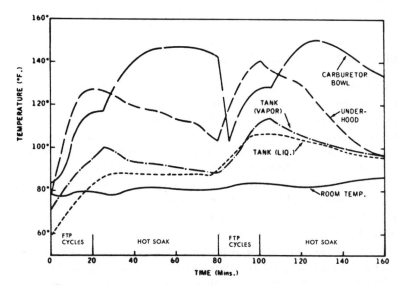

Figure 6.6. Typical Federal Test sequence temperature profiles. (Figure from Reference 3.)

crease in volume and the tank expels some hydrocarbon vapor air mixture. In addition, because the vapor pressure of each constituent of the gasoline increases with temperature, additional vaporization of each fuel component occurs until the vapor pressure is satisfied for the constituent at the new temperature. Thus additional vapor must be expelled from the tank on this account.

The basic factors governing the mass of fuel evaporated from a heated fuel tank are:

- the initial and final fuel temperatures
- the volume of the tank not filled with fuel
- the composition of the fuel, especially the light C_4 and C_5 ends
- the presence of a pressure relief cap
- the area of the liquid-vapor surface
- the length of time or degree of agitation of the tank near its maximum temperature.

The last two factors govern the speed at which equilibrium is attained.

Simplified Vapor-Liquid Equilibrium

A number of simple concepts will demonstrate the basic physical factors involved in the evaporation of fuel into the vapor space of the fuel tank. Additional material may be found in Van Wylen[4] or similar thermodynamics books.

IDEAL GAS BEHAVIOR

The vapors in the tank may be assumed to behave as ideal gases. Thus the equation of state for each component in the vapor (both air and fuel) can be written

$$P_i V = n_i \overline{R} T$$

where

P_i = pressure exerted by component i (partial pressure)
V = total volume of tank vapor space
n_i = moles of component i in gas phase (equals mass of i divided by molecular wt of i)
$\overline{R}$ = universal gas constant
T = absolute temperature

The total pressure exerted by all the components of the vapor space equals the sum of the individual partial pressures. Thus

$$P = P_{air} + P_{butane} + P_{pentane} + \cdots\cdots\cdots$$

Normally P, the total tank pressure, equals ambient pressure unless a pressure cap is used on the tank.

Case A — Pure Fuel

When a pure fuel such as isooctane is in the tank, the partial pressure of the fuel P_{iso} in the vapor space is equal to the vapor pressure of the fuel at the tank temperature. Figure 6.7 shows the vapor pressure of isooctane as a function of temperature. If the tank were at 60°F, the fuel vapor partial pressure would be about 0.6 psia. If the ambient pressure were 14.7, then the partial pressure of the air would have to be 14.1, if a pressure cap were not used. Now if the tank temperature were increased to 100°F, the partial pressure of the isooctane would increase to about 1.7 (some liquid would evaporate) and enough of the mixture of fuel and air vapor already in the tank would be expelled so the partial pressure of the air would be 13.

Case B — Commercial Multicomponent Fuel

The addition of other components to the fuel adds a good deal of complexity to the problem. Each fuel component exerts some pressure in the vapor space. Raoult's rule, which assumes both ideal liquid and gas behavior, says that the partial pressure P_i of each vapor constituent is equal to the product of the mole fraction

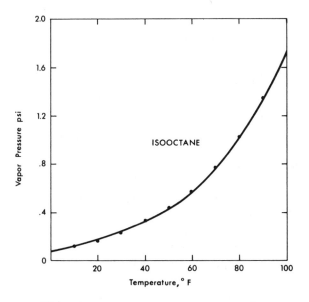

Figure 6.7. Effect of temperature on vapor pressure of isooctane. (Data from Reference 8.)

of this component in the liquid, X_i, and the vapor pressure of the pure substance at the tank temperature. Consequently,

$$P = P_{air} + X_{butane} \times P_{butane}^{vapor} + X_{heptane} \times P_{heptane}^{vapor} + \cdots$$

Thus the fuel-generated vapor pressure depends on the presence in the liquid of highly volatile (high vapor pressure) constituents and the amount of each constituent present. For example, butane has a vapor pressure of 51 psi at 100°F. If the fuel contained 5 mole per cent, the contribution of butane to the tank pressure would be 2.55 psi. If the fuel contained only 1 mole per cent, it would contribute only 0.51 psi.

It is clear that from an evaporative emission point of view, it is undesirable to have fuel components in any significant amount which have high vapor pressures at low temperatures. Also, from a reactivity point of view it is better to have paraffins such as butane and pentane rather than olefins such as butene and pentene.

Figure 6.8 shows the vapor pressure at 100°F of some paraffins and olefins. When viewed on semilog plot, there is an almost linear relationship between vapor pressure and the number of carbon atoms in the molecule. Small molecules have high vapor pressures. Figure 6.9 shows a vapor pressure curve for regular gasoline.

Reid Pressure Correlation

Because fuel tank loss results from an equilibrium evaporation process around 100°F, it has been experimentally found that the fuel tank loss in grams can be correlated with the Reid vapor pressure, a volatility test conducted at 100°F. Figure 6.10 from Jackson[1] shows the correlation for the vehicle whose carburetor losses were shown in Figure 6.1. The car had a fuel tank of 25 gallons capacity which was filled with 10 gallons of fuel for the test (40% full). The Federal Evaporative Test Procedure was used and the maximum tank temperature increased from 60 to 86° in the test. For this particular vehicle, the tank loss would be about 62 grams for a RVP of 9.5 which is typical of California fuels. Indolene brand emission test fuel has a RVP between 8.7 and 9.2 when specified for evaporative emission testing.

EXAMPLE 1

A hypothetical example illustrates the interplay of the various basic factors. Suppose the car has a fuel tank of 25 gallons with 10 gallons of liquid fuel such as in Jackson's experiment and that the

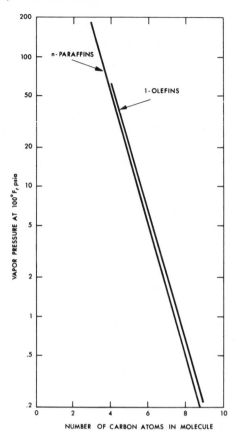

Figure 6.8. Vapor pressure of pure fuels vs. carbon number.

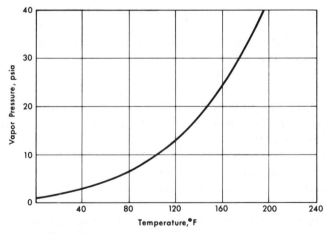

Figure 6.9. Effect of temperature on vapor pressure of regular gasoline. (Data from Reference 9.)

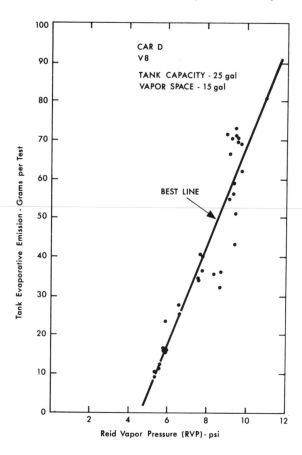

Figure 6.10. Effect of fuel volatility on amount of fuel tank emission. (Redrawn from Reference 1.)

peak temperature is 86°F. For this situation, the tank vapor loss would be 62 grams, as we saw for an average summer fuel of RVP 9.5.

Case A

Suppose that a less volatile fuel with a RVP of 7 was used. This could be accomplished by removing 65% of the butane from a typical Los Angeles gasoline.[1] What would be the new evaporative loss?

Answer: 30 grams, a 52% reduction.

Case B

Suppose that the fuel tank contained only 5 gallons of fuel but that the temperature remained the same. What is the tank loss?

Answer: The vapor space is now 33% larger. Consequently more fuel must evaporate to satisfy equilibrium. Figure 6.11 shows the vapor volume effect calculated for a particular set of tests. In going from 40% to 25% tank fill, the curve suggests that tank emissions increase linearly in the ratio of 30/23.8. Therefore the new loss would be $62 \times 30/23.8 = 78$ grams, a 29% increase. In general the peak tank temperature also increases as the amount of fuel in the tank decreases. Thus in practice the evaporative loss increases more than linearly with liquid volume decrease.

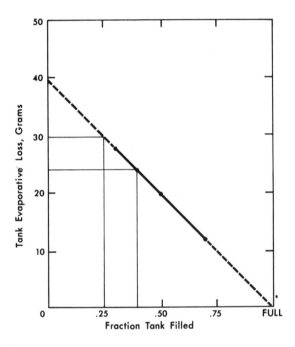

Figure 6.11. Calculated effect of tank fill on evaporative loss. Initial tank temperature 60°F, peak temperature 84°F, 20 gallon tank, RVP 9.5. (Data from Reference 10.)

Case C

Suppose that by rerouting the exhaust pipe, the peak tank temperature was reduced to 82°F. What is the evaporative loss?

Answer: Figure 6.12 shows the calculated effect of peak tank temperature. Reducing temperature from 86 to 82°F reduces losses in the ratio of 20.9/27.2. The new loss would be $62 \times 20.9/27.2 = 46$ grams, a 26% reduction. Slight variations in peak tank temperature lead to large variations in the test data.

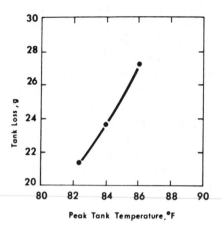

Figure 6.12. Calculated effect of peak tank temperature on tank evaporative loss. Initial tank temperature 60°F, 20 gallon tank, 40% fill, RVP 9.5. (Data from Reference 10.)

Loss Composition

As mentioned previously the composition of the tank losses strongly reflects the volatile components of the fuel. Figure 6.4 also shows the correlations between fuel tank C_4 and C_5 olefins and those in the evaporative emissions. Note the particularly strong correlation for the C_4 olefins. These volatile constituents as a group have the highest vapor pressures of any fuel components. A fuel which contains 4% C_4 has a tank loss containing 16% C_4. The reactivity of the tank emission is shown in Figure 6.5.

EXAMPLE 2

Using the set up of Example 1 but modifying the fuel so that all the C_4 and C_5 olefins are replaced by C_4 and C_5 paraffins would mean that the RVP and grams loss would remain the same. What is the reactivity reduction of the evaporated tank emissions, if the original fuel contained 5 mole per cent total C_4 and C_5 olefins?

Answer: Figure 6.5 shows that the reactivity of the original fuel was 5 per 100 grams of evaporated loss whereas with zero olefins it would be about 2.7, a 46% reduction in smog-forming potential.

Other Factors

Design factors affecting the evaporative losses include the peak tank temperature, the area of the liquid vapor surface, and the amount of agitation. From the foregoing discussion, it is obvious that any design change which reduces the peak tank temperature will reduce the tank loss. Such modifications include tank insulation, lower surface to volume ratio of tank, and better tank orientation or location for reduced heat pickup from solar radiation or other heat source such as the exhaust system.

The surface area for evaporation and tank agitation are factors which influence the speed with which equilibrium is achieved. If the amount of evaporated fuel lags the fuel temperature increase in the tank, then the total loss will be reduced, for the tank temperature will reach its peak and then drop before the amount predicted by equilibrium considerations will be evaporated. Design factors influencing the speed at which equilibrium is achieved included:

(a) the liquid-vapor surface area. An hourglass-shaped tank approaches equilibrium slowly when the liquid level is near the waist.

(b) degree of agitation. The establishment of concentration gradients in the liquid or vapor will slow evaporation. Agitation of the tank by driving the vehicle over a rough road will speed up the evaporation loss.

(c) baffles in the tank. These can reduce losses by maintaining concentration gradients.

Calculation of Evaporative Emissions

Because carburetor and fuel tank losses are similar to simple distillation and evaporation processes, established analytical techniques can be used to predict their amount and composition with good accuracy. Since this aspect of evaporative emission is beyond the scope of this text, the student is referred to References 6 and 7 for a detailed discussion of such analytical techniques.

REFERENCES

1. Jackson, M. W., and R. L. Everett. "Effect of Fuel Composition on Amount and Reactivity of Evaporative Emissions," SAE PT-14, 802 (1967–70).
2. Martens, S. W., and K. W. Thurston. "Measurement of Total Vehicle Evaporative Emissions," SAE PT-14, 191 (1967–70).
3. Clarke, P. J., et al. "An Adsorption-Regeneration Approach to the Problem of Evaporative Control," SAE PT-14, 756 (1967–70).
4. Van Wylen, G. J., and R. E. Sonntag. "Fundamentals of Classical Thermodynamics," (New York: John Wiley and Sons, 1967).

5. Deeter, W. F., et al. "An Approach for Controlling Vehicle Emissions," SAE Preprint 680400 (1968).
6. Muller, H. L., et al. "Determining the Amount and Composition of Evaporation Losses from Automotive Fuel Systems," SAE **PT-12**, 402 (1963–66).
7. Wade, D. T. "Factors Influencing Vehicle Evaporative Emissions," SAE Preprint 670126 (1967).
8. Obert, E. F. *Internal Combustion Engines*, 3rd ed. (Scranton, Pa.: International Textbook Co., 1968).
9. Maxwell, J. B. *Data Book on Hydrocarbons* (New York: van Nostrand Co., 1958).
10. Koehl, W. J. "Mathematical Model for Prediction of Fuel Tank and Carburetor Evaporation Losses," SAE Preprint 690506 (1969).

7

PRESENT AND FUTURE EMISSION CONTROL SYSTEMS FOR GASOLINE ENGINES

To meet the need for continuing reduction of emission levels from gasoline engine powered vehicles, efforts must be concentrated in the four areas of engine design, fuel system design, exhaust treatment devices, and evaporative emission devices. It is the purpose of this chapter to discuss some of the more important current and potential future control systems for these vehicles. Laboratory tests have demonstrated that there are many different methods for reducing exhaust and evaporative emissions. Some have been discussed in earlier chapters. The control systems that finally find their way into production vehicles depend on production feasibility and cost compared to alternative solutions.

Gasoline Engine Design

Crankcase Emission

Formerly the blowby gases from the cylinders into the crankcase were vented directly to the atmosphere by the road draft tube—dashed lines in Figure 7.1. These gases have high concentrations of unburned fuel, lubricating oil vapor and partially reacted hydrocarbons. Also present in varying amounts are H_2, CO, CO_2, H_2O, O_2, N_2, and NO. It has been estimated that the blowby gases contributed 20–25% of all hydrocarbon emissions from uncontrolled vehicles.

Table 7.1 shows a comparison between blowby gas composition and exhaust gas composition. The high O_2 concentration result is evidence of a relatively large amount of raw mixture escaping by the compression rings into the crankcase during the compression and early combustion processes. Figure 7.2 shows the mass emission of unburned hydrocarbon from the crankcase compared to

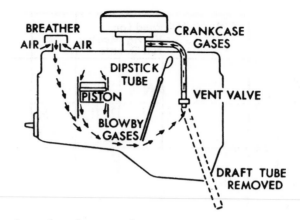

Figure 7.1.   Internal crankcase ventilation system.

that from the exhaust of one uncontrolled vehicle. In this case they are clearly about the same order of magnitude.

The addition, in 1963, of the positive crankcase ventilation system shown schematically in Figure 7.1 virtually eliminated all the blowby losses. In later years the breather cap was connected to the clean side of the air cleaner and purge rates increased. This has taken care of any possible large increase in blowby from older engines which could have backed up through the breather cap into the atmosphere. All cars are now equipped with such "closed" PCV systems shown in Figure 7.3.

Control of the volume of recirculated blowby is achieved by a

Table 7.1

**Orsat Analyses of Exhaust
and Blowby Gases**

	Volume per cent		
	CO_2	O_2	CO
Rich Air/Fuel (12.6)			
Exhaust Gas	11.0	0.7	4.6
Blowby Gas	1.5	17.9	0.4
Lean Air/Fuel (16.4)			
Exhaust Gas	13.0	2.6	0.5
Blowby Gas	1.8	18.4	0.3

Data from Reference 1.

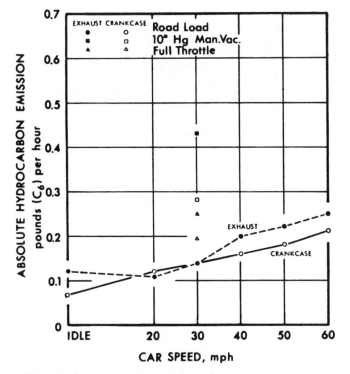

Figure 7.2. Crankcase and exhaust hydrocarbon emission. (Figure from Reference 1.)

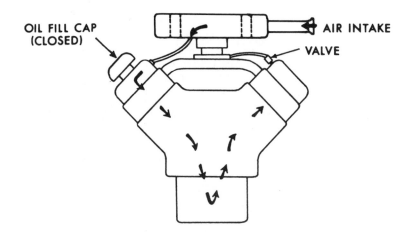

Figure 7.3. Closed manifold PCV system.

vacuum sensitive valve with a variable orifice. The valve, called the PCV valve, must

- eliminate excessive flow at idle and other high vacuum operating points. This would bypass the function of the carburetor and lead to poor engine performance at these conditions.
- provide adequate capacity at WOT where blowby is high and vacuum is low.

Figure 7.4 shows the engine blowby as a function of speed and load and a typical valve characteristic. Ideally the valve should just match the blowby flow. Figure 7.5, a schematic of a typical valve, shows the valve position under high and low vacuum operation. When vacuum is high, the valve is pulled to the right, restricting the flow to match the blowby curve of Figure 7.4.

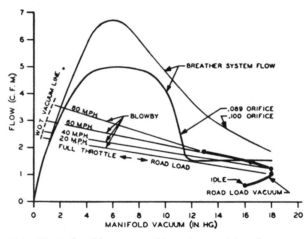

Figure 7.4. Typical calibration problem in matching flow control valve to engine blowby characteristics. (Figure from Reference 3.)

Present crankcase ventilation systems have completely eliminated the crankcase as a source of atmosphere contamination. No additional future control is required.

Exhaust Emission Reduction

UNBURNED HYDROCARBONS AND CARBON MONOXIDE

Most of the gasoline engine design factors that affect the exhaust emissions were discussed in Chapter 5. Lean mixture oper-

ENGINE OFF IDLE OR CRUISE ACCELERATION

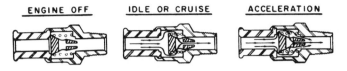

Figure 7.5. PCV valve. (Figure from Reference 2.)

ation, retarded spark timing, reduced compression ratio, lower valve overlap and lower surface to volume ratio combustion chambers are the major engine modifications made for control of hydrocarbon and carbon monoxide emission. Higher temperature thermostats have been used in some cases to reduce hydrocarbon emissions. Many of these changes reduce the thermal efficiency of the engine and thus increase the heat rejection to the coolant. This requires an increase in the cooling system capacity. The higher exhaust temperature resulting from the reduced efficiency and the presence of oxygen in the exhaust due to leaning the mixture may increase valve burning problems and exhaust system deterioration.

Hydrocarbon and CO emissions have been further reduced by decreasing manifold vacuum at idle. This has been accomplished by increasing idle speed and retarding idle timing, both of which require larger throttle openings. On some vehicles dual diaphragm distributors have been used which permit substantial retard at idle without causing excessive retard at WOT, which would result in a peak power loss. The problem arises because distributor vacuum is essentially zero at both idle and WOT with ported spark. Thus excessive retard would be applied at the WOT condition as well as at idle. Decreasing vacuum at idle decreases exhaust dilution which lowers HC emissions and allows a leaner stable idle which decreases HC and CO further. These changes also promote exhaust after-reaction.

Increasing throttle opening at idle coupled with leaner idle operation (near chemically correct) has increased autoignition (dieseling) problems. Dieseling results from deposit ignition which is enhanced when dilution is reduced (and combustion potential increased). Moreover, autoignition of the fuel is optimized near chemically correct mixture ratios as Figure 2.20 and Figure 3.3 suggest. To eliminate dieseling after shut down, some cars have a throttle positioner which allows the throttle to completely close when the ignition is turned off.

Hydrocarbon emission under high vacuum deceleration conditions has been decreased by either limiting dilution with throttle crackers or dashpots, or by fuel shut off devices. The effectiveness of such devices is shown in Figure 7.6.

One recent innovation is the transmission controlled spark valve. This valve routes the manifold vacuum signal to the distributor only in direct drive and gives no advance in lower gears. Retarding the spark in this manner does not depreciate fuel economy too much unless there is a great deal of stop and go driving. However, this reduces HC, NO, and aldehyde emissions significantly.

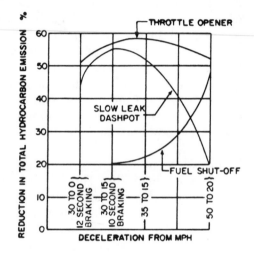

Figure 7.6.   Typical reduction in hydrocarbon emission from principal types of devices. (Figure from Reference 4.)

OXIDES OF NITROGEN CONTROL

NO, the principle oxide of nitrogen exhaust emission, is formed in the combustion chambers at peak temperature and is increased as oxygen availability is increased. Lean mixtures which minimize CO and HC maximize NO. Reducing peak combustion temperature is the only practical way to reduce NO formation in the chamber for a fixed mixture composition. This can be achieved by retarding the spark or diluting the incoming fuel-air mixture. Dilution may be achieved by either injecting an inert fluid such as water into the fresh mixture or by recirculating a portion of the exhaust gas.

Water injection has been experimentally proven to be effective in reducing NO as shown in Figure 7.7a. Per cent NO reduction is shown as a function of water injection rate divided by fuel rate. At

1 lb of water per 1 lb of fuel, a 60% reduction was achieved. Theoretically a slight benefit in BSFC may result with water injection as shown in Figure 7.7b. Since NO is high during high load operation (such as acceleration), water injection may be re-

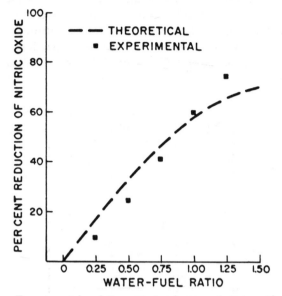

Figure 7.7a. Experimental and theoretical reduction of nitric oxide with water injection; fuel-air equivalence ratio – 1.0. CFR Engine. (Figure from Reference 5.)

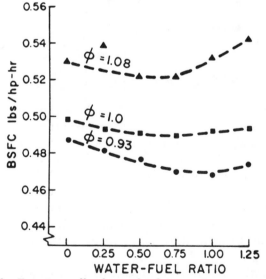

Figure 7.7b. Experimentally observed influence of water injection bsfc; inlet manifold pressure – 14.7 psia (nominal); compression ratio – 8.5:1; ignition – 28 deg btdc. CFR Engine. (Figure from Reference 5.)

quired during this time only. Engineers tend to dislike water injection because it requires a large water tank which the customer must keep filled in order to make the emission control system effective. Freezing, oil dilution and rust are additional problems.

Exhaust gas recirculation, EGR, is a much more promising method for reduction of NO. In this system exhaust is recirculated, often from the crossover, directly into the intake manifold. Figure 7.8 shows one method. Here two tubes recirculate exhaust gas from the crossover to each side of the manifold. Good cylinder to cylinder distribution of gas is essential for maximum benefit. Figures 7.9a and 7.9b show calculated theoretical benefits of exhaust gas recirculation. At a chemically correct air-fuel ratio, 70% NO reduction can be obtained with 20% recycle. Theoretically this depreciates fuel economy only 3% as shown in Figure 7.9b. Figure 7.10 shows vehicle data at 30 mph for different recycle rates. The data reflect an automatic carburetor. A noticeable fuel economy penalty was observed in the vehicle.

A major problem of EGR is poor driveability caused by an increase in residual gases. This often necessitates richer mixtures. In addition, excessive intake system deposit build-up and increased oil sludging occur.

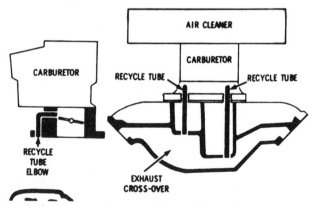

Figure 7.8. Carburetor recycle system. (Figure from Reference 6.)

OTHER APPROACHES

Many engineers think that additional emission gains through engine modifications may be small compared to the cost or performance penalties of other control methods. Undoubtedly further research will uncover new techniques. One promising but potentially expensive and complicated technique is variable valve timing which provides internal exhaust gas recirculation directly.[14]

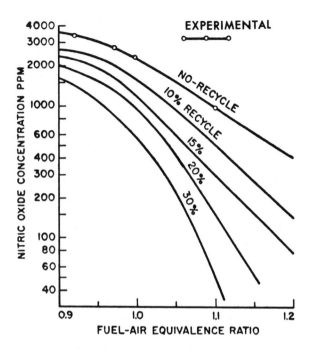

Figure 7.9a. Variation of exhaust nitric oxide with fuel-air equivalence ratio, CR 8:1. (Figure from Reference 7.)

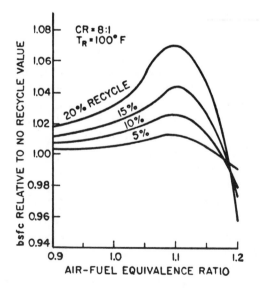

Figure 7.9b. Influence of recycle on bsfc. (Figure from Reference 7.)

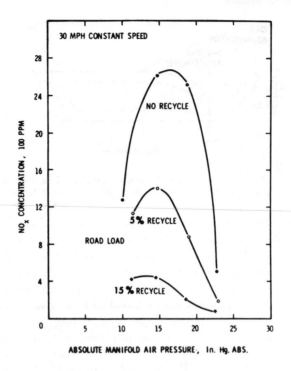

Figure 7.10. Effect of load on NO$_x$ for different recycle rates. (Figure from Reference 6.)

Fuel System Design

Fuel system design for low exhaust emission has centered around improvements in carburetor design and manufacture. Leaner average operation has been achieved through better atomization and mixing of the fuel with the air. Smaller primary venturii can achieve this by increasing air velocity which promotes mixing, increases the rate of evaporation, and enhances the metering signal (GM Quadrajet). In addition, carburetor tolerances have been cut. The rich limit carburetor is now set only 6% richer than lean limit rather than 12% as it was formerly. Each carburetor is checked on a flow stand and an adjustment is made to control the off-idle mixture ratio. Finally, the idle adjustment itself has been limited so that excessively rich mixtures at idle cannot be obtained. Figure 7.11 indicates the two set points.

It is well known that carburetor metering is changed when ambient air temperature is changed. This arises because fuel flow rate is a function of venturi air velocity and not of both velocity

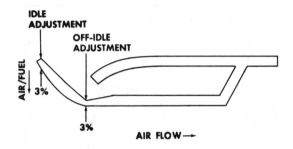

Figure 7.11. A 3% tolerance band can be maintained at two points in the metering curve with assembly line adjustments. (Figure from Reference 11.)

and density. This means that delivered mixtures are too rich when carburetor air temperature is high and air density low. Normally the carburetor calibration for a car is established in a cool ambient temperature (around 35°F) to provide surge-free operation there. In warmer ambients the mixture becomes too rich. Most emission control systems preheat the air to 100–110°F so that the carburetor air temperature is about the same winter and summer. Thus a leaner summer calibration can be obtained without poor winter driveability. On some vehicles a throttle override is added which permits cold air to bypass the air preheater and enter directly the air cleaner when the throttle is opened wide. Air preheaters have minimized carburetor icing problems and have eliminated the need for the exhaust crossover valve on some engines.

Promising designs for better mixture preparation and distribution in future engines include the three barrel carburetor and dual induction manifold system. These devices are discussed by Bartholomew in Reference 8. The three barrel carburetor has a very small diameter primary venturi which meters idle and off-idle fuel requirements up to 70 mph. No separate idle system is used. At 70 mph the two larger rear barrels open to provide full power.

The dual manifold system employs the principle of high velocity in the intake manifold for good mixing and increased evaporation. A separate small diameter manifold is used to provide idle and road load up to 70 mph mixtures to the engine. It feeds off the primary barrel of the three barrel carburetor. A separate large diameter manifold system is used for full power and feeds off the secondary barrels. The mixture from the primary runners can be directed into the cylinder in such a way that increased combustion chamber swirl results.

Figure 7.12 shows Bartholomew's manifold. Figure 7.13 shows

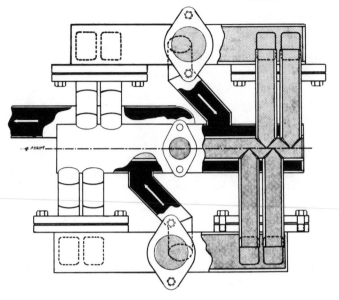

Figure 7.12. Dual mixture-induction system for large V8 engine. (Figure from Reference 8.)

another less successful dual manifold design. Figure 7.14 shows comparative hydrocarbon emissions from the standard and Bartholomew's dual induction system. If surge-free operation can be made lean enough, then all three emission constituents can be reduced.

Fuel injection has been suggested as a means for improving fuel distribution and lean mixture driveability, thereby decreasing HC and CO emission through leaner operation, especially during warm-up. Volkswagen has developed a commercial electronically-controlled injection system for some of their engine-vehicle combinations. This system is described in Reference 15. In general, under warmed-up operation, experience suggests that only a modest hydrocarbon reduction can be achieved with fuel injection. However, CO can be reduced to 0.2% or less because leaner surge-free operation is possible.

Fuel injection is best for improving full load power where maximum volumetric efficiency is required. Accurate metering of the small amount of fuel required for road load and idle operation in an individual cylinder presents a formidable problem for the fuel injection engineer. This is the critical operating range for emission reduction. In a vehicle which has good manifold heating, a carburetor could provide better warmed-up fuel preparation and distribution at light loads. European vehicles, which have little

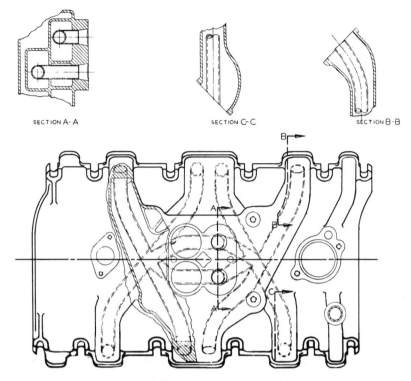

SECTION A-A   SECTION C-C   SECTION B-B

Figure 7.13. Dual manifold. (Figure from Reference 9.)

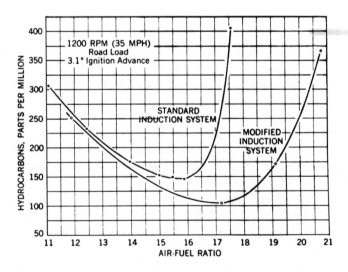

Figure 7.14. Effect of design of mixture-induction system on hydrocarbon emission. Large V8 engine. (Figure from Reference 8.)

manifold heating, apparently are improved with fuel injection. Deposit build-up on the fuel nozzles as mileage increases may seriously upset the fuel delivery balance between cylinders, leading to increased emissions and poor driveability. As a result, increased maintenance may be a problem with fuel injection. At the time of this writing, the major attribute of fuel injection is fast and lean warm-up. Also, atmospheric pressure and temperature compensation may be easier than with a carburetor.

Exhaust Treatment Devices

To date the most successful exhaust treatment technique used commercially has been air injection into the exhaust system. To meet extremely low emission levels proposed for the mid- and late 1970's, it is likely that some additional exhaust treatment devices will be required. Both catalytic and thermal exhaust reactors have the potential for very low emissions. Laboratory tests have demonstrated that vehicle emissions from the Federal test can be reduced to the following levels with such systems:

HC—less than 50 ppm
CO—less than 0.3 mole %
NO—less than 500 ppm.

Improvements will be needed to meet the more stringent Federal 1975 and 1976 requirements.

Catalysts

Several catalysts have shown ability to oxidize hydrocarbons and CO in the exhaust. Usually a noble metal such as platinum, or an oxide, is needed as a part of the catalyst formulation. Catalysts are often granular alumina pellets made with very high surface area per unit volume. The catalyst material is deposited upon the surface of the pellet. Typical catalysts may have as much as 500,000 ft^2 of surface area per lb of material. The catalyst container may look much like a muffler and be located in the conventional muffler position. Catalyst volume may run between 200 and 400 in^3. Figure 7.15 shows one container design. Typically six to eight pounds of catalyst are used. Location as close to the engine as possible is desirable for minimum heat loss although over heating is also a problem.

The benefit of the catalyst is that it permits the oxidation reactions to occur rapidly at relatively low temperatures. In general

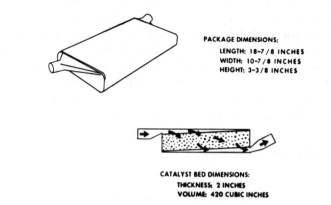

PACKAGE DIMENSIONS:
LENGTH: 18-7/8 INCHES
WIDTH: 10-7/8 INCHES
HEIGHT: 3-3/8 INCHES

CATALYST BED DIMENSIONS:
THICKNESS: 2 INCHES
VOLUME: 420 CUBIC INCHES

Figure 7.15. A catalytic converter. (Figure from Reference 10.)

the curves of Figure 7.23 for thermal reactors apply except that higher reaction efficiency (high specific reaction rate) occurs at lower temperatures. Figure 7.16 shows comparative temperature and reactor efficiency as a function of elapsed time on the Federal cycle. Fast warm-up (low thermal inertia and good heat conservation) are important for good emission reduction on the cycle.

One problem with catalysts is that they deteriorate with mileage. Figure 7.17 shows this effect for the hydrocarbons. Often the deterioration is produced by lead compounds in the exhaust which plug the bed and coat the active catalyst surface. In this test the catalyst is deactivated after 12,000 miles with Indolene 30 gasoline containing 3 cc TEL. Figure 7.18 shows that this particular catalyst was not as greatly deactivated in its ability to remove CO. Some catalyst deterioration occurs even without TEL in the fuel.

Catalysts may use air injection to complete combustion or they may operate without air utilizing excess oxygen from lean engine mixtures if good heat conservation is achieved. There is evidence that some catalysts accumulate oxygen during lean operating modes, such as cruise. This oxygen then reacts during richer modes, such as idle when there is a deficiency of oxygen in the exhaust.

Catalytic reduction of NO is more of a problem. A chemically reducing environment is required and this means rich engine operation and a fuel economy penalty. Many NO catalysts have been found to produce ammonia,[18,19] a very toxic compound.

All catalysts may emit trace metalic compounds as the catalyst support breaks up in normal driving. Possible health aspects must

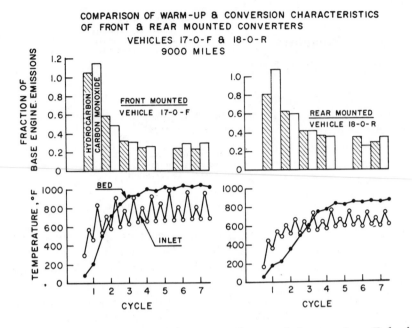

Figure 7.16. Temperatures and emissions from catalytic converters — Federal test cycle. (Figure from Reference 11.)

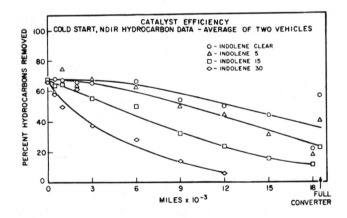

Figure 7.17. Catalyst hydrocarbon efficiency vs. miles. (Figure from Reference 11.)

be considered. Monolithic catalysts are much better in this respect.

Thermal Reactors

BASIC PRINCIPLES

One of the methods used in production to reduce hydrocarbon and CO emissions is air injection into the exhaust system.[13] Oxides of nitrogen are not reduced; in fact, they may be increased if sufficiently high exhaust temperature results from the combustion of the CO and hydrocarbons with the added air or if the injected air enters the cylinder during the overlap period, thereby leaning the mixture in the cylinder. To achieve a high degree of exhaust system oxidation of HC and CO a high exhaust temperature coupled with sufficient O_2 and residence time to complete the combustion is needed. If a flame is established, the heat generated by the combustion of the CO and hydrocarbons keeps the reaction going.

Because of its abundance, the carbon monoxide in the exhaust provides most of the combustion-generated heat. Quite often CO concentrations of several per cent are measured (1% = 10,000 ppm). On the other hand, HC concentrations are only a few hundred ppm. As a result, thermal reactors are developed most easily for rich carburetion. Brownson and Stebar[16] have studied thermal

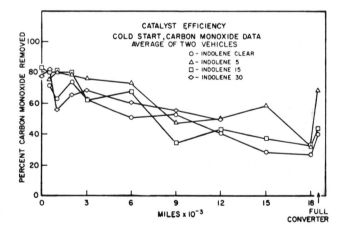

Figure 7.18. Catalyst carbon monoxide efficiency vs. miles. (Figure from Reference 11.)

reactor performance for a reactor coupled to a single cylinder CFR engine. In their work an insulated exhaust mixing tank of 150 in³ was used for some tests. They determined that the basic factors governing the combustion of CO and hydrocarbons in the exhaust system are composition of the reacting mixture, temperature and pressure of the mixture, and residence time of the mixture or time available for reaction.

Figure 7.19 shows the hydrocarbon and CO emissions as a function of air-fuel ratio and injected air flow rate. The emission concentration results were corrected for the added air. Injected air flow rate is indicated as a percentage of the engine air volume flow rate. The insulated 150 in³ exhaust mixing tank was used.

The minimum HC concentrations occurred at rich mixtures. When too much air was injected, especially at lean mixtures, excessive cooling of the exhaust increased HC concentrations to above those with no air. Thus the normal oxidation process was apparently inhibited by this cooling. The effect of air injection on CO concentration was somewhat different. Exhaust CO was uniformly low at most rich air-fuel ratios. A small increase in CO occurred slightly richer than stoichiometric. At stoichiometric mixtures and leaner, CO was very low. Best results occurred for rich mixtures with air injection at 20–30% of inlet air flow. The leanest air-fuel ratio for best emission reduction was 13.5:1. Normally engine operation at such a rich mixture would reduce fuel economy 10%.

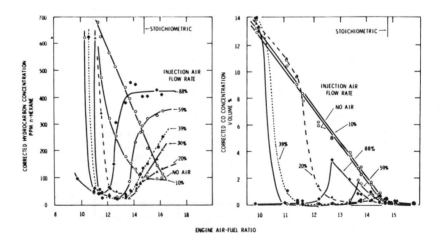

Figure 7.19. Effect of air-fuel ratio and injection air flow rate on exhaust hydrocarbon and CO concentration. 1200 RPM, 9″ Hg. Vac., MBT spark. Insulated 150 in exhaust manifold. (Figure from Reference 16.)

To further study the peculiar shape of the CO curve with air injection, a quartz window was installed in the exhaust system. For each air injection rate tried, a blue-white luminous flame was observed for all mixture ratios to the left of the small CO peak up to the rich mixture where the large CO increase occurred near 11:1. The very low emissions with rich mixtures and air injection arose from a "fire" in the exhaust system. For mixtures leaner than the small CO peak, nonluminous oxidation occurred and CO emission reduction was relatively poor.

OPTIMIZATION OF AIR INJECTION RATE

At each air-fuel ratio there exists one minimum air injection rate that provides maximum emission reduction. Minimum air flow is desired in order to reduce pump power requirement, size and cost. Figure 7.20 shows the optimum air injection rate for the data of Figure 7.19 for both HC and CO emissions. It is apparent that air injection was not highly effective in reducing CO emission unless luminous burning (flame) occurred. This did not happen when the mixture ratio provided by the carburetor was chemically correct or leaner.

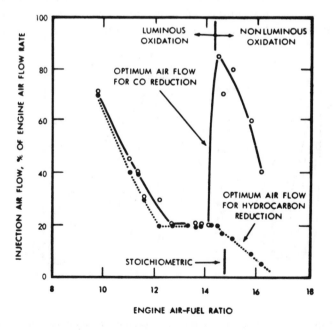

Figure 7.20.   Effect of air-fuel ratio and type of oxidation on injection air flow requirements. (Figure from Reference 16.)

EXHAUST TEMPERATURE AND PRESSURE

Figure 7.21 shows the result of a small (80°F) exhaust temperature reduction at 14:1 air-fuel ratio. As a result of the temperature decrease, luminous burning could not be established and minimum CO concentration required a 90% air flow rather than a 20% flow. A result such as this demonstrates the possible dependence of the required air injection rate on ambient temperature and prior engine operation (state of warm-up). Conversely these data also show that small changes in engine condition might produce large changes in air injection effectiveness.

Exhaust system insulation may be necessary to achieve high reaction rates in engines with well-cooled exhaust ports. Insulation also helps to reduce emissions during warm-up by accelerating warm-up rate.

At mixtures significantly leaner than stoichiometric in the range of 16 to 17.5:1, air injection is not needed to supply O_2; in fact it would only cool the exhaust to too low a temperature for any reaction to occur. On the other hand, at such lean mixtures only extremely good heat conservation can produce temperatures high enough for appreciable reaction. Warren[17] has studied this lean region and has concluded that with improved carburetion it is

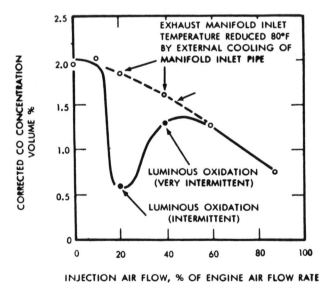

Figure 7.21. Importance of temperature in promoting luminous oxidation. (Figure from Reference 16.)

possible to achieve surge-free vehicle operation at 17 to 17.5:1 and leaner. When this can be achieved, both HC and CO exhaust emissions are reduced to extremely low values (HC less than 50 ppm, CO less than 0.1%, Federal Emission Tests) if exhaust temperature is maintained high enough through proper insulation. Unfortunately oxides of nitrogen are high at 17:1. Even leaner operation is necessary to reduce all three emission components. Promising work in this direction is currently underway.

For lean mixtures, Warren[17] has derived the following equation for the concentration of hydrocarbons leaving the exhaust system:

$$C_o = C_i \exp \left(\frac{- K_r O_2 P^2 V}{K_3 T^2 W} \right)$$

where C_o = conc. of HC leaving exhaust system

C_i = conc. of HC leaving cylinders and entering exhaust system

K_r = specific reaction rate, ft³/lbm-mole/sec

K_3 = constant

O_2 = oxygen concentration in exhaust gases, volume per cent

P = exhaust pressure (psia)

V = exhaust system volume available for reaction, ft³

T = absolute temperature, °R

W = mass flow rate of air, lb/sec.

Note the importance of the pressure term. Increasing exhaust system back pressure promotes after-reaction. However, commercially the possible back pressure increase is small.

Figure 7.22 shows the effect of temperature on specific reaction rate, K_r, calculated from the above equation by Warren from his experimental data. The nearness of his curve to a straight line suggests the equation is a good approximation for the overall reactions occurring. Note that a decrease in exhaust temperatures from 1100 to 1000°F decreases the reaction rate by a factor of 10.

EXHAUST SYSTEM VOLUME–RESIDENCE TIME EFFECTS

Figure 7.23 shows the effect of temperature and reactor volume on exhaust hydrocarbon concentration at an O_2 input concentration of 3%. Reactor volume may be viewed as the volume of the

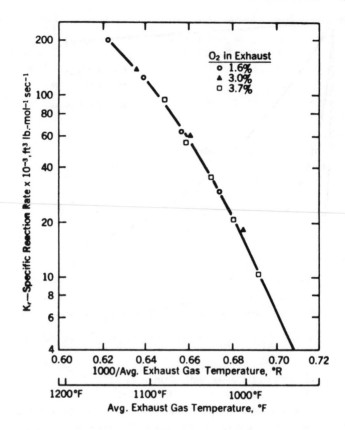

Figure 7.22. Effect of temperature on exhaust reaction rate. Single-cylinder engine, 1350 rpm. (Figure from Reference 17.)

exhaust system which is insulated and at the high temperature needed for reaction. Note that if the exhaust temperature were 1400°F, only twice the convention system volume is required for virtually complete elimination of the hydrocarbons. On the other hand, if the temperature were only 1200°F, eight times the volume would achieve only a 76% reduction. A pair of conventional exhaust manifolds has about 0.09 ft³ of volume.

Increasing the exhaust system volume increases the residence time during which reactions can occur. This is a benefit, providing the added surface area does not result in excessive cooling. Thus when large volume exhaust manifolds are to be used, they must be well insulated.

The importance of residence time in connection with exhaust gas temperature and composition was theoretically shown by

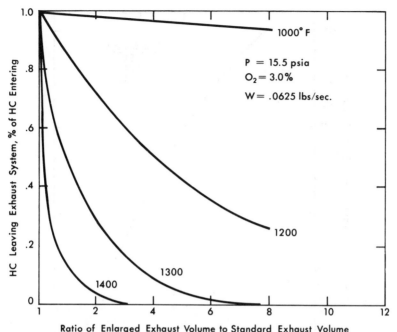

Figure 7.23. Calculated effect of volume and temperature on exhaust reaction. (Private communication, J. Warren, Ethyl Corporation.)

Schwing[20] for exhaust system oxidation of carbon monoxide and hydrocarbons. His results show how the extent of oxidation is determined by a balance between the rate of reaction and residence time and the energy liberated by combustion. Schwing's approach can be used as a design base for thermal reactors which are well mixed. The reader is referred to Reference 23 for a fundamental discussion of reactor engineering, and to References 24 and 25 for an application of these fundamentals to a multicylinder engine thermal reactor system.

Figure 7.24 shows the volume advantage which Brownson found when he added increased insulated exhaust volume at a mixture ratio of 14.5:1. In this case, CO and HC reduction are sought. Significant HC reductions were noted as volume was increased. No CO reduction was found for this nonluminous oxidation mixture ratio. Figure 7.25 shows that at a rich mixture of 12.3:1 both CO and HC were reduced to virtually zero with 150 in^3 of added insulated volume. Moreover, the minimum air injection rate requirement was decreased as added volume increased.

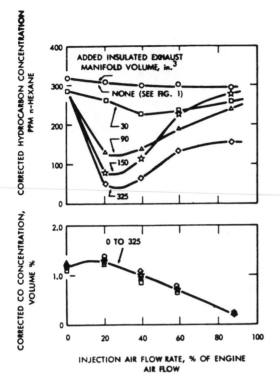

Figure 7.24. Effect of injection air flow rate and added insulated exhaust manifold volume on hydrocarbon and CO concentrations at 14.5 air-fuel ratio (nonluminous oxidation). (Figure from Reference 16.)

Without insulation, at 12.3:1 no decrease was noted in either emission constituent in spite of the volume increase. This result suggests that the exhaust oxidation occurring in the unmodified engine was in the port and immediately downstream thereof. The increased surface area of the added uninsulated volume downstream allowed enough cooling to stop the reactions that might otherwise have proceeded within this added volume had the exhaust temperature been sufficiently high.

In conclusion, increasing the residence time of the exhaust by increasing volume improves both the CO and HC oxidation effectiveness of air injection and reduces the injected air flow requirement provided that good heat conservation is maintained. This conclusion applies to both rich and lean carburetion. In fact, as Warren's data demonstrate, if surge-free carburetion can be made lean enough no air injection is required. At this point in time, no commercial carburetor has been developed which can do this. It is difficult to achieve good exhaust clean up near stoichiometric with or without air injection.

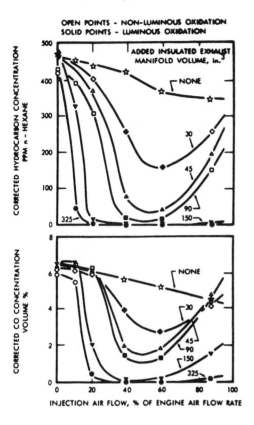

Figure 7.25. Effects of injection air flow rate and added insulated exhaust manifold volume on hydrocarbon and CO concentrations at 12.3 air-fuel ration. (Figure from Reference 16.)

VEHICLE MOUNTED SYSTEM

Thermal reactors for vehicles are normally larger than catalytic reactors because they must have higher residence time to offset lower reaction rates. Reactors may run with or without air injection depending upon engine carburetion. The most effective reactors are those that run rich with air injection. Rich engine operation produces low NO and high CO and H_2 emissions. Vehicle experience shows that combustion of the CO and H_2 with the injection air generates temperatures high enough to oxidize virtually all the unburned hydrocarbons. Getting very low CO values from reactors is more difficult than with catalysts. Much evidence exists to suggest that multicylinder engine thermal reactors are poorly mixed, leading to trace CO and HC exiting the reactor.

Figure 7.26 shows one proposed multicylinder reactor design. It has radiation shields in the exhaust ports and a high temperature

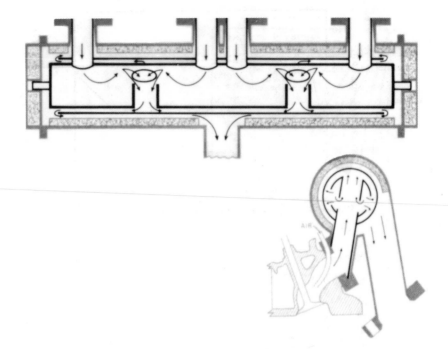

Figure 7.26.   Type III Shielded exhaust manifold reactor. (Figure from Reference 12.)

center core of about 100 in³ volume for each four cyliners. Overall reactor size is 4-1/2″ diameter × 22″ length. Two reactors are required for a V-8 engine. This reactor requires rich engine operation (10% fuel economy loss) with air injection.

Figure 7.27 shows Federal test emission levels as a function of mileage accumulation. Leaded gasoline was used. The potential for low emissions from such reactor systems is obvious. Like catalysts, low thermal inertia and good insulation promote good exhaust clean up during warm-up. Figure 7.28 shows reactor core temperature as a function of time on the test cycle. Figure 7.29 shows the HC and CO with the exhaust reactor system compared to a standard air injection system.

Exhaust Treatment Device Summary

Exhaust treatment oxidation devices are capable of reducing exhaust HC and CO to very low levels. Such reactors do not reduce NO; in fact they may increase it. However, those reactor

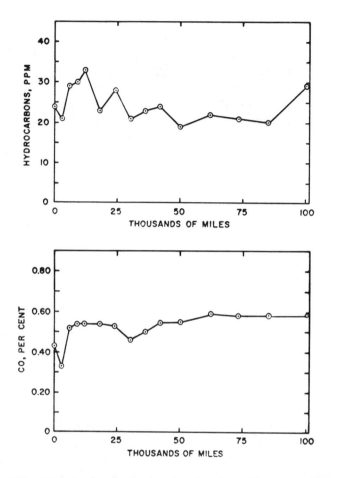

Figure 7.27. Emission levels of car equipped with an exhaust manifold reactor system. (Figure from Reference 12.)

systems employing rich carburetion emit relatively low NO because the engine emission of NO is low with rich mixtures. Lean reactors without air injection may reduce NO if surge-free vehicle operation can be as lean as 17 or 18:1. Catalytic reduction of NO is a different problem. The reduction of NO to N_2 and O_2 requires a chemical reduction process as opposed to the oxidation process required to consume CO and HC. Reactions involving both CO and NO leading to CO_2 and N_2 are possible. With rich operation a reducing catalyst with no air injection could be used upstream of an oxidizing catalyst with air injection in order to reduce all three components.[22] The ideal catalyst would reduce all three components.

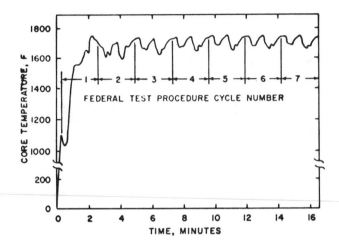

Figure 7.28.   Reactor core temperature during Federal Test Procedure. (Figure from Reference 12.)

One promising system which is very effective for CO and HC and moderately effective for NO is a small air-injected thermal reactor in series with an oxidizing catalytic bed.[22] The thermal reactor permits fast catalyst warm-up through rapid oxidation of CO, H_2 and HC during startup. Exhaust gas recirculation controls NO after warm-up when mixtures are leaned.

Table 7.2 attempts to define the advantages and problems of oxidizing exhaust treatment devices. It must be kept in mind that catalyst use would likely require nonleaded fuels barring a technological breakthrough in catalytic materials. Thermal reactors do not require special fuels.

Evaporative Control Devices

Evaporative control systems are designed to virtually eliminate the hydrocarbon vapors emitted by the carburetor and fuel tank during both running and hot soak. Present (1972) standards are 2 g/test or 4 g/day. During running, fuel tank vapors are inducted and burned in the engine. Carburetor running losses are vented to the intake system.

During hot soaks, vapors from the fuel tank are routed to a storage device. Carburetor vapors may be vented to the storage system or retained internally in the carburetor or induction system

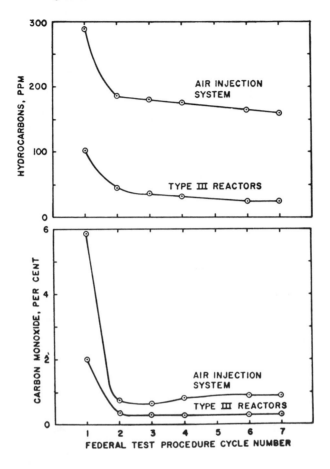

Figure 7.29. Performance of exhaust manifold reactors during the Federal Test Procedure. (Figure from Reference 12.)

volumes. Upon restart, filtered air is drawn through the stored vapors and the mixture is metered into the intake system and burned in the engine. (This can lead to a small increase initially in the exhaust HC and CO.) In this manner the storage device is purged. In some systems purging is not done at idle to prevent overrich mixtures there. The fuel tank filler cap is effectively sealed by using a moderate pressure 2 psi cap. As the tank empties, a relief valve allows air to enter and prevent tank collapse.

Two storage systems are used. One is a cannister containing activated charcoal located in the engine compartment, Figures 7.30 and 7.31. Activated charcoal has an affinity for hydrocarbons

Table 7.2

Thermal and Catalytic Comparison

Oxidizing systems	Catalytic reactors	Thermal reactors
Possible Advantages		
Reduces HC and CO	80–90%	80–90%
Reduces NO	no	no
Reduces aldehydes	50% or more	50% or more
Use same design for all vehicles	hopefully	hopefully
Long life	up to 50,000 miles?	up to 100,000 miles?
Possible Disadvantages		
Cost	high	high
Volume	high	higher
Engine mounting required	no	yes
Weight added	some	significant
Container durability problem	yes	yes
Potential over temp. problem	yes	yes
Raises engine compartment temp.	depends on location	yes
Requires non-leaded fuel	probably	no
Requires air injection	some do	some do
Lowers fuel economy	no	probably yes (depends on mixture requirement)
Decreases power	depends on back pressure	depends on back pressure
Loss of catlytic material due to attrition	yes	no
May emit other toxic material	yes	no

and on a recycle basis can store 30–35 g fuel per 100 g charcoal without breakthrough. Typically 700–800 g charcoal are used in a vehicle system. This is adequate unless a high volatility fuel is used. Often a fuel volatility limit of 10 psi RVP or less is recommended for optimum system performance.

The other system uses the crankcase to store the vapors. Under soak conditions, vapors are introduced at the breather cap, Figure

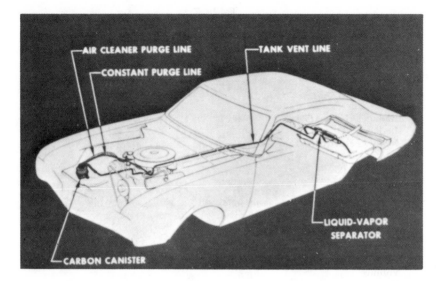

Figure 7.30. Charcoal storage system for a vehicle. (Figure from Reference 21.)

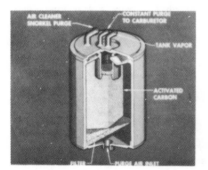

Figure 7.31. Detail of canister containing activated carbon. (Figure from Reference 21.)

7.32, where they settle into the crankcase. Purging is through the positive crankcase ventilation system. The capacity of the crankcase to store vapors is expected to depend on the vapor volume of the crankcase and the specific way the vapors are put into and removed from the crankcase. Equivalent fuel storage can be achieved in this manner. However, vapor breakthrough is more of a problem, and it is more difficult to achieve an extremely high degree of evaporative control with a crankcase storage system. Initially, concern over the effect of excessive oil dilution on engine life was expressed. However, during cold weather operation extensive dilution of engine oil results normally from liquid fuel

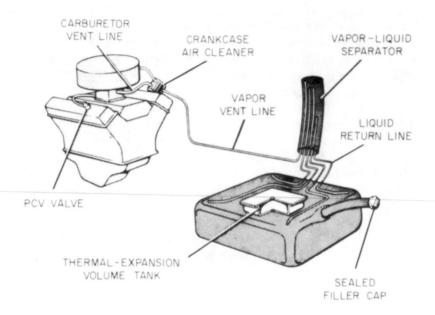

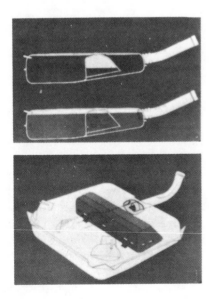

Figure 7.32. Crankcase storage system for a vehicle. (Figure from Reference 21.)

Figure 7.33. Tank design for thermal expansion of fuel. (Figure from Reference 21.)

in the cylinder seeping into the crankcase, and no additional problems were encountered with crankcase storage.

One problem with any storage system is the possibility of liquid fuel entering the storage device. To preclude this, vapors are vented at several tank locations or the tank is constructed so that at least one vent line carries vapor regardless of vehicle attitude up to 30°. Ball check valves, Figure 7.30, or a vapor liquid separator, Figure 7.32, assure that only fuel vapors reach the storage device.

In addition, a dead volume in the gas tank allows for thermal expansion of a full fuel tank. About 10% of the tank volume is partially walled off from the remainder of the tank. Tank designs such as Figure 7.33 are used. When the tank is first filled, this volume remains nearly empty. After a period of time, the fuel fills the additional volume, thereby leaving room for expansion in the rest of the tank. Otherwise expansion could force liquid fuel into the charcoal canister or the crankcase.

References

1. Bennett, P. A., et al. "Reduction of Air Pollution by Control of Emission from Automotive Crankcases," SAE **TP-6**, 224 (1964).
2. Tracy, C. B., and W. W. Frank. "Fuels, Lubricants, and Positive Crankcase Ventilation System," SAE **PT-12**, 451 (1963–66).
3. Templin, R. J. "Discussion of Reference 2," SAE **TP-6**, 249 (1964).
4. Dietrich, H. H. "Automotive Exhaust Hydrocarbon Reduction During Deceleration by Induction System Devices," SAE **TP-6**, 254 (1964).
5. Nicholls, J. E., et al. "Inlet Manifold Water Injection for Control of Nitrogen Oxides," SAE Preprint 690018 (1969).
6. Benson, J. D. "Reduction of Nitrogen Oxides in Automobile Exhaust," SAE Preprint 690019, (1969).
7. Newhall, H. F. "Control of Nitrogen Oxides by Exhaust Recirculation," SAE Preprint 670495 (1967).
8. Bartholomew, Earl. "Potentialities of Emission Reduction by Design of Induction Systems," SAE **PT-12**, 192 (1963–66).
9. Homfeld, M. F. "Discussion of Reference 8," SAE **PT-12**, 210 (1963–66).
10. Schaldenbrand, H., and J. H. Struck. "Development and Evaluation of Automobile Exhaust Catalytic Converter Systems," SAE **TP-6**, 274 (1964).
11. Weaver, E. E. "Effects of Tetraethyl Lead on Catalyst Life and Efficiency in Customer Type Vehicle Operation," SAE **PT-14**, 429 (1967–70).

12. Cantwell, E. N., et al. "A Progress Report on the Development of Exhaust Manifold Reactors," SAE PT-14, 286 (1967–70).

13. Steinhagen, W. K., et al. "Design and Development of the General Motors Air Injection Reactor System," SAE PT-12, 146 (1963–66).

14. Kirby-Meacham, G. B. "Variable Cam Timing as an Emission Control Tool," SAE Preprint 700673 (1970).

15. "Electronically Controlled Gasoline Injection Systems," Robert Bosch Corp. Technical Bulletin (January 15, 1968).

16. Brownson, D. A., and R. F. Stebar. "Factors Influencing the Effectiveness of Air Injection in Reducing Exhaust Emissions," SAE PT-12, 103 (1963–66).

17. Warren, J. A., et al. "Potentialities of Further Emissions Reduction by Engine Modifications," SAE Preprint 680123 (1968).

18. Hunter, J. E. "Effect of Catalytic Converters on Automotive Ammonia Emissions," General Motors Research Pub., GMR-1061, (March, 1971).

19. Bernstein, L. S., et al. "Application of Catalysts to Automotive NO_x Emissions Control," SAE Preprint 710014 (1971).

20. Schwing, R. C. "An Analytical Framework for the Study of Exhaust Manifold Reactor Oxidation," SAE PT-14, 368 (1967–70).

21. "Evaporative Emission Control Systems," SAE Journal, 77 (10), 47 (1969).

22. Campau, R. M. "Low Emission Concept Vehicles," SAE Preprint 710294 (1971). Also included in IIEC, A Cooperative Research Program for Automotive Emission Control, SAE SP-361.

23. Levenspiel, Octave. *Chemical Reactor Engineering* (New York: John Wiley and Sons, 1968).

24. Blenk, M. H., and R. G. E. Franks. "Math Modeling of an Exhaust Reactor," SAE Preprint 710607 (June, 1971).

25. Patterson, D. J., et al. "Kinetics of Oxidation and Quenching of Combustibles in Exhaust Systems of Gasoline Engines," 2nd annual progress report on Project CAPE-8-68, submitted to CRC, 1971.

8

DIESEL ENGINE COMBUSTION EMISSIONS AND CONTROLS

Part I   Introduction

A review of the literature on combustion engine emissions shows that most of the previous work has been concerned with emission formation in spark-ignition engines. Few studies have been directed to the mechanisms of emission formation in the diesel engine. We know that wall quenching, incomplete combustion and scavenging are the main sources of unburned hydrocarbon emission in the spark ignition engine with its homogeneous mixture. This was discussed in detail in Chapter 4. This chapter discusses the potential sources of unburned hydrocarbons and the other emissions, in the diesel engine, with its heterogeneous mixture. The emissions considered are the unburned hydrocarbons, nitrogen oxides, aldehydes, carbon monoxide, smoke particulates, and the odor constituents.

Since all these emissions are a result of the combustion process, it is necessary at this point to study the mechanisms of combustion in diesel engines. This combustion process is very complex and its detailed mechanisms are not well understood. Autoignition occurs at several locations in the combustion chamber where there is a combustible mixture. Meanwhile in some other locations the fuel may still be in the liquid phase. Under most engine operating conditions, ignition starts while some portion of the fuel has not yet been injected. The proportion of fuel present in the combustion chamber at the start of combustion to the total amount of fuel injected greatly affects the combustion process. Also the distribution of the fuel within the combustion space has a great effect on the mechanisms of combustion and emission formation. This distribution depends mainly on the injection process and the air motion.

The first part of this chapter will be concerned with the process of injection, air swirl, and spray formation. This will be followed by a study of the ignition delay and a model for the combustion and emission formation in direct-injection engines. The effect of design and operating variables on emission formation in direct-injection and indirect-injection engines will be discussed. Finally, a comparison between the emission characteristics of the different engines will be made. Many of the combustion and emission phenomena apply to both the direct-injection and indirect injection engines. These will be discussed in Parts II–VI and will not be repeated in Part VII, which deals with the indirect-injection engine.

Part II   Spray Formation

During the injection process liquid fuel is discharged from the injector nozzle under a high pressure differential. This differential varies with time. Figure 8.1 shows a typical trace of upstream fuel line pressure as a function of crank angle degrees in a direct injection engine. This pressure depends on the pump and injector characteristics. The downstream pressure is the cylinder pressure. This depends on many factors such as the compression ratio, inlet air condition, engine design, and speed. A typical cylinder pres-

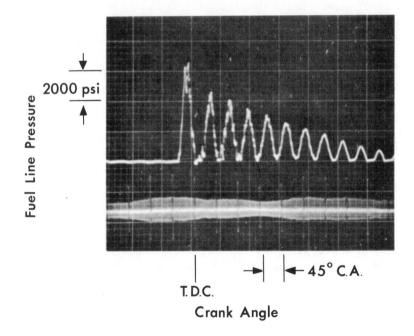

Figure 8.1.   Fuel line pressure vs. crank angle.

sure record is shown in Figure 8.2 for an open chamber engine, C.R. = 16.59, under a supercharging pressure of 15 psig. The injector opening pressure and the maximum injection pressure vary from one engine to another and depend to a great extent upon the type of combustion chamber used. In prechamber engines the fuel pressures are in general lower than in open chamber engines. In the former, mixing of fuel and air results mainly from combustion generated motion. In the latter, the mixing of the fuel and air depends mainly upon the spray atomization and penetration and the air motion. Various types of nozzles are used. In the present study we will consider the simple case of spray formation in plain orifices with single and multiple holes.

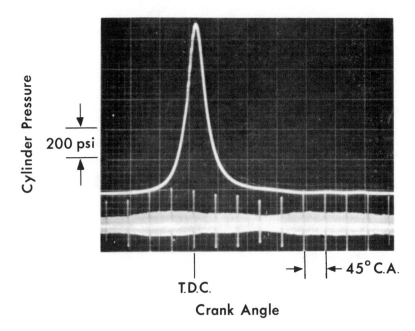

Figure 8.2. Cylinder pressure for one complete engine cycle.

Spray Formation in Stagnant Air

Figure 8.3 shows a spray formed by injecting a liquid in stagnant air. After the jet leaves the nozzle it becomes completely turbulent at a very short distance from the point of discharge.[1] Due to jet-turbulence, the emerging jet becomes partly mixed with surrounding air. Particles of the air are carried away by the jet. As a result the mass-flow increases in the x-direction. Con-

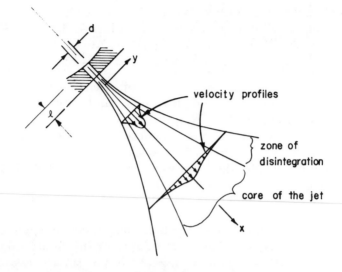

Figure 8.3. Fuel spray formation in stagnant air.

currently the jet spreads out in the y-direction. By applying the principle of conservation of momentum, we find that the jet velocity decreases. Also, the velocity of the jet will further decrease as it moves in the x-direction because of frictional drag. Figure 8.3 suggests the velocity distribution at two cross sections. The fuel velocity is highest at the centerline and decreases to zero at the interface between the zone of disintegration (or the conical envelope of the spray) and the ambient air.

Spray Atomization

The degree of atomization increases with the distance x from the nozzle tip as a result of the break up of the big droplets. Droplet break up continues whenever the Weber Number exceeds a critical value. The Weber Number is defined as the ratio of inertia body forces to surface tension forces and is given by:

$$W_e = \frac{\rho d^2 V^2}{\sigma_d} \qquad (8.1)$$

where ρ = mass density
d = droplet diameter
V = the upstream velocity
σ = surface tension

Hinze[2] found that the critical Weber Number is 10.

The degree of atomization can be indicated by the "Sauter Mean Diameter," d_s. d_s is the drop size which has the same surface-volume ratio as the total spray, and is given by:

$$d_s = \frac{\Sigma n d^3}{\Sigma n d^2} \qquad (8.2)$$

where n is the number of drops in a size group of mean diameter d.

Good spray atomization is very important for the proper operation of high speed open chamber diesel engines because the time available for combustion is limited. One effect of spray atomization is an increase in the heating rate of the liquid droplets. This results not only from an increase in the surface to volume ratio but also from an increase in the heat transfer coefficient. The increase in the surface to volume ratio can be illustrated if we consider a fuel droplet of 0.008" diameter. (This value represents the order of magnitude of the nozzle hole diameter in many high speed automotive direct injection diesel engines.) If this droplet is broken up into droplets of 20 microns diameter, the surface to volume ratio would increase about 10,000 times. The increase in heat transfer coefficient with increased atomization can be shown by considering the Nusselt number for the simple case of a sphere in stagnant air. For this case Ranz and Marshall[3] suggest:

$$Nu = \frac{hd}{k} = 2 \qquad (8.3)$$

where k = the thermal conductivity. Equation 8.3 shows that the heat transfer coefficient, h, is inversely proportional to the droplet diameter, d. In the previous example, h for the 20 micron droplet would be about 10 times that for the 0.008" droplet. Thus it can be concluded that spray evaporation is greatly promoted by atomization.

The shape of the jet and the droplet size distribution depend mainly upon the nozzle pressure differential, the geometry of the nozzle hole, the air density, and fuel properties such as viscosity and surface tension. Droplet size distribution was obtained by Sass[4] for three different nozzle diameters under a fuel pressure of 280 atmospheres (4116 psia) and an air pressure of 10 atmospheres (147 psia). Under these conditions, the droplet sizes as shown in

Figure 8.4 ranged from a diameter of about 2 microns to 40 microns. The effect of nozzle diameter on the mean droplet size is shown in Figures 8.5a and 8.5b. Figure 8.5a shows that the mean droplet diameter increases linearly with the nozzle diameter. Fig-

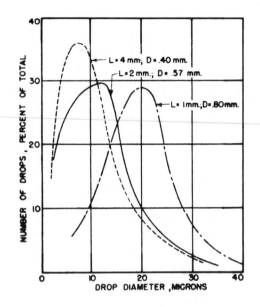

Figure 8.4. Effect of nozzle diameter on distribution of size of drops. Injection pressure 280 atm., chamber pressure 10 atm. (Figure from Reference 4.)

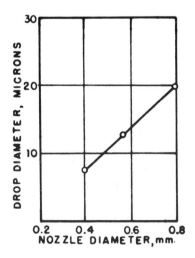

Figure 8.5a. Effect of nozzle diameter on average size of drops. Injection pressure 280 atm., chamber pressure 10 atm. (Figure from Reference 4.)

ure 8.5b shows the change in the droplet size distribution for different nozzle diameters. The effect of the chamber pressure on the average drop diameter is shown in Figure 8.6. The mean diameter decreases with the increase in the chamber pressure because of the increase in air density.

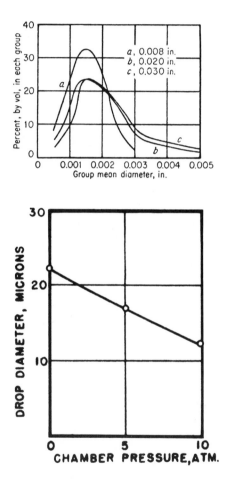

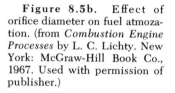

Figure 8.5b. Effect of orifice diameter on fuel atmozation. (from *Combustion Engine Processes* by L. C. Lichty. New York: McGraw-Hill Book Co., 1967. Used with permission of publisher.)

Figure 8.6. Effect of chamber pressure on average size of drops. Nozzle diameter 0.57 mm., injection pressure, 280 atm. (Data from Reference 4.)

The effect of an increase in fuel injection pressure on the decrease of the droplet size is shown in Figures 8.7a and 8.7b. The droplet sizes in Figures 8.4 and 8.7 approximate those occurring at the start of injection in naturally aspirated diesel engines. With supercharging, it is expected that the average droplet size will decrease.

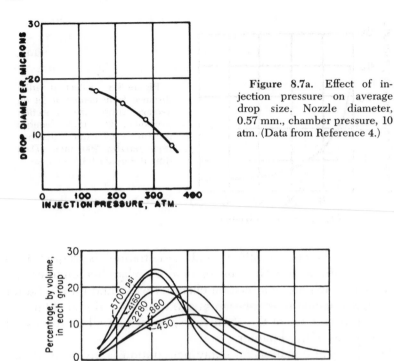

Figure 8.7a. Effect of injection pressure on average drop size. Nozzle diameter, 0.57 mm., chamber pressure, 10 atm. (Data from Reference 4.)

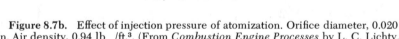

Figure 8.7b. Effect of injection pressure of atomization. Orifice diameter, 0.020 in. Air density, 0.94 lb $_m$/ft.³. (From *Combustion Engine Processes* by L. C. Lichty. New York: McGraw-Hill Book Co., 1967. Used with permission of publisher.)

The radial droplet size distribution in a fuel spray was given by Mehlig[6] for a spray under an injection pressure of 60 atm. and a chamber pressure of 2.7 atm. This is shown in Figure 8.8. Similar distributions are expected to occur at each axial position x from the nozzle. Figure 8.8 shows that the large droplets, 40μ, are located near the center and the small droplets, 2μ, are at the periphery of the spray.

On the average, the distance between centers of the fuel droplets varies from a minimum at the centerline of the spray to a maximum at the edge of the spray.

SPRAY PENETRATION

The spray penetration is measured by the distance to which the tip of the fuel spray penetrates in the combustion chamber. For

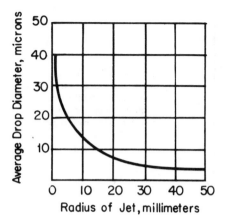

Figure 8.8. Effect of radial distance from center of jet on average drop size. Injection pressure, 60 atm., chamber pressure, 2.7 atm., distance from nozzle, 300 mm. (Data from Reference 6.)

large open-chamber engines high penetration is required to efficiently utilize the air. For small open chamber engines the spray may reach the combustion chamber walls and form a liquid film. The mechanisms of combustion of this liquid film are different from those of the atomized spray. This will be discussed in a later part of this chapter.

An empirical equation for spray penetration is given by Parks, Polonski and Toye.[7]

$$s = \frac{200\,d}{1+\rho_a} \left\{ \frac{\rho_a\sqrt{\Delta P}}{d_o}[1-(1-\frac{d}{d_o})1.12 \times 10^{-3}(T-70)]^{0.6}t^{0.6} \right\} \quad (8.4)$$

where s = penetration, in.
d = orifice diameter, in.
ρ_a = gas density relative to atmosphere
t = time
ΔP = pressure drop across orifice psi
T = gas temperature, °F
d_o = reference orifice diameter
= 0.0236 in (0.6 mm).

Equation 8.4 shows that the penetration at a given time, t, depends primarily upon the jet velocity which is proportional to $\sqrt{\Delta P}$, combustion chamber air density, ρ_a, and the orifice diameter, d. The effect of the different factors on spray penetration is shown in Figures 8.9 and 8.10. Figure 8.9 shows the effect of injection pressure on spray-tip penetration. Higher injection pressures increase the spray-tip penetration. The rate of increase decreases with the increase in pressure. Figure 8.10 shows the effect of air density on penetration. An increase in density reduces the penetration.

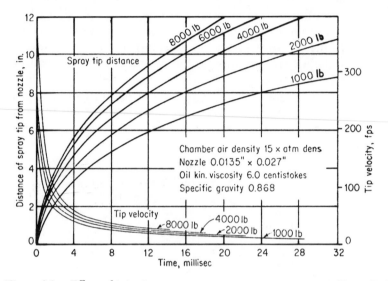

Figure 8.9. Effect of injection pressure on spray-tip penetration. (From P. H. Schweitzer, Penetration of oil sprays, Penn. State Coll. Eng. Expt. Sta. Bull. 46, 1937.

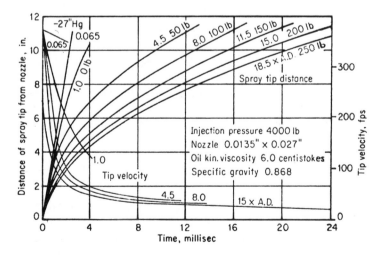

Figure 8.10. Effect of air density in combustion chamber on spray-tip penetration. (From P. H. Schweitzer, Penetration of oil sprays, Penn. State Coll. Eng. Expt. Sta. Bull. 46, 1937.)

Spray Formation in Swirling Air

AIR MOTION IN DIESEL ENGINES

One of the important design parameters in any diesel engine is the turbulence in the combustion chamber at the time of fuel injection and during the combustion process. This is particularly important in open chamber engines where the fuel is injected in the bulk of the air. In prechamber engines the fuel is injected in a portion of the air and the flow of the products of combustion from the prechamber to the main chamber is responsible for mixing the partially oxidized products and air in the main chamber. In this case the flow velocity is a function of many factors such as the area of the restriction between the prechamber and the main chamber, the rate of injection, the air pressure and temperature, and the ratio of the volumes of the two chambers. In swirl-type indirect injection engines, mixing is achieved by preinjection air motion which adds to the combustion-produced turbulence.

In open chamber engines the air velocity has two components: (a) air swirl and (b) air radial flow (squish).

1. Air Swirl. Swirl is created during the intake stroke by inducing the air into the cylinder through a shaped intake port such as that shown in Figure 8.11 which is tangential to the piston. The air swirl produced in the cylinder may be estimated from the air

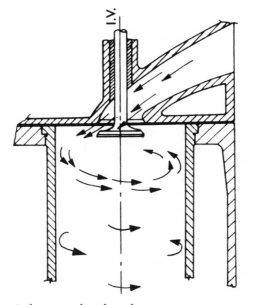

Figure 8.11.   Induction-induced swirl.

flow rate, its temperature and pressure, the air of flow through the valve, and the distance from the valve centerline to the cylinder centerline. The induced swirl can be augmented during compression by transferring the air to the recess in the piston or in the cylinder head.

2. Air Radial Flow. This is known in the literature as the "squish," and is illustrated in Figure 8.12. As the piston approaches T.D.C., the air flows radially inward toward the combustion chamber recess. The radial streams from the opposite sides meet one another, and are therefore deflected upward into the chamber. After reaching the end of the chamber, the air flows

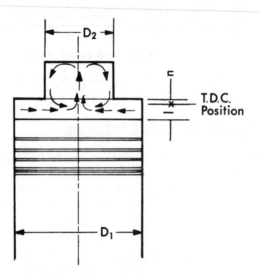

Figure 8.12.   Air radial flow.

radially outward toward the outer walls, then downward toward the open end. Here the air is met by air flowing radially inward from between the cylinder and piston, and is carried around again, producing a toroidal movement within the combustion chamber. Alcock[9] suggests a method for the calculation of the air velocity in the combustion chamber of diesel engines. Figure 8.13 shows the swirl and radial (squish) velocities in a 4.5″ × 5.25″ engine at 840 rpm. From this figure, it can be observed that the air motion is due mainly to the swirl component. The effect of the swirl component on the spray formation will be discussed later in this chapter. Normally the effect of the squish component is so small that it can be neglected.

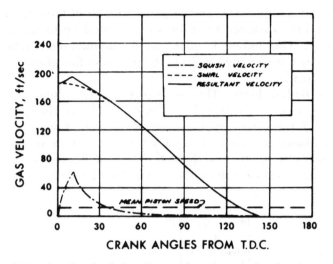

Figure 8.13. Spiral and radial air flow in a combustion chamber due to primary turbulence.

Part III   Ignition Delay in D.I. Engines

The combustion in an actual engine consists of the combustion of a single spray or a group of sprays. If we plot the gas pressure in the cylinder versus the crank angle degrees, as shown in Figure 8.14, we notice that there is a period, after the start of injection, during which the pressure appears to follow the compression curve. At the end of this period the pressure rises at an increasing rate until the maximum pressure gradient is reached in the cylinder. It is interesting to notice that the ignition delay is much longer than the period during which the active combustion takes place. This is particularly the case under part load operation. Also fuel injection continues during the ignition delay. It is obvious that the longer the delay period, the greater will be the amount of fuel accumulated in the combustion chamber before the start of combustion. This results in higher rates of pressure rise and maximum gas pressures and temperatures.

There is great emphasis attached to ignition delay in diesel engine combustion because ignition delay affects:

1. the rate of pressure rise and the maximum gas pressure. These in turn affect engine noise, vibrations and mechanical stresses.
2. the maximum gas temperature. This affects the NO_x emission, the thermal loads on the cooling system, and the temperature and thermal stressing of the combustion chamber walls.

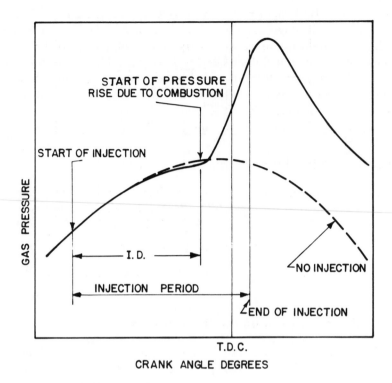

START OF PRESSURE
RISE DUE TO COMBUSTION

START OF INJECTION

GAS PRESSURE

I. D.

INJECTION PERIOD

NO INJECTION

END OF INJECTION

T.D.C.
CRANK ANGLE DEGREES

Figure 8.14. Cylinder pressure in an open chamber diesel engine with and without fuel injection.

Processes That Take Place During I.D.

The processes that take place during the ignition delay can be divided into physical and chemical processes. The physical processes are:

1. spray disintegration and droplet formation
2. heating of the liquid fuel and evaporation
3. diffusion of the vapor into the air to form a combustible mixture.

The chemical processes are:

1. decomposition of the heavy hydrocarbons into lighter components
2. preignition chemical reactions between the decomposed components and oxygen.

It is difficult to draw a distinct line separating the physical and chemical processes since they do overlap. The chemical processes start after the fuel vapor comes into contact with the air. However, at the very early stage of combustion, the mass of fuel vapor which undergoes chemical reaction is very small compared to the mass necessary to cause a detectable pressure rise. Therefore, the first part of the ignition delay is considered to be dominated by the physical processes which result in the formation of a combustible mixture. The second part of the ignition delay is considered to be dominated by the chemical changes which lead to autoignition.

Ignition Delay Definitions

Ignition delay has been defined many ways. Researchers agree that the start of fuel injection is the beginning of the delay period. The differences in definition arise from the criteria used to determine the end of delay, that is, the start of combustion. Figure 8.15

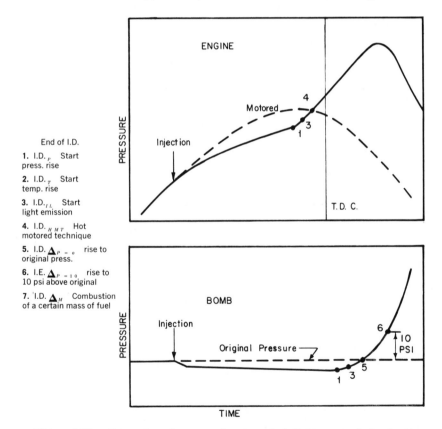

End of I.D.

1. I.D.$_P$ Start press. rise

2. I.D.$_T$ Start temp. rise

3. I.D.$_{IL}$ Start light emission

4. I.D.$_{HMT}$ Hot motored technique

5. I.D. $\Delta_{P=0}$ rise to original press.

6. I.E. $\Delta_{P=10}$ rise to 10 psi above original

7. I.D. Δ_M Combustion of a certain mass of fuel

Figure 8.15. Comparison between the several definitions used for ignition delay in bombs and engines.

lists seven definitions used. A discussion of these definitions is given in Reference 10.

The two most commonly used definitions are the pressure rise and illumination delays. The end of the pressure rise delay is defined by the point at which pressure rise caused by combustion is detected on a cylinder pressure time record. At this point sufficient exothermic reactions have occurred to cause a detectable increase in the gas pressure. The illumination delay, marked by the emission of visible radiation, is due to chemiluminescence or thermal radiation.[11] Chemiluminous radiation is believed to result from the excitation of the formaldehyde molecules, and thermal radiation is due to the high temperature carbon atoms in the flame.

Experimental evidence shows that these two combustion phenomena, illumination and pressure rise, do not occur simultaneously.[12] Illumination usually occurs after a measurable pressure rise, or in other words, the illumination delay period is longer than the pressure rise delay. This is shown in Figure 8.16 for an open combustion chamber.

In a detailed study of the ignition delay[12] it has been found that the pressure rise delay is more reproducible. Also, it has the greater engineering significance in engine design, especially as related to stresses and noise. In the present chapter all reference will be to the pressure rise delay.

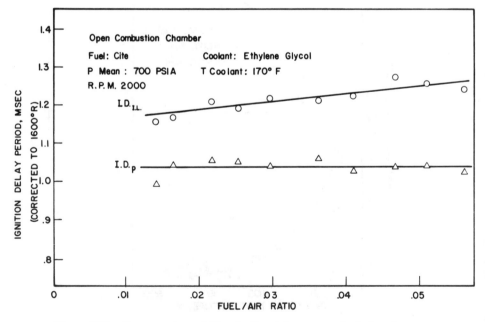

Figure 8.16. Pressure rise and illumination delays versus fuel-air ratio.

Rate-Controlling Processes in the Preignition Reactions

One of the main controversies about diesel combustion is the relative role of physical and chemical changes during the pre-ignition processes. This controversy exists because the fuel is injected in the cylinder as a liquid and it should evaporate before combustion. Spray disintegration and droplet formation have been found to take a very short time compared to the ignition delay period. A comparison between the time taken by the other physical processes such as heating, evaporation and diffusion, and that taken by the preignition chemical reactions follows.

Figure 8.17 shows the experimental results of the pressure rise delay for three fuels: diesel No. 2, CITE (Compression Ignition Turbine Engine fuel), and gasoline. These results were obtained in an open chamber, single cylinder research engine. The engine

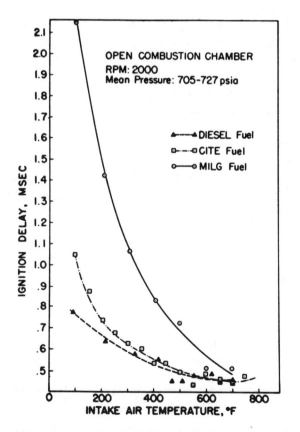

Figure 8.17.   Effect of gas temperature on ignition delay ID $_p$ for different fuels.

was run at a constant speed of 2000 rpm under steady conditions. The details of the test conditions and procedures are given in Reference 12. The integrated mean pressure during the ignition delay was kept constant at about 700 psia in order to eliminate the effect of the pressure changes on the ignition delay. The inlet air temperature was varied over a range from about 100°F to 750°F.

Figure 8.17 shows that, at any intake air temperature, gasoline fuel (of the highest volatility) has the longest ignition delay. At an intake temperature of 106°F the gasoline has an ignition delay of 2.14 milliseconds, while diesel No. 2 fuel has 0.75 millisecond, or about one-third of that for gasoline. There is no doubt that the rate of the physical processes, such as evaporation, increase with the fuel volatility. Therefore, if physical processes control the ignition delay, one would expect the ignition delay for the gasoline to be shorter than that for the other fuels.

From these results it can be concluded that the chemical processes are the rate controlling processes during the delay period. This conclusion is supported by experimental results in bombs and other engines. Figure 8.18, showing typical bomb results published by Hurn et al.,[13] illustrates the changes in air pressure which follow fuel injection in both an inert gas and in an oxidizing atmosphere. The drop in pressure results from the drop in the air temperature caused by the heat transfer from the air to the evaporating liquid fuel. These experiments were made at relatively low pressures, where the latent heat of evaporation is much higher than the increase in sensible heat. Therefore, as an approximation, it can be assumed that the ratio of the drop in pressure $(P_0 - P_\infty)$, at any time, to the total pressure drop $(P_0 - P_\infty)$ is equal to the ratio of the mass of the fuel evaporated to the total mass of the fuel injected. The pressure of the inert gas decreased with time and asymptotically reached a constant value, P_∞, where all the fuel could be assumed to be vaporized. In the oxidizing atmosphere the pressure followed that in the inert gas to the point where about 80% of the fuel was evaporated. Before this point it could be assumed that significant exothermic reactions had not yet started. If combustion occurred it would have caused the pressure trace to deviate from that of the inert gas because the ratio of the energy of combustion to the latent heat of evaporation is in the order of 100. This means that if only about 1/100 of the evaporated fuel had burned, it would have caused the pressure to reach the original pressure, P_0. One can conclude that the rate of evaporation is much faster than the rate of the chemical preignition reactions.

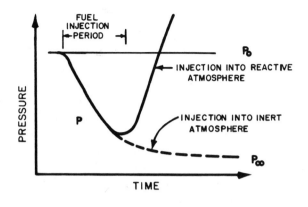

Figure 8.18. Fuel injection in inert and reactive atmospheres.

Figure 8.19 shows the ignition delay measured by Hurn *et al.*[14] in a bomb for fuels with and without additives. The only difference between the two curves is the addition of 2% n-amyl nitrate to the fuel. It is expected that the 2% additive would not greatly affect the physical processes of spray formation, evaporation, and vapor diffusion. But the additive had a great effect on the ignition delay. The ignition delay was reduced by about 45% at 900°F, and 27% at 1050°F. The reduction in the ignition delay is due to the increase in the rate of preignition chemical reactions.

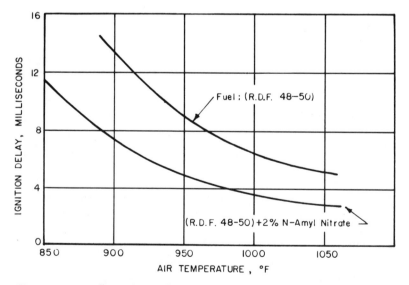

Figure 8.19. Effect of a fuel additive on the ignition delay. (Figure from Reference 19.)

Preignition Chemical Reactions

Very little is known about the detailed mechanisms of the reactions leading to the autoignition of hydrocarbon fuels in air. Even the reactions leading to the autoignition of simple hydrocarbons such as methane (CH_4) are not known. However, a study of the published data on diesel combustion indicates that two types of lumped reactions take place during the ignition delay. Garner *et al.*[15] sampled the gas in the combustion chamber of a diesel engine during the early stages of the combustion process. They found that for four different liquid hydrocarbons, peroxides and aldehydes were formed during the ignition delay and reached their peak concentration just before the start of pressure rise caused by combustion. This is shown in Figure 8.20. Also, they found that for high cetane number fuels the peak concentration of these intermediate compounds occurred earlier than with lower cetane number fuels.

Therefore we can consider the reactions taking place during the ignition delay to be divided into the following two stages:

Chain Reactions

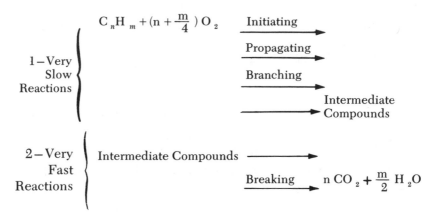

First, very slow reactions occur which form intermediate compounds such as peroxides and aldehydes. Then, once a critical concentration of these intermediate compounds has been formed, very fast chain reactions occur which lead to autoignition and the final products of combustion. If the critical concentration of the intermediate compounds is not reached in any part of the combustion chamber, for example in the very lean areas at the leading

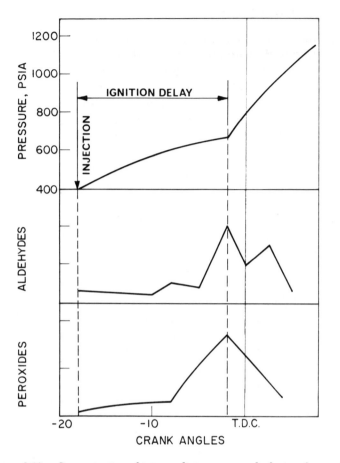

Figure 8.20. Concentration of intermediate compounds during the combustion process.

edge of the spray or in the very rich areas in the core, partial oxidation products such as the aldehydes will be formed without being completely burned.

Part IV   A Model for the Mechanisms of Combustion and Emission Formation in a Fuel Spray Injected into Swirling Air In Direct-Injection Engines

Fuel-Air Distribution in the Spray

Figure 8.21 is a schematic diagram for a fuel spray injected into swirling air. The small droplets are carried away with the air and

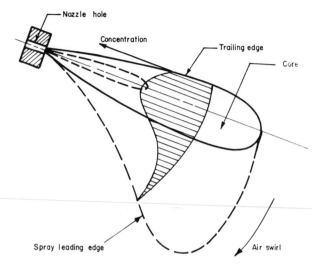

Figure 8.21. Schematic diagram for a fuel spray injected into swirling air.

form the leading edge of the spray. The relatively large droplets are concentrated in the core and the trailing edge of the spray. The average distance between the droplets changes with location in the spray, being greatest in the leading edge of the spray.

If we plot the local fuel-air ratio on a mass basis against the angle from the centerline of the injector hole, and take into consideration all the fuel present—whether it is in the liquid or the vapor phase—we get a distribution similar to that shown in Figure 8.21. This distribution varies with the radial distance from the nozzle hole. However, the leading edge of the spray always contains the smallest droplets, which are the first to evaporate. A theoretical analysis of the time required for complete evaporation of these small droplets shows that the time of evaporation of a 15μ n-dodecane droplet is less than one millisecond within the environment of the diesel combustion chamber.[16]

In actual engines the ignition delay is about one millisecond, and the actual fuel is a distillate which consists of more volatile and heavier compounds than n-dodecane. Therefore, most of the small droplets which are carried away with the swirling air may be assumed to be completely evaporated before ignition.

The smaller the droplet diameter the farther it will be carried away from the core, by the swirling air. Thus the mixture near the leading edge of the spray may be assumed to consist of premixed fuel-vapor and air before ignition. In the core the big droplets are concentrated, and they are expected to be in the liquid phase at the start of ignition.

Spray Regions

The spray may be divided into several regions depending upon the fuel-air distribution and the mechanism of combustion in each region. These are lean flame region (LFR), lean flame-out region (LFOR), spray core, spray tail, after-injection, and fuel deposited on the walls.

LEAN FLAME REGION (LFR)

The concentration of the vapor in the air between the core and the leading edge of the spray is not homogeneous, and the local fuel-air ratio may vary from zero to infinity. Ignition nuclei will be formed at several locations where the mixture is most suitable for autoignition. Photographic studies on spray combustion in diesel engines[17,18] show that ignition starts near the leading edge (downwind) of the spray. This is illustrated in Figure 8.22. Once ignition

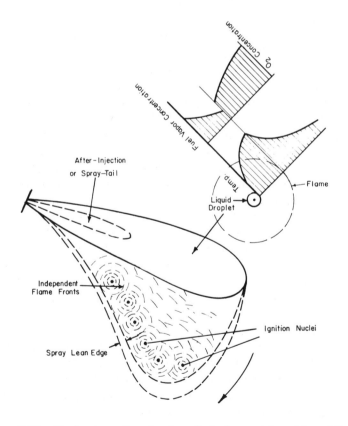

Figure 8.22. Mechanisms of combustion of a fuel spray injected in swirling air.

starts, small independent nonluminous flame fronts propagate from the ignition nuclei and ignite the combustible mixture around them; as an alternative, this area may undergo microvolume two-stage combustion.[19]

This mixture, on a mass average basis, is leaner than the stoichiometric mixture. The region in which these independent flames propagate or microvolume combustion occurs will be referred to as the "Lean Flame Region" (LFR). In this region, combustion is complete and nitric oxide may be formed at high local concentrations. Under very light loads, the temperatures may not be high enough to produce high nitric oxide concentrations at this early stage of the combustion process.

LEAN FLAME-OUT REGION (LFOR)

Near the far leading edge of the spray (downwind), the mixture is too lean to ignite or support combustion. This region will be referred to as the "Lean Flame-Out Region" (LFOR). Within this region, one would expect some fuel decomposition and partial oxidation products. The decomposition products consist of lighter hydrocarbon molecules. The partial oxidation products may contain aldehydes and other oxygenates. It is believed that this region is one of the main contributors to the unburned hydrocarbons in the exhaust. It corresponds to the quench zone in S.I. engines in terms of the formation of unburned hydrocarbons. The width of the LFOR depends upon many factors including the temperature and pressure in the chamber during the course of combustion, the air swirl, and the type of fuel. In general, higher temperatures and pressures extend the flames to leaner mixtures,[20,21] and thus reduce the LFOR width. Increases in temperature and pressure occur during the combustion of the rest of the spray. Thus, the width of the LFOR region varies and depends upon all factors which affect the cylinder gas pressure and temperature. Such factors include the overall fuel-air ratio, turbocharging, and coolant temperature.

At the borders between the LFOR and LFR, primary reactions take place and hydrocarbons are attacked and reduced to CO, H_2, H_2O, and the various radical species (H, O, OH). Other lighter unburned hydrocarbons are formed. Fristrom and Westenberg[22] suggested that a paraffin molecule in a lean fuel flame undergoes a reaction according to the following scheme:

$$OH + C_nH_{2n+2} \rightarrow H_2O + C_nH_{2n+1} \rightarrow C_{n-1}H_{2n-2} + CH_3 \quad (8.5)$$

They indicated that since hydrocarbon radicals higher than ethyl are thermally unstable the initial radical C_nH_{2n+1} usually splits off CH_3, forming the next lower ethylenic compound as in Equation 8.5. The unsaturated hydrocarbons formed are attacked rapidly by oxygen atoms in this region, forming oxygenated hydrocarbons. If the reaction is completed, as in the LFR, recombination reactions occur and produce CO_2 and H_2O. However, if the flame is extinguished as in the LFOR, then unburned hydrocarbons, oxygenated hydrocarbons, CO and other intermediate compounds are left without being completely burned.

SPRAY CORE

Following ignition and combustion in the LFR, the flame propagates toward the core of the spray. In the region between the LFR and the core of the spray, the fuel droplets are larger. They gain heat by radiation from the already established flames and evaporate at a higher rate. The increase in temperature will also increase the rate of vapor diffusion because of the increase in molecular diffusivity. These droplets may be completely or partially evaporated. If they are completely evaporated, the flame will burn all the mixture with the rich ignition limit. The droplets which are not completely evaporated will be surrounded by a diffusion-type flame as illustrated in Figures 8.22 and 8.23. The rate of combustion of these droplets depends upon many factors which govern the rate of evaporation and diffusion of the fuel vapor to the flame, and the rate of diffusion of oxygen to the flame. The combustion in the core of the jet depends mainly upon the local fuel-air ratio. Under part-load operation, this region contains adequate oxygen; combustion is expected to be complete and to result in high NO_x production. The temperature of the flame depends upon both the mixture temperature before the start of the droplet combustion and the heat of combustion which is mainly a function of the heavy compounds of fuel used. The flame zone temperature is one of the major factors affecting the NO_x formation.

Near full-load conditions, incomplete combustion occurs in many locations in the fuel-rich core. Fristrom and Westenberg[22] suggested that in fuel-rich saturated-hydrocarbon flames the initial reaction is simply the H-atom stripping, according to the following scheme:

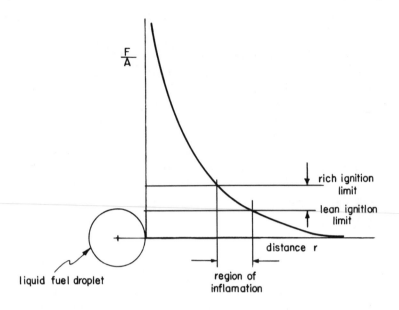

Figure 8.23. Fuel-air ratio distribution around an evaporating droplet before combustion.

$$H + C_nH_{2n+2} \longrightarrow H_2 + C_nH_{2n+1} \qquad (8.6)$$

Recombination reactions between the hydrocarbon radicals may occur, and hydrocarbons heavier or lighter than the original fuel molecules may be formed. This may explain the observations made by Barnes[23] and Milks *et al.*[24] that in diesel engines with a single compound hydrocarbon fuel, the exhaust emissions contained molecules with more and with fewer carbon atoms than the original fuel. In addition to unburned hydrocarbons, carbon monoxide, oxygenated compounds, and carbon may be formed near full-load. Nitrogen oxides are formed at low concentration under these conditions.

SPRAY-TAIL

The last part of the fuel to be injected usually forms large droplets because of the relatively small pressure differential acting on the fuel near the end of the injection process. This is caused by a combination of decreased fuel injection pressure and increased cylinder gas pressure. Also, the penetration of this part of the fuel is usually poor. This portion is referred to as the spray tail. Under high load conditions, the spray tail has little chance to get into regions with adequate oxygen concentration. However, the temperature of the surrounding gases is high (near the maximum cycle temperature), and the rate of heat transfer to these droplets is fairly high. These droplets therefore tend to evaporate quickly and decompose. The decomposed products contain unburned hydrocarbons and a high percentage of carbon molecules. Partial oxidation products include carbon monoxide and aldehydes.

AFTER-INJECTION

Under medium and high loads, many injection systems produce after-injection. When this occurs the injector valve opens for a short time after the end of the main injection. In general, the amount of fuel delivered during after-injection is very small compared to the whole amount of fuel injected. However, it is injected late in the expansion stroke, under a relatively small pressure differential, and with very little atomization and penetration. This fuel is quickly evaporated and decomposed, resulting in the formation of CO, carbon particles (smoke), and unburned hydrocarbons and oxygenated hydrocarbons. An extensive study of the effect of after-injection on exhaust smoke is given in Reference 25.

FUEL DEPOSITED ON THE WALLS

Some fuel sprays impinge on the walls. Because of the shorter spray path and the limited number of sprays this is especially the case in small, high speed D.I. engines. The rate of evaporation of the liquid film depends on many factors including gas and wall temperatures, gas velocity, gas pressure, and properties of the fuel. Previous studies by El Wakil *et al.*[26] showed that the liquid droplets reach an equilibrium temperature during evaporation and remain at this temperature until they are completely evaporated. For the liquid film, the wall temperature is generally lower than the equilibrium temperature for many compounds in the fuel. Also, the surface area for mass transfer is smaller with the liquid film than if the liquid were atomized into many droplets. Therefore, the rate of evaporation of the liquid film is expected to be less than the corresponding rate for the droplets, and it is expected that this liquid film will be the last to be evaporated. The vapor concentration is maximum on the liquid surface and decreases with increased distance from the surface. If we assume that the surrounding gas has a high relative velocity and contains enough oxygen, the flame will propagate to within a small distance from the wall. Combustion of the rest of the fuel on the walls will depend upon the rate of evaporation and mixing of fuel and oxygen. If the surrounding gas has a low oxygen concentration or the mixing is not appropriate, evaporation will occur without complete combustion. Under this condition, the fuel vapor will decompose and form unburned hydrocarbons, partial oxidation products, and carbon particles.

As the piston moves on the expansion stroke, the gases flow outward radially in an inversed squish motion to fill the expanding space between the piston top and the cylinder head. In shallow-bowl combustion chambers, most of the combustion process takes place in the bowl. In deep bowl types, the reversed squish flow is significant and will help the mixing of incomplete combustion products and oxidants during the expansion stroke. In both cases the swirl motion will continue but, because of frictional losses, at a lower rotational velocity than that on the compression stroke. The combination of inverted squish and swirl produces heterogeneous eddies and tends to draw the fuel vapor and the partial oxidation products, including carbon which has been formed from fuel deposited on the bowl walls. Photographic films by Scott[18] showed eddies and heavy smoke clouds outside the bowl from the areas where the sprays impinge the wall. These eddies are heterogeneous, and upon combustion they burn with a luminous flame because of the presence of carbon particles.[27]

Based upon the above model, the progression of combustion in the spray and the pressure and temperature development in the cylinder may be represented as shown in Figure 8.24. The emission formation expected in the different regions of the spray without fuel impingement on the walls may be summarized as shown schematically in Figure 8.25.

Part V   Heat Release Rates in D.I. Engines

Many studies have been made by Lyn,[27,28] Austen,[29] and Grigg[30] to determine the heat release rate from pressure traces obtained in open-chamber diesel engines. Figure 8.26 shows sample traces of the gas pressure, rate of heat release, and cumulative heat release. The details of the work done to obtain these traces are given in Reference 28. The negative heat release after the start of injection, at 22° BTC, is a result mainly of the heat transfer from the hot air to the liquid fuel. During the I.D. the spray is formed and the droplets at the leading edge of the spray

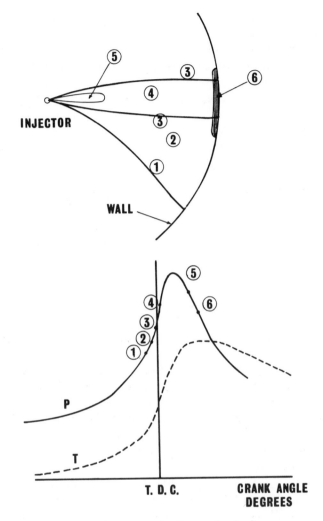

Figure 8.24. Progression of spray combustion, and cylinder pressure and temperature in a direct injection engine.

are the first to evaporate, forming a nonhomogeneous fuel-vapor-air mixture. As mentioned earlier, complete evaporation of these droplets takes place in much less time than the I.D. period.

Lyn observed that ignition occurred at 13° BTDC and the rate of burning reached its peak at about 10° BTDC; that is, it took three crank angle degrees to reach the peak. The end of the I.D., 13° BTDC, can be considered to coincide with the start of combustion in the LFR. It is interesting to note that the flame observed, up to

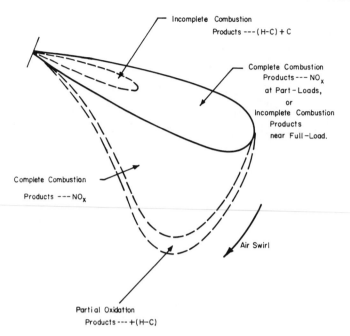

Incomplete Combustion
Products --- (H–C) + C

Complete Combustion
Products --- NO$_x$
at Part – Loads,
or
Incomplete Combustion
Products
near Full –Load.

Complete Combustion

Products --- NO$_x$

Air Swirl

Partial Oxidation
Products --- +(H–C)

Figure 8.25.   Emission formation in a fuel spray injected in swirling air.

10° BTDC, was of very low luminosity, indicating that the burning was essentially confined to the premixed part of the jet.

Figure 8.26 shows that at the point of maximum heat release rate, point B, the cumulative heat release is about 5% of the total computed heat release. This reflects the approximate amount of fuel burned soon after ignition as a percentage of the total amount of fuel in this particular case.

The first appearance of the orange-colored luminous flame was observed at 10° BTDC, but did not spread to surround the tip of the jet until 7° BTDC. During the rest of the combustion process (near the core of the jet) the flame was observed to have high luminosity because of the presence of carbon particles. High luminosity is a characteristic of diffusion-type flames.

Part VI   Effect of Some Design and Operating Variables on D.I. Engine Emissions

The concentration of the different emission species in the exhaust is the result of their formation, as discussed in the above model, and their elimination or further formation in the cylinder and exhaust system.

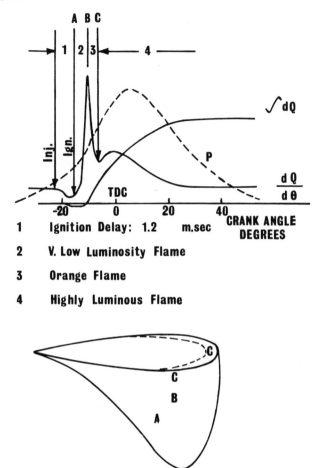

1   **Ignition Delay: 1.2**   **m.sec**

2   **V. Low Luminosity Flame**

3   **Orange Flame**

4   **Highly Luminous Flame**

Figure 8.26. Typical traces for gas pressure, rate of heat release, cumulative heat release. (Figure after Reference 28.)

$$\text{Exhaust Emissions} = \left\{ \begin{array}{c} \text{Emission} \\ \\ \text{Formation} \end{array} \right\} \begin{array}{c} + \\ \\ - \end{array} \left\{ \begin{array}{c} \text{Further} \\ \text{Formation} \\ \text{Elimination} \end{array} \right\} \begin{array}{c} + \\ \\ - \end{array} \left\{ \begin{array}{c} \text{Further} \\ \text{Formation} \\ \text{Elimination} \end{array} \right\} \quad (8.7)$$

in   in   in

the spray   the cylinder   the exhaust

                                   system

In general, "Further Formation" applies to the nitric oxide and "Further Elimination" applies to the incomplete oxidation products. The further formation and elimination reaction rates are functions of the oxygen (or oxidants) concentration, the local mixture temperature, mixing, and residence time.

Unburned Hydrocarbons

The unburned hydrocarbons in the diesel exhaust consist of either original or decomposed fuel molecules, or recombined intermediate compounds. A small portion of these hydrocarbons originate from the lubricating oil.

In the spray, the unburned hydrocarbons are related to the LFOR, spray core, fuel on the walls, spray tail and after-injection. The mechanisms of formation and oxidation of the hydrocarbon molecules depend upon most of the engine operating variables. The effects of some of these variables are studied in the following sections.

FUEL-AIR RATIO

In diesel engines, if the changes in volumetric efficiency are neglected, the mass of air per cycle is almost constant. The change in load is accomplished by controlling the amount of fuel injected. This produces variations in fuel distribution in the spray, amount of fuel deposited on the walls, cylinder gas pressure and temperature, and injection duration. In general, an increase in fuel-air ratio results in a decrease in the portion of the fuel in the LFOR as a ratio of the total fuel injected and an increase in that portion in the core and on the walls.

An increase in fuel-air ratio affects the oxidation reactions in many ways. It results in longer periods of injection, and if injection timing and rate are kept constant, more fuel is injected later in the cycle. In general this results in a shorter reaction time for the last part of the injected fuel. An increase in fuel-air ratio also results in lower oxygen concentration. These two factors tend to decrease the rate of the elimination reactions. However, higher gas temperatures are reached because more fuel is burned and because there is a drop in the percentage of heat losses to the coolant.[31] This tends to increase the elimination reactions rate.

At very light loads and idling conditions, it can be assumed that the fuel spray does not reach the walls and that its concentration in the core is small. Under these conditions the unburned hydrocarbon emissions originate mainly from the LFOR. The increase in the local temperature of this region, due to subsequent combustion of the rest of the spray, is very small, and the elimination reaction rates are very slow. These reactions are further reduced because of the very low concentration of the fuel molecules as they diffuse in the air around this region. The ratio of the unburned hydrocarbon formed in this region to total fuel injection is the highest at idling. This ratio decreases with the increase in fuel-air ratio due to the factors discussed above.

At part loads, the increase in fuel-air ratio causes more fuel to be deposited on the walls and produces higher concentrations in the core. The unburned hydrocarbons formed in these regions increase. However, there is sufficient oxygen in the mixture so that, with increased temperature, the oxidation reactions are promoted and the hydrocarbon emissions are reduced. The reduction in the unburned hydrocarbon emissions (corrected to the stoichiometric ratio) with the increase in fuel-air ratio or load has been observed by Hurn,[32] Marshall and Hurn,[33] and Perez and Landen.[34] The results of Reference 32 are shown in Figure 8.27.

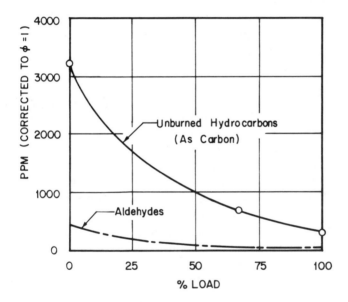

Figure 8.27.   Effect of load on unburned hydrocarbons and aldehydes.

It should be noted that in the study of emissions in heterogeneous combustion systems, such as diesel engines, the observed concentration may be misleading, particularly at part loads. This is due to the effect of dilution by excess air. For example, some reported data show that the concentration of the incomplete combustion products increases with the increase in load or fuel-air ratio. After correcting these data for the effect of dilution, the opposite trend is observed, as discussed in the present model.

The emission data may be judged as a mass fraction of the fuel, corrected to $\phi = 1$, or as a specific emission rate in mass per brake horsepower. The specific emission takes into account the mechanical efficiency of the engine.

At the full load and overload conditions, an increase in fuel-air ratio results in the formation of more unburned hydrocarbon molecules in the core and near the walls. Under these conditions, the contribution of the LFOR to the total emission is expected to be very small. The oxidation reactions are also limited because of lack of oxygen, in spite of the very high temperatures reached. This explains the increase in the unburned fraction of the fuel at full load observed by Marshall and Hurn.[33]

The molecular structure of the unburned hydrocarbon emissions may vary with fuel-air ratio. At idling and light loads, the hydrocarbon emissions are related to the LFOR and are mainly composed of the original fuel molecules because the molecules have little chance to decompose later in the cycle due to the relatively low gas temperatures reached under light loads.

At high loads the hydrocarbon emissions originate from the fuel molecules in the core and on the walls. Under these conditions, the temperatures reached in the cycle are fairly high and cause decomposition of some of the original fuel molecules. Since the fuel-air ratio in the core and near the walls is generally rich, there is a great possibility that some recombination reactions may occur between the hydrocarbon radicals and the intermediate compounds.[22] This results in higher concentrations of the heavier hydrocarbons. Figure 8.28 shows the difference between the mole concentration of the different molecules at full load and no load. The data of this figure were obtained from Reference 32. It should be noted that at full load the molecules with 6 to 12 carbon atoms were reduced, but the molecules with 1 to 4 and 18 to 24 carbon atoms were increased. This implies that the medium-size molecules were decomposed to lighter molecules and that the intermediate compounds were recombined to form heavier molecules.

The process of recombination of the hydrocarbon compounds and radicals may also result in compounds having a different molecular structure than the original fuel. This has been reported by Bascom *et al.*[36] and Aaronson and Matula.[37] Aaronson and Matula found that a large number of aromatic hydrocarbons were synthesized during the heterogeneous combustion of pure cetane-air mixtures in an air-aspirating spray burner and in a Cooperative Fuel Research, CFR, diesel engine. In the CFR engine the

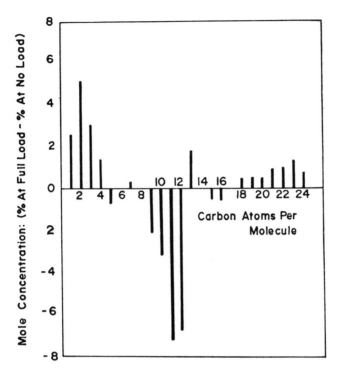

Figure 8.28. Effect of load on distribution of unburned hydrocarbon emissions in a D.I. engine.

aromatic hydrocarbons were formed from the straight chain fuel used because the lubricating oil did not contain any cyclic hydrocarbon compounds.

TURBOCHARGING

At any fuel-air ratio, turbocharging, apart from its effect on spray formation, increases the average gas temperature over the whole cycle. With the same oxygen concentration, the increase in the average temperature causes the rate of oxidation reactions to increase and the concentration of the unburned hydrocarbon emissions to be reduced. This is enhanced by further oxidation reactions in the exhaust manifold and the turbocharger. With turbocharging, higher exhaust temperatures are also reached, the reaction time is increased, and mixing is improved. The reduction of the unburned hydrocarbon emissions with turbocharging has been observed by Perez and Landen[34] as shown in Figure 8.29 for both the D.I. and indirect-injection, I.D.I., engines.

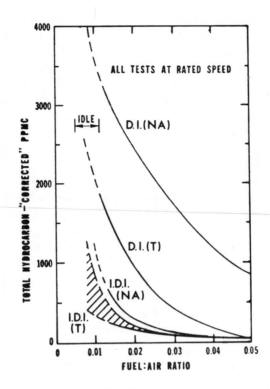

Figure 8.29. Effect of fuel-air ratio on the unburned hydrocarbon emissions in D.I. and I.D.I. engines. N.A.: naturally aspirated; T: turbocharged. (From Reference 34.)

INJECTION TIMING

An advance in injection timing was found by Khan and Grigg to increase the unburned hydrocarbon emissions.[38] Apparently, the longer ignition delay allows more fuel vapor and small droplets to be carried away with the swirling air, producing a wider LFOR. Another factor suggested by Khan and Grigg[38] is the increase in fuel impingement on the walls.

SWIRL

An increase in swirl in the D.I. engine improves the mixing process and the hydrocarbon oxidation processes. Excessive swirl may, however, produce a wider LFOR or an overlap of the sprays and an increase in unburned hydrocarbon emissions.

The swirl in D.I. engines may be changed by varying the ratio of the bowl diameter, d, to its depth, l. This ratio, d/l, is known as the aspect ratio. Conservation of moment of momentum causes the deep bowl pistons to tend to have a higher swirl than the shallow bowl pistons. The variation in the aspect ratio has been found by Watts and Scott[17] to have little effect on the fuel economy; it may, however, affect the emission formation. The data published on this are insufficient; however, the comparisons made by Bascom *et al.*[36] show that the unburned hydrocarbon emissions were higher in the deep bowl than in the shallow bowl (Mexican-hat) pistons.

OTHER FACTORS.

Other factors which affect the unburned hydrocarbon emissions are related to the injection system design, timing, and rate of injection. Merrion[39] reported the results of tests on injectors with different (sac) volumes between the needle seat and the nozzle holes. He found that a reduction in the sac volume greatly reduced the unburned hydrocarbon emissions. Apparently the fuel remaining in the sac seeps out through the injector holes during the expansion stroke. This fuel has very little chance to mix with the oxidants before the exhaust valves open.

Carbon Monoxide

Carbon monoxide is one of the compounds formed during the intermediate combustion stages of hydrocarbon fuels.[22] As combustion proceeds to completion, oxidation of CO to CO_2 occurs through recombination reactions between CO and the different oxidants. If these recombination reactions are incomplete because of lack of oxidants, low gas temperatures, or short residence time, CO will be left.

During the early stages of spray combustion in D.I. diesel engines, CO is believed to be formed at the borders between the LFOR and LFR. But since the local temperature is not high enough, little oxidation to CO_2 takes place. Later on, during the combustion process, the local temperature may increase and promote the oxidation reactions.

In the LFR, the carbon monoxide formed as an intermediate compound is immediately oxidized because the oxygen concentration and the gas temperature are adequate. In the core of the spray and near the walls, CO is formed at a high rate. The rate of its elimination depends mainly upon the local oxygen concentration, mixing, local gas temperature, and the time available for oxidation.

The CO formed near the borders of the LFOR, as a ratio of the total fuel in the spray, depends upon the fuel-air ratio. At light loads this ratio is high because the gas temperature is low and very little oxidation takes place. An increase in load, or fuel-air ratio, results in lower CO emissions because of the increase in gas temperatures and elimination reactions. This has been observed by Perez and Landen[34] and by Marshall and Hurn[33] for the corrected CO concentration. The increase in fuel-air ratio beyond a certain limit may reduce the elimination reactions, despite the increase in temperature, because of the low oxidants concentration and the short reaction time. This results in high CO emissions with increase in load, as shown in Figure 8.30.

By using a shrouded inlet valve Khan and Grigg[38] studied the effect of swirl on CO emissions. They found that the optimum swirl for best economy is almost the same as that at which the CO concentration is minimum. This is believed to be due to the improved elimination reactions caused by the better mixing.

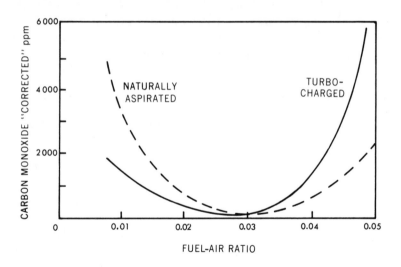

Figure 8.30. Effect of fuel-air ratio on carbon monoxide emission in a D.I. engine. (From Reference 34.)

Aldehydes

In the fuel spray before ignition, the aldehyde concentration is expected to be high around the ignition nuclei in the LRF and low in the LFOR. After the small flame fronts are established they pass through the LFR and burn the aldehydes, leaving those in the LFOR without oxidation. Like the unburned hydrocarbons, these aldehydes can be eliminated later in the cycle because the combustion of the rest of the spray causes a temperature rise. This, too, depends on the oxygen concentration. At light loads, the increase in fuel-air ratio enhances the oxidation reactions and results in a decrease in aldehyde emission concentration. This has been observed by Hurn,[32] Elliott,[40] Merrion,[39] and Marshall and Hurn.[33] The data of Hurn are plotted in Figure 8.27. At heavy loads the increase in fuel-air ratio, beyond a certain value, may result in higher temperatures but lower oxygen concentration. This may result in an increase in aldehyde emissions as observed by Merrion[39] and by Marshall and Hurn.[33]

Odor

Diesel odor has been the subject of many investigations during the last few years, particularly as related to odor-producing species and instrumentation.[41-47]

In a recent study, Spindt *et al.*[45] identified many mono- and polyoxygenated partial oxidation products and certain fuel fractions as being the odor-producing compounds. These occur at very low concentrations in the exhaust.

According to Reference 41 the principal components responsible for the characteristic oily-kerosene portion of diesel exhaust odor are alkyl benzenes, indans, tetralins and indenes. The contribution of the alkyl naphthalenes, which constitute a major portion of the mass of the oily-kerosene fraction, to the odor perception may be through a synergistic effect. The unburned fuel in the exhaust is very likely to contribute heavily to the oily-kerosene odor.

Somers and Kittredge[44] indicated that alkyl-substituted benzene and naphthalene type compounds have been related to the oily-kerosene odor quality and that oxygenated aromatic structures have been related to the smoky-burnt odor quality. O'Donnell and Davnieks[42] found from mass spectral data that in addition to the partial oxidation hydrocarbon compounds, sulfur species are among the more important odor contributors.

Many human panel techniques have been used to measure odor intensity. These techniques include a sniff box with different dilution ratios, natural dilution in a large building, or a Turk kit.[47, 48]

Data published by Merrion[39] showed that the odor intensity increased with load, decreased with improving the design of the injection system, and did not vary appreciably with engine speed.

Rounds and Pearsall[49] and Merrion[39] suggested that there may be some weak correlation between formaldehyde emission and odor intensity. Stahman *et al.*[46] found that with the use of some types of catalytic reactors the odor levels and the oxygenated compounds were reduced with no significant influence on the engine perform-ance parameters.

Barnes[23] found that large differences in exhaust odor intensity were achieved by altering the intake atmosphere conditions to an engine. The engine used was a single cylinder, four-stroke cycle diesel engine using n-heptane as fuel. The artificial atmospheres supplied to the engine were comprised of oxygen plus an inert gas or air. The inert gases used were argon, helium, nitrogen, and carbon dioxide. These mixtures of inert gases and oxygen have different lean ignitability limits. Barnes found that there is a corre-lation between the odor levels and the lean flammability limits, LFL.

The LFL ratio is defined as the ratio of percentage of fuel by volume at the LFL with the mixture to the percentage with air. A LFL ratio more than unity means that the fuel-oxidizer ratio is richer at the LFL than in air. Barnes[23] concluded that for such mixtures a larger portion of the injected fuel would be too lean to burn and would be partially oxidized. He observed that this was particularly true at idling and light loads.

In terms of the model developed in this chapter for the emis-sions in D.I. engines, the volume of the LFOR increases for the mixtures with high LFL ratio. This results in more fuel in that region and an increase in the concentration of the partially oxi-dized products.

Trumpy *et al.*[50] studied the effect of inlet temperature and equivalence ratio on odor production from premixed n-heptane-air mixtures in a motored spark ignition CRF engine. The results are shown in Figure 8.31a. The pressure traces showed that below the lower line no energy was released during the compression stroke, and the odor was that of n-heptane only. In the area between the two lines, smoke, odor and eye irritation species were found in the exhaust. Under these conditions the pressure traces showed energy release indicating oxidation reac-tions. Above the upper line, autoignition occurred in two stages, as shown in Figure 8.31b. This reduced the concentration of the partially oxidized products. Trumpy *et al.* concluded that the smoke, odor, and eye irritants are formed when the second stage combustion is quenched.

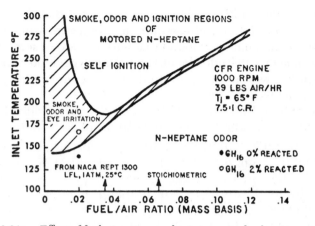

Figure 8.31a. Effect of fuel-air ratio on odor in premixed n-heptane-air mixture with and without self-ignition. (From Reference 50.)

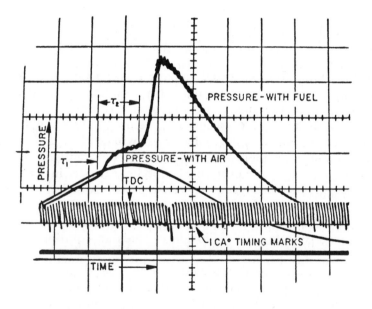

Figure 8.31b. Pressure time trace showing self-ignition. (From Reference 50.)

Smoke Particulates

Different types of particulates are emitted from diesel engines under different modes and operating conditions. These particulates can be divided into the following:

    1. Liquid particulates appear as white clouds of vapor emitted

under cold starting, idling, and low loads. These consist mainly of fuel and a small portion of lubricating oil, emitted without combustion; they may be accompanied by partial oxidation products. These white clouds disappear as the load is increased.

2. Soot or black smoke is emitted as a product of the incomplete combustion process, particularly at maximum loads.

3. Other particulates include lubricating oil and fuel additives.

The present study will be limited to the soot or black smoke.

The black smoke emission consists of irregularly shaped, agglomerated fine carbon particles.[51] According to current theories, these carbon particulates can be formed from the hydrocarbon fuels in the presence or absence of oxygen.

In the presence of oxygen, as in the LFR and in the core under light loads, pyrolysis of the fuel molecules may take place to form carbon. Carbon formation was observed during the early stages of combustion in the LFR by Alcock and Scott.[53] Later, these carbon particles are completely burned due to the presence of enough oxygen.

In the spray core, especially under heavy loads, the oxygen concentration is low, the gas temperature is high, and the concentration of the high boiling point components is high, as discussed on page 264. These are easier to decompose than the lighter compounds. Pyrolysis of the molecules may take place and lead to the formation of acetylene and hydrogen.[52] The simultaneous condensation and dehydrogenation of acetylene results in solid carbon. The presence of oxygen may cause partial oxidation reactions to take place and result in a high concentration of CO. According to Behrens[54] and Kassel[55] carbon may be formed if the ratio of carbon monoxide to carbon dioxide exceeds an equilibrium constant.

Smoke particles are also formed from the fuel deposited on the walls[18] by the same mechanism described for the spray core under heavy loads. The carbon particles formed according to the previous mechanisms may be oxidized later in the turbulent flames formed during the combustion process. The extent of the oxidation reactions depends upon the oxygen concentration in the vicinity of the surface of the soot particles, temperature, and residence time.

The smoke intensity in the diesel exhaust is greatly affected by many parameters. By controlling them, smoke intensity may be reduced.

EFFECT OF FUEL

Previous experimental results showed that higher cetane number fuels which are suitable for high speed transportation engines have a tendency to produce more smoke (References 25, 56, 57, 58). This is shown in Figure 8.32 and is believed to be due to the lower stability of these fuels. This results in higher rates of carbon formation during the combustion process since more fuel is injected after the end of I.D.[59] An interesting experiment was made by Rost[60] in which he measured the smoke intensity with regular gasoline and with additive treated gasoline of a cetane number equal to that of the regular diesel fuel. His results showed that the smoke intensity increased as a result of the additive and was almost equal to that of the regular diesel fuel. Similar observations on the increase of smoke intensity with the increase in the cetane number are reported by Broeze and Stillebroer.[61]

Rost's experiment indicates that the fuel volatility has little effect on smoke reduction. Golothan's results[56] showed that for a given cetane number less smoke is produced with more volatile fuels. Other results by Savage[62] showed an opposite trend. Thus, no definite conclusion can be drawn from the available experimental data on the effect of volatility on smoke. The change in the fuel spray characteristics in each of the engines used with the more volatile fuel is believed to be one of the primary reasons for this disagreement.

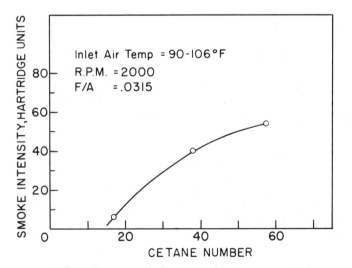

Figure 8.32. Effect of centane number on smoke intensity in a D.I. engine.

INJECTION TIMING

Advancing the start of injection in D.I. engines with all other parameters kept constant results in longer delay periods, more fuel injected before ignition, higher temperatures in the cycle, and earlier ending of the combustion process. The residence time is therefore increased. All these factors have been found to reduce the smoke intensity in the diesel exhaust.[58] However, earlier injection results in more combustion noise, higher mechanical and thermal stresses, and higher NO emissions.

In a recent study, Khan[38] found that very late injection reduces the smoke. The timing after which this reduction occurs is that at which the minimum I.D. occurs. He suggested that one of the factors that contributes to the reduction in smoke at the retarded timing is the reduced rate of formation caused by the decrease in the temperature of the diffusion flames as most of these flames occur during the expansion stroke. Similar results are shown in Figure 8.37.

RATE OF INJECTION

Higher initial rates of injection have been found to be effective in reducing the exhaust smoke.[38] As discussed above, an early ending of the injection process will improve the elimination reactions of the carbon particles.

INJECTION NOZZLE

The size of the nozzle holes and the ratio of the hole length to its diameter have an effect on smoke concentration. A larger hole diameter results in less atomization and increased smoke.[38] An increase in the ratio of the hole length to its diameter beyond a certain limit also results in increased smoke.[38]

INLET AIR TEMPERATURE

An increase in inlet air temperature results in higher gas temperature during the entire cycle. This affects both the mixture formation and the chemical reactions which contribute to the carbon formation.

The effect on the mixture formation is related to the spray characteristics, mainly penetration and atomization, evaporation and diffusion. The increase in the gas temperature at a given pressure reduces the penetration.[63] This has been found to be more significant for more volatile fuels.[64] The reduction in gas density associated with the increase in temperature at constant pressure will result in smaller spray cone angles.[65] These factors result in high local concentrations of the fuel droplets near the nozzle. The increase in the rate of evaporation and diffusion with temperature will result in the formation of overrich mixtures near the nozzle where mixing is not as effective as near the walls. Higher temperatures also increase the decomposition reactions. All these factors lead to increased smoke intensity. Khan's results[59] showed an increase of smoke intensity with temperature at the different injection timings tested.

In some less-volatile fuels the effect of increased intake air temperature may accelerate the oxidation reactions at a higher rate than that of the decomposition reactions. This produces a reduction in smoke intensity with the increase in temperature as explained in Reference 25.

AFTER-INJECTION

After-injection, sometimes called secondary injection, is different from dribbling. Dribbling is caused by fuel leakage past the valve seat when the valve is closed. It has a negative effect on smoke intensity, unburned hydrocarbon emissions, carbon monoxide, and engine operation. In after-injection the needle valve is lifted off the seat as shown in Figure 8.33. The effect of the increase in the amount of after-injection on the smoke intensity as obtained by Reference 25 is shown in Figure 8.34.

The reduction in after-injection may be achieved by injection system design modifications. These modifications may be guided by theoretical studies based on computer simulation of the injection process.[66,67,68]

OTHER APPROACHES TO CONTROL SMOKE EMISSIONS

Other approaches to reduce diesel smoke include fumigation[46] and smoke suppressant fuel additives. Barium-type additives were found to have little or no effect on power, odor, or gaseous emissions in naturally aspirated D.I. engines.[43] Catalytic reactors were found to have a little effect on smoke reduction.[46]

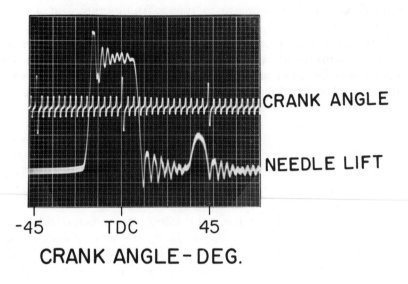

CRANK ANGLE - DEG.

Figure 8.33.   Needle lift diagram showing after-injection.

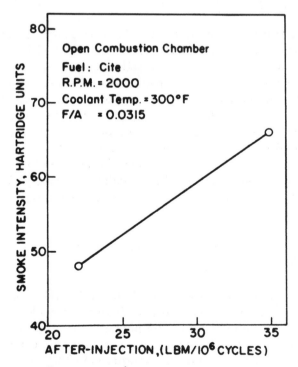

Figure 8.34.   Effect of after-injection on smoke intensity.

Nitric Oxide

Nitric oxide is formed during the combustion process at various concentrations in all the spray regions. Many mechanisms for nitric oxide formation in combustion systems have been proposed (References 69, 70, 71, 72). The most widely accepted mechanism is that of Zeldovich.[69]

$$O_2 \rightleftharpoons 2O \tag{8.8}$$

$$O + N_2 \rightleftharpoons NO + N \tag{8.9}$$

$$N + O_2 \rightleftharpoons NO + O \tag{8.10}$$

The chain reactions are initiated in Equation 8.8 by the atomic oxygen which is formed from the dissociation of oxygen molecules at the high temperatures reached in the combustion process. According to this mechanism, the nitrogen atoms do not start the chain reaction because their equilibrium concentration during the combustion process is relatively low compared to that of atomic oxygen. Therefore, in diesel combustion the local NO formation in the spray is related to the local oxygen atom concentration. This is a function of the local concentration of the oxygen molecules and the local temperature.

In the diesel engine, NO is not formed during the compression stroke even under high supercharging conditions because of the relatively low temperatures reached. Although NO is not formed in the LFOR during the early stages of combustion, raising the air temperature in this region may cause some NO to be formed here later in the cycle after the combustion of the rest of the spray.

Newhall and Shahed[73] found that in flames, NO is formed at higher rates with rich mixtures than with stoichiometric or lean mixtures. The final concentration, however, is maximum with a slightly lean mixture. Therefore the NO formation in the LFR may start at a lower rate than in the richer regions of the spray but will reach much higher concentrations.

The results of Newhall and Shahed[73] also showed that most of the NO formation occurs during the post-flame reactions. Accordingly, the LFR may be one of the major contributing regions to NO formation since it is the first part of the spray to burn and has the longest post-flame residence time.

The temperature rise caused by the combustion of the fuel in the core and on the walls may contribute to the NO formation in two ways. First, it increases the average temperature in the cylinder and results in higher concentrations of NO in the LFOR and LFR. Second, it may result in very high flame temperatures in the core. The NO formed in the core will also be influenced by the local oxygen concentration. For example, if the oxygen concentration in the core increases, such as when more holes are used to deliver the same amount of fuel, the NO formed in the core is expected to increase.

As the gas temperature decreases during the expansion stroke, the NO concentration does not decrease to the equilibrium concentration. Starkman and Newhall[74] and Lavoie *et al.*[72] found that in reciprocating engines the NO removal processes during the expansion stroke are very slow; thus NO concentration remains nearly constant during expansion.

EFFECT OF FUEL-AIR RATIO

The effect of the overall fuel-air ratio on the NO emission and the related engine parameters is shown in Figure 8.35 for a single cylinder D.I. research engine. A detailed description of this engine is given in Reference 31. The observed NO concentration in the exhaust increased with the increase in fuel-air ratio and reached a maximum at a ratio of about 0.048. It should be noted that the observed NO concentration does not represent the extent of NO formation by the combustion process because of the dilution with excess air. The NO concentration, corrected to the stoichiometric ratio, is plotted in Figure 8.35 and shows that, within the range of fuel-air ratios used in the experiments, it decreased with the increase in fuel-air ratio. Decreasing the fuel-air ratios below 0.02 may decrease the NO concentration due to the relatively low temperature reached. This is illustrated by the dotted line in Figure 8.35.

The increase in fuel-air ratio resulted in an increase in the maximum mass-average gas temperature as indicated in Figure 8.35 by the increase in the maximum pressure and the exhaust gas temperature. It seems that this increase in the maximum mass-average gas temperature did not cause a corresponding increase in the NO formation. This suggests that the NO emission in this engine is primarily related to the local combustion of the LFR. Also, the increase in NO concentration due to the subsequent combustion of the fuel in the core and on the walls may not be the main contributing factor to NO formation in this engine.

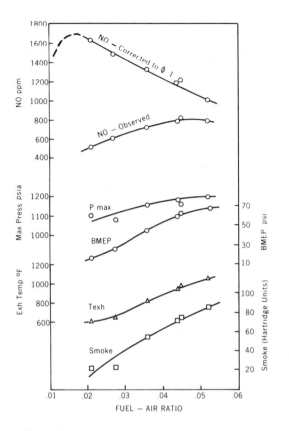

Figure 8.35. Effect of fuel-air ratio on nitric oxide emission and other performance parameters.

EFFECT OF TYPE OF FUEL

Figure 8.36 is a plot of the nitrogen oxides concentration for two fuels having cetane numbers of 35 and 59, as obtained by McConnell.[75] The injection timing was advanced for the low cetane number fuel to account for its longer delay period. This kept the start of combustion at the same point in the cycle for each fuel. With low cetane fuel, the I.D. is longer than with the other fuel and more fuel is present in the LFR when combustion starts. This larger quantity of fuel produces a higher gas temperature upon combustion early in the cycle, and more NO is formed in the LFR.

The increase in the formation of nitrogen oxides with the decrease in cetane number of the fuel may be attributed to the effect

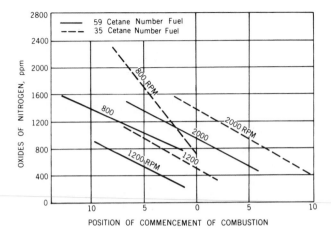

8.36.   Effect of centane number on nitric oxide emission. (From Reference 75.)

the preignition radicals have on the mechanism of NO formation. This has been discussed by Fenimore.[76] Similar effects have been observed by Meguerian[77] with fuels of higher octane number during the combustion of homogeneous mixtures.

EFFECT OF INJECTION TIMING

The effect of injection timing on the NO emissions and other related engine parameters is shown in Figure 8.37 for the single cylinder D.I. research engine of Figure 8.35. Figure 8.37 shows that injection advance results in longer I.D. because the fuel is injected in air at lower temperatures and pressures. However, since the increase in I.D. in crank degrees is less than the injection advance, autoignition occurs earlier in the cycle. Longer I.D. causes more fuel evaporation and mixing in the LFR and high NO concentration. The NO formation in the other regions of the spray increases with injection advance due to the high temperatures reached.

Late injection is one of the effective ways of reducing NO emissions; however, this results in a loss in BMEP and fuel economy as shown in Figure 8.37.

EFFECT OF SWIRL

The effect of swirl on the emissions in a D.I. engine was studied by Khan and Grigg[38] as discussed earlier. They found that the

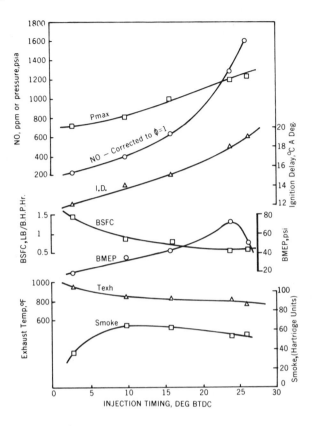

Figure 8.37. Effect of injection timing on nitric oxide emission and other performance parameters.

shroud position which produces minimum CO also results in the highest NO concentration in the exhaust.

EFFECT OF TURBOCHARGING

Figure 8.38 shows the NO_x concentration with and without turbocharging at various fuel-air ratios, as obtained by Mc-Connel.[75] Near the higher fuel-air ratios (60% air usage), turbocharging resulted in higher NO_x concentration. Figure 8.39 shows the same data as Figure 8.38 but the NO_x concentrations are plotted versus the fuel delivery in mm³/cycle.

EFFECT OF INTAKE AIR CHARGE DILUTION

One of the methods used to reduce the NO emissions in the

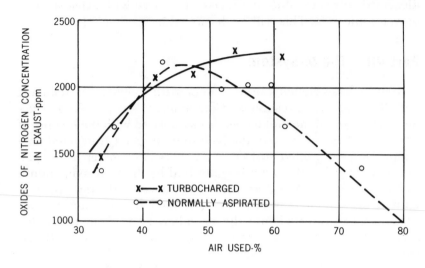

Figure 8.38. Effect of turbocharging on nitrogen oxides emission. (From Reference 75.)

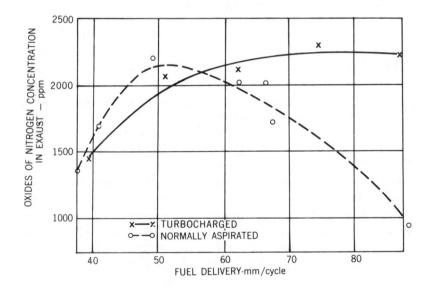

Figure 8.39. Effect of turbocharging on nitrogen oxides emission. (From Reference 75.)

diesel exhaust is to dilute the intake air charge with exhaust gases or water injection. This will be discussed in Section XII.

Part VII   The M-System

Meurer[79] developed the M-system with the idea of reducing both the preignition reactions of the autoignition process and the decomposition of the fuel molecules associated with the heating of heterogeneous mixtures. In the M-system, the fuel is injected on a temperature-controlled surface of a spherical chamber in the piston. The rate of evaporation is controlled by the wall temperature and the air swirl. After the fuel vapor mixes with the air, it is ignited by several ignition sources formed by injecting a small percentage of the fuel into the chamber, away from the walls. More detailed information on this system may be found in References 8, 78 and 79.

The swirl and radial velocity components in the M-system are higher than those in the other types of open-chamber engines. The NO emission characteristics of an engine of the M-system are given in Figure 8.45, and will be compared with the other engines in Part X.

Part VIII   Indirect-Injection Engines (I.D.I.)

Indirect-injection engines, known as prechamber or divided chamber engines, have many different designs as detailed in References 8 and 78. The performance of the I.D.I. engine depends upon many factors including the ratio of the prechamber volume to the total clearance volume, the eddies and gas flow patterns in the prechamber and main chamber, size and direction of the throat, piston recesses, and the surface temperatures.

In the swirl type, the volume of the prechamber is about 50% or more of the total clearance volume. Swirl motion is produced in the prechamber during the compression stroke by the flow of air through a tangential throat. The swirl increases during the compression stroke and reaches its maximum a few degrees before Top Dead Center (T.D.C.). The swirl measured by Lyn[80] in a Comet Mark V, by using a Schlieren technique, reached its maximum at seven degrees before T.D.C. and was about 21 times the engine speed. The swirl helps to mix the fuel and air before the start of combustion in the prechamber. After ignition the flame moves toward the center of the prechamber because of the increase in the buoyant force acting on the hot products of combustion in the centrifugal field created by the swirl.[81] Nagao[82] found that the direction of injection with respect to the throat has a great effect on engine performance and smoke emissions. Other performance characteristics of the swirl chamber may be found in References 8 and 78.

In the other types of I.D.I. engines, the volume of the prechamber and the area of the throat are smaller than in the swirl type. In these designs the turbulence produced in the prechamber during the compression stroke is milder than that in the swirl type. The main turbulence is produced after the start of combustion by the flow of the products from the prechamber into the main chamber where the combustion is completed.

The extent of combustion in the prechamber of any type of I.D.I. engine depends primarily upon prechamber volume compared to the total clearance volume. Bowdon[83] found that in swirl chambers the ratio of the heat released in the prechamber to the total heat released was the same as the ratio of the prechamber volume to the total clearance volume.

The exhaust emissions in the indirect injection engines may be considered to take place in two stages: first, upon combustion in the prechamber, and second, after the gases from the prechamber mix with the air in the main chamber. The extent of the reaction in each stage depends upon the concentration of the fuel and oxidants, temperature, mixing, and residence time in each chamber. These factors change with the engine design and operating variables.

Part IX   Effect of Some Design and Operating Variables on I.D.I. Engine Emissions

Effect of Load

Figure 8.40 shows the effect of load on the rates of heat input, heat release, and cylinder pressure. This figure is compiled from figures published by Bowdon *et al.*[83] for a swirl type I.D.I. engine at constant speed and injection timing. During part load operation, as the load is increased, more fuel is injected later in the cycle. It can be assumed that the oxygen concentration in the prechamber decreases as more fuel is injected. Therefore, the increase in fuel injection with load may reduce the extent of burning of the last portions of the fuel injected into the prechamber. The unburned hydrocarbons and CO formation in the prechamber may therefore

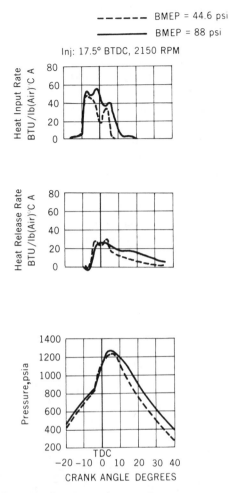

Figure 8.40. Effect of load on heat release and pressure in an I.D.I. engine.

increase with load, but their rate of oxidation in the main chamber may likewise increase. This is primarily due to the higher temperature reached in the main cylinder during the expansion stroke, as can be seen from the pressure traces of Figure 8.40. This may result in lower HC and CO emissions in the exhaust.

At fairly high loads, near the smoke limit, the rates of the oxidation reactions in the main chamber might not be high enough to eliminate the increased amounts of HC and CO discharged from the prechamber. This is due to the small oxygen concentration and residence time, in spite of the very high temperatures reached. This may result in increased HC and CO emis-

sions near the smoke limit. Moreover, the high temperatures promote the decomposition reactions which result in increased smoke
intensity.

Figures 8.41 and 8.42 show maps of the hydrocarbon and CO
emissions, respectively, at various loads and speeds in a Comet
Mark V I.D.I. engine. These figures were obtained from Reference 84. At any constant speed it is noticed that the concentrations
of these emissions decrease with the increase in load from
no-load. Their concentrations then increase as further increases in
load approach the smoke limit. It should be noted here that the
concentrations given in Figures 8.41 and 8.42 are not corrected to
the stoichiometric ratio and that those near no-load should be
multiplied by a factor up to six in order to compare them with
those at full load. The decrease in the unburned hydrocarbons and
CO emissions with the increase in load from no-load has also been
observed by Perez and Landen[34] for other types of D.I. and I.D.I.
engines. This has been shown in Figure 8.29.

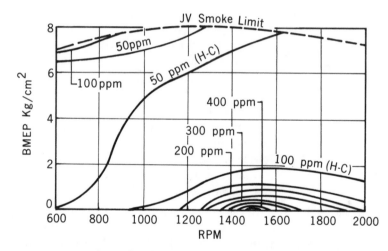

Figure 8.41. Unburned hydrocarbon emissions in an I.D.I. Comet V engine.
(From Reference 84.)

In I.D.I. engines both the prechamber and main chamber contribute to NO formation. At light loads the NO emissions are
related mainly to the combustion in the prechamber, where a
greater portion of fuel is burned. This portion decreases with the
increase in load. At higher loads the mixture formed in the prechamber is rich, combustion is incomplete, and the NO formation
in the prechamber is not the primary contributor to the NO concentration in the exhaust.

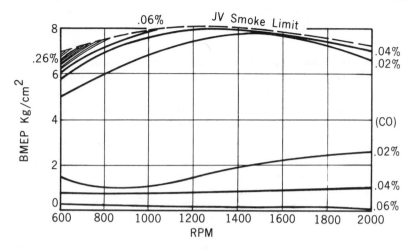

Figure 8.42. Carbon monoxide emissions in an I.D.I. Comet V engine. (From Reference 84.)

As the incomplete combustion products expand and pass through the throat, they mix with each other. Because of the lack of oxygen, however, chemical reactions are not likely to occur at an appreciable rate in the throat and the temperature may not increase. At very rich mixtures, the flow through the throat may even cause cooling of the mixture as the pressure decreases.

The increase in the temperature and NO formation in the main chamber depend upon the amount of incompletely burned compounds discharged from the prechamber, the oxygen concentration, and the timing of the discharge. The increase in load results in more unburned compounds to be discharged in the main chamber, and higher temperatures. But this causes a decrease in oxygen concentration. Higher loads also result in a later discharge in the main chamber and a relatively smaller temperature rise after combustion due to the expansion work. The rate of expansion (piston velocity) increases as the piston moves away from T.D.C. in the first part of the expansion stroke. Accordingly, it is expected that the increase in load beyond a certain limit should result in lower NO concentrations. This limit depends mainly upon the chamber design, engine speed and injection timing. Figure 8.43 shows the variation in the observed NO emissions in ppm for the engine of Figures 8.41 and 8.42.

Effect of Speed

Figure 8.44 shows the effect of speed, at constant injection

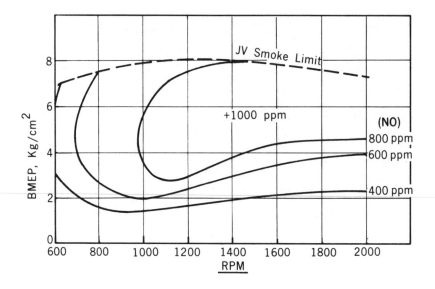

Figure 8.43. Nitric oxide emission in an I.D.I. Comet V engine. (From Reference 84.)

timing, on the rates of heat input, heat release, and cylinder pressure for the swirl chamber engine of Figure 8.40. The B.M.E.P. was constant within about ±10%.

For the same B.M.E.P., more fuel is injected per cycle to account for the decrease in mechanical efficiency at higher speeds. At such speeds the rates of injection are higher, and in spite of the shorter delay period, the amount of fuel injected before T.D.C. is larger. All these factors result in earlier discharge of the gases from the prechamber and higher temperatures in the main chamber. Under the conditions of Figure 8.44, therefore, the increase in speed is expected to improve the elimination reactions in the main chamber, to reduce the hydrocarbons and CO and to increase the NO concentration.

In I.D.I. engines under actual running conditions, the change in speed may affect many of the other engine parameters, particularly the injection timing. The emission formation will therefore be a result of the variation in speed as well as of the other parameters. Figures 8.41, 8.42, and 8.43 show the variation in the observed HC, CO and NO emissions, respectively, at various speeds and at optimum injection timing for a swirl chamber engine.

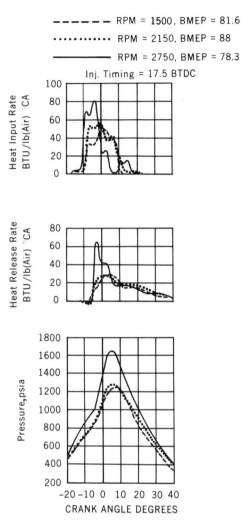

Figure 8.44. Effect of speed on heat release and cylinder pressure in an I.D.I. engine.

Part X   Comparison Between the Emission Characteristics of M-System, D.I. and I.D.I. Diesel Engines

NO Emission

The NO emissions, in grams per horsepower-hour, are given for the three types of high speed diesel engines in Figures 8.45, 8.46,

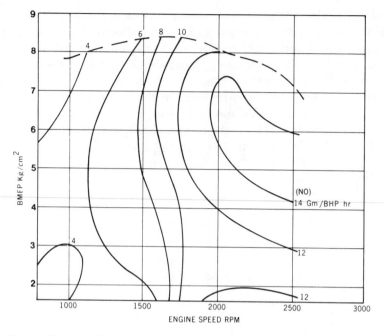

Figure 8.45. Specific nitric oxide emission in an M-system engine. (From Reference 85.)

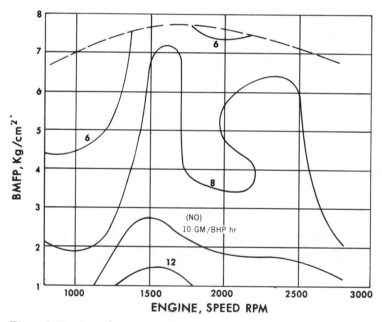

Figure 8.46. Specific nitric oxide emission in a D.I. engine. (From Reference 85.)

and 8.47. These figures are obtained from Reference 85. Figure 8.45 is for an engine using the M-system, Figure 8.46 is for a D.I. engine and Figure 8.47 is for an I.D.I. engine. All three are four-cylinder and water-cooled engines. The dotted lines in the figures indicate the smoke limit in each engine.

It should be noted that the level of the NO emissions near the smoke limit in the I.D.I. engine is lower than that in the D.I. or M-system engines. This may be caused by the relatively higher fuel-air ratio during combustion in the prechamber, and the relatively lower maximum temperatures reached during combustion in the main chamber.

The NO emissions at a given B.M.E.P. in the I.D.I. engine are not as sensitive to engine speed as in the other types. The M-system engine results show the sensitivity of the NO emissions to engine speed at any B.M.E.P.

Emissions Based on a 13-Mode Cycle

A comparison between the brake specific emissions, on a 13-mode cycle, of D.I. and I.D.I. diesel engines was made by Marshall and Fleming[86]; the results are given in Table 8.1. These results show that (1) the I.D.I. engine produced the lowest CO,

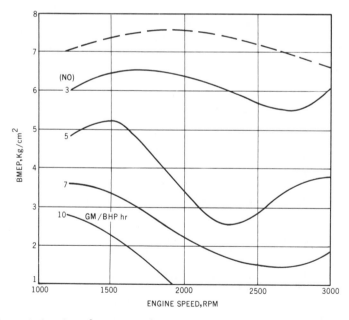

Figure 8.47. Specific nitric oxide emission in an I.D.I. engine. (From Reference 85.)

Table 8.1

Comparison Between the Brake Specific Emissions in Different Types of Diesel Engines, Over a Modified 13-Mode Test Cycle[a]

Engine and code identification	Power bhp	Emissions, g/bhp-hr					Odor
		Carbon monoxide	Nitric oxide (as NO_2)	Hydro-carbons (as CH_2)	Aldehydes (as HCHO)	Particu-lates	
4-CYCLE, NATURALLY-ASPIRATED, D.I.							
A	34.5	10.0	8.7	1.9	0.5	0.6	4.5
B	53.6	4.2	6.7	3.1	0.4	0.6	3.6
C	57.1	5.8	19.8	3.0	0.4	0.1	4.0
D	58.1	4.9	16.7	3.1	–	–	4.4
E	68.1	5.6	9.5	2.3	0.3	0.2	4.5
F	73.1	5.7	6.9	0.6	–	–	3.0
4-CYCLE, TURBOCHARGED, D.I.							
G	77.1	3.9	17.8	3.1	0.2	0.2	3.8
H	85.7	4.9	11.7	2.6	0.2	0.3	3.6
4-CYCLE, TURBOCHARGED, I.D.I							
I	88.6	2.3	6.1	0.3	0.1	0.4	3.3
2-CYCLE, D.I.							
J	46.7	6.1	14.7	0.7	–	–	3.3

[a]Data from Reference 86.

NO, hydrocarbons, and aldehydes, and (2) the odor levels were not greatly different for any of the engines tested.

Part XI   Comparison Between the Emissions from Diesel and Gasoline Engines

Springer[87] compared the emissions measured from a four-cylinder gasoline and a diesel-powered Mercedes 220 passenger car. The diesel engine had an I.D.I. combustion chamber. The odor, smoke, and gaseous emissions from the diesel-powered car were measured by using methods developed for heavy-duty diesel trucks and buses. Comparative tests of the gasoline and diesel vehicles were also made by using the 1972 Federal Test Procedure for CO, hydrocarbons, and NO. This test is discussed in Chapter 10.

The results showed that the hydrocarbons, acrolein, and aldehydes seemed to correlate well with odor ratings. The 1972 test procedures revealed that the diesel produced about 30% as much HC, 5% as much CO, and about 50% as much NO_x as the gasoline.

Springer[87] reported that for these two engines, partial oxygenates such as acrolein, aliphatic aldehydes, and formaldehyde were substantially lower from the diesel than from the gasoline engine. The results of these tests should not be used to draw general conclusions in comparing the emissions in diesel and gasoline engines. More tests are needed before such conclusions are made.

Part XII   NO Emission Control

Many controls may be used to reduce the NO emissions in diesel engines. These may, however, affect the combustion process, increase the concentration of other emission species, and affect engine performance.

The control of NO emissions in diesel engines should be made during the combustion process. The exhaust treatment techniques used to control NO emissions from gasoline engines employ a catalyst in the presence of CO.[88,89] These techniques are not effective in diesel engines because of the presence of excess oxygen in the exhaust, even under full load conditions.

As discussed earlier, reduction in NO formation during the actual combustion process may be achieved by reducing either the maximum temperatures reached, the oxygen concentration or the residence time. This may be obtained by any of the following methods or a combination of them.

Injection Timing

The retard of injection has been found to be very effective in reducing the NO emissions in both the D.I. and I.D.I. diesel engines.[75],[84],[85],[90] This is due mainly to the reduction in both the maximum temperatures reached in the different parts of the combustion chamber and the residence time. McConnell[75] and others found that retarding the injection timing is more effective for the direct injection engines than for the indirect injection engines. This is shown in Figure 8.48, for two engines of the same bore and stroke.

Springer and Dietzmann[43] found that retarding the injection timing in a D.I. engine had no apparent effect on odor or CO and increased the unburned hydrocarbons.

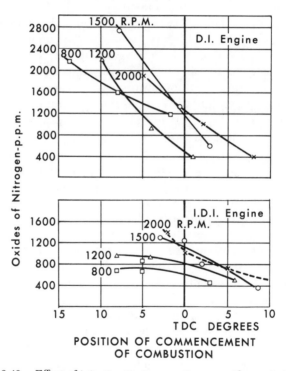

Figure 8.48. Effect of injection timing on nitrogen oxides emission in D.I. and I.D.I. engines. (From Reference 75.)

Water Addition

Diluting the charge by adding water affects both the emission formation and elimination in D.I. and I.D.I. engines.

D.I. Engines

Adding water is expected to change the lean ignition limit and to increase the LFOR width and the HC and CO formation. It may also reduce the elimination reactions due to the drop in the maximum temperatures reached. This would result in a further increase in the HC and CO emissions.

Increasing inlet air humidity in a D.I. engine was found by Springer and Dietzmann[43] to significantly reduce NO and to increase smoke. Its effect on hydrocarbons and CO was minor except at full load.

Valdamanis and Wulfhorst[90] compared the effect of introducing water in the fuel as an emulsion to water inducted with the intake air in a D.I. engine. As the ratio of water to fuel increased, the ignition delay increased, and injection had to be advanced to obtain peak power. The increase in ignition delay and injection advance for optimum power were greater with the emulsified fuel than with induced water. It is believed that the NO emission in these tests was affected by two factors: the effect of water on reducing the maximum temperatures and oxygen concentration, and the effect of injection advance on the maximum temperatures reached. These two factors resulted in an increase in NO emissions with the emulsified fuel and a decrease in NO emissions with the inducted water.

The combined effects of water addition and injection advance (for optimum power) in Valdamanis tests affected the other emissions in different ways. It resulted in a reduction in smoke and an increase in unburned hydrocarbon emissions.

The effect of water injection on the emissions in the M-system was observed by Abthoff and Luther.[85] They found that water injection reduced the NO emissions and increased the CO emissions, as shown in Figure 8.49.

I.D.I. ENGINES

In I.D.I. engines, water injection may result in more HC and CO formation in the prechamber and less elimination in the main chamber. The effect of water injection on a swirl type I.D.I. engine, Comet V, was studied by Torpey, *et al.*[91]; the results are given in Figure 8.50. In general, water injection decreased the NO, increased CO, HC, and B.S.F.C., particularly near fuel load.

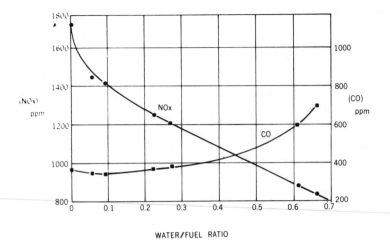

WATER/FUEL RATIO

Figure 8.49. Effect of water addition on the emissions in an M-system engine. (From Reference 85.)

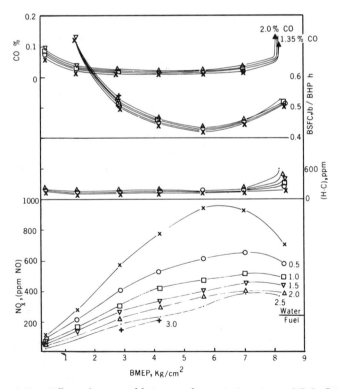

BMEP, Kg/cm^2

Figure 8.50. Effect of water addition on the emissions in an I.D.I. Comet V engine. (From Reference 91.)

Exhaust Gas Recirculation

The reduction in NO emission in diesel engines by exhaust gas recirculation is believed to be due to the increase in the heat capacity of the charge, as has been found in gasoline engines.[92,93] The exhaust gas recirculation affects the combustion and emissions in the D.I. and I.D.I. engines in a manner similar to water injection. The effect of percentage exhaust gas recirculation on the NO and unburned hydrocarbon emissions and fuel consumption for a swirl type I.D.I. engine has been studied by Torpey, *et al.*[91] and is shown in Figure 8.51. The increase in percentage exhaust gas recirculation reduced the NO emissions for the entire B.M.E.P. range. Its effect on increasing HC and B.S.F.C. was significant near full load.

Similar effects of the exhaust gas recirculation on reducing the NO emissions have been observed by Abthoff and Luther[85] in another type of indirect injection engine.

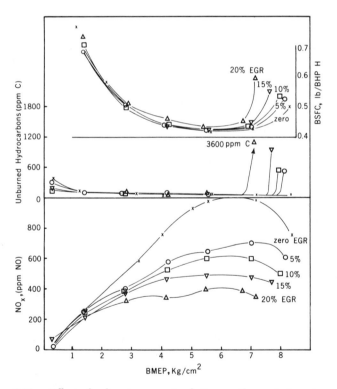

Figure 8.51. Effect of exhaust gas recirculation on the emissions in an I.D.I. Comet V engine. (From Reference 91.)

McConnell[75] studied the effect of reducing the oxygen concentration on the per cent reduction in oxides of nitrogen by using different diluents. Figure 8.52 shows the effect of charge dilution by carbon dioxide, nitrogen, and exhaust gases on NO reduction.

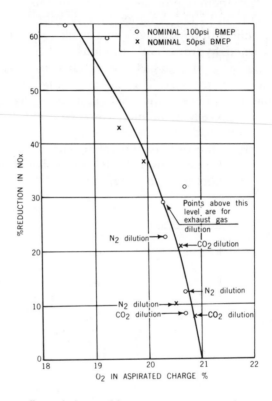

Figure 8.52. Effect of charge dilution on nitrogen oxides emissions. (From Reference 75.)

REFERENCES

1. Schlichting, H. *Boundary Layer Theory* (New York: McGraw-Hill Book Co., Inc., 1955).
2. Hinze, J. O. "Critical Speeds and Sizes of Liquid Globules," Appl. Sci. Res. Al (1949).
3. Ranz, W. E., and W. R. Marshall. "Evaporation from Drops," Chem. Eng. Prog. 48 (3), 141 (1952).
4. Sass, F. *Compressorless Diesel Engines* (Berlin: Julius Springer, 1929).

5. Elliott, M. A. "Combustion of Diesel Fuel Oils," ASME National Oil and Gas Power Conference, ASME, New York (1947).

6. Mehlig, H., "On the Physics of Fuel Jets in Diesel Engines," ["Zur Physik der Brennstoffstrahlen in Dieselmaschinen"], Automob-tech. Zeitschrift, 37, (1934).

7. Parks, M. V., C. Polonski, and R. Toye. "Penetration of Diesel Fuel Sprays in Gases," SAE 660747 (1966).

8. Lichty, L. C. *Combustion Engine Processes* (New York: McGraw-Hill Book Co., 1967).

9. Alcock, J. F. "Air Swirl in Oil Engines," Proc., I.M.E., **128**, 123 (1934).

10. Henein, N. A., and J. A. Bolt. "Ignition Delay in Diesel Engines," SAE Trans. 76 (1968) p 27.

11. Lewis, B., and G. von Elbe. "Combustion Flames and Explosions of Gases," (New York: Academic Press, 1961).

12. Henein, N. A., and J. A. Bolt. "Correlation of Air Charge Temperature and Ignition Delay for Several Fuels in a Diesel Engine," SAE 690252, (1969).

13. Hurn, R. W., J. O. Chase, C. F. Ellis, and K. J. Hughes. "Fuel Heat Gain and Release in Bomb Autoignition," SAE Trans. **64**, 703 (1956).

14. Hurn, R. W., and K. J. Hughes. "Combustion Characteristics of Diesel Fuels as Measured in a Constant-Volume Bomb," SAE Quarterly Trans. **6** (1), 25 (1952).

15. Garner, F. H., F. Morton, J. B. Saunby. "Preflame Reactions in Diesel Engines, Part V," J. Inst. Petrol. **47**, 175 (1961).

16. Henein, N. A. "Combustion and Emission Formation in Fuel Sprays Injected in Swirling Air," SAE Paper No. 710220 (1971).

17. Watts, R., and W. M. Scott. "Air Motion and Fuel Distribution Requirements in High-Speed Direct-Injection Diesel Engines," Diesel Engine Combustion Symposium, Proceedings, Institution of Mechanical Engineers, London, **184** (Pt 3J), 181 (1970).

18. Scott, W. M. "Looking in on Diesel Combustion," SAE **SP-345** (1968).

19. Henein, N. A., and J. A. Bolt. "Kinetic Considerations in The Auto ignition and Combustion of Fuel Sprays in Swirling Air," CIMAC 9th International Congress on Combustion Engines, paper No. A-7, Stockholm, Sweden (May, 1971). Also, ASME publication 72-DGP-8, April, 1972.

20. Friedman, R., and W. Johnson. "The Wall Quenching of Laminar Propane Flames as a Function of Pressure, Temperature, and Air-Fuel Ratio," J. Applied Physics, **21** (8), 791 (1950).

21. Schmidt, Fritz, A. F. *The Internal Combustion Engine,* R. W. Stuart Mitchell and J. Horne, translators (London: Chapman and Hall, 1965) p 78.

22. Fristrom, R. M., and A. A. Westenberg. *Flame Structure* (New York: McGraw-Hill, 1965) p 350.

23. Barnes, G. J. "Relation of Lean Combustion Limits in Diesel Engines to Exhaust Odor Intensity," SAE **PT-14**, 144 (1967–70).

24. Milks, D., C. W. Savery, J. L. Steinberg, and R. A. Matula. "Studies and Analysis of Diesel Engine Odor Production," Clean Air Congress of the International Union of Air Pollution, Washington, D.C. (December, 1970).

25. Henein, N. A., and J. A. Bolt. "The Effect of Some Fuel and Engine Factors on Diesel Smoke," SAE Paper No. 690557 (1969).

26. El-Wakil, M. M., P. S. Myers, and O. A. Uyehara. "Fuel Vaporization and Ignition Lag in Diesel Combustion," SAE Trans. **64**, 713 (1956).

27. Lyn, W. T. "Study of Burning Rate and Nature of Combustion in Diesel Engines," 9th Symposium (International) on Combustion, (New York: Academic Press, 1963) pp 1069–1082.

28. Lyn, W. T. "Calculations of the Effect of Rate of Heat Release on the Shape of Cylinder-Pressure Diagram and Cycle Effiiciency," Proc. Instn. Mech. Engrs. (A.D.), **1**, 34 (1960–61).

29. Austen, A. E. W., and W. T. Lyn. "Relation Between Fuel Injection and Heat Release in a Direct-Injection Engine and the Nature of the Combustion Processes," Proc. Instn. Mech. Engrs. (A.D.), **1**, 47 (1960–61).

30. Grigg, H. C., and M. H. Syed. "The Problem of Predicting Rate of Heat Release in Diesel Engines," Paper 18, Symposium on Diesel Engine Combustion, Proceedings, Instn. Mech. Engrs., London, **184** (3J), 192 (1970).

31. Bolt, J. A., and N. A. Henein. "Diesel Engine Ignition and Combustion," The University of Michigan, Contract No. DA-20-018-AMC-1669(T), Final Report 06720-11-F (February, 1969) p 542.

32. Hurn, R. W. "Air Pollution and the Compression-Ignition Engine," 12th Symposium (International) on Combustion, (Pittsburgh, Pa.: The Combustion Institute, 1969), pp 677–687.

33. Marshall, W. F., and R. W. Hurn. "Factors Influencing Diesel Emissions," SAE 680528 (1968).

34. Perez, J. M., and E. W. Landen. "Exhaust Emission Characteristics of Precombustion Chamber Engine," SAE **PT-14**, 478 (1967–70).

35. Johnson, J. H., E. J. Sienicki, and O. F. Zeck. "A Flame Ionization Technique for Measuring Total Hydrocarbon in Diesel Exhaust," SAE **PT-14**, 130 (1967–70).

36. Bascom, R. C., L. C. Broering, and D. E. Wulfhorst. "Design Factors that Affect Diesel Emissions," 1971 SAE Lecture Series, "Engineering Know-How in Engine Design." (March, 1971).

37. Aaronson, A. E., and R. A. Matula. "Diesel Odor and the Formation of Aromatic Hyrocarbons during the Heterogeneous Combustion of Pure Cetane in a Single-Cylinder Diesel Engine," 13th Symposium (International) on Combustion (Pittsburgh, Pa.: The Combustion Institute, 1971) pp 471–481.

38. Khan, I. M., and H. C. Grigg. "Progress of Diesel Combustion

Research," paper no. A-18, CIMAC, 9th International Congress on Combustion Engines, Stockholm, Sweden (May, 1971).

39. Merrion, D. F. "Effect of Design Revisions on Two-Stroke Cycle Diesel Engine Exhaust," SAE PT-14, 496 (1967–70).

40. Elliott, M. A. *Diesel Fuel Oils—Production, Characteristics and Combustion,* (New York: ASME, 1948) pp 57–120.

41. "Chemical Identification of the Odor Components in Diesel Engine Exhaust," Arthur D. Little Inc., Final report to CRC and NAPCA, C-71407, C-71475, CRC Project: CAPE-7-68 (1–69), HEW Contract no. CPA-22-69-63 (June, 1970).

42. O'Donnell, A. and A Dravnieks. "Chemical Species in Engine Exhaust and their Contributions to Exhaust Odors," IIT Research Institute, Chicago, Ill., report no. IITRI C6183-5 (November, 1970).

43. Springer, K. J., and H. E. Dietzmann. An Investigation of Diesel-Powered Vehicle Odor and Smoke," Part IV, Southwest Research Institute, San Antonio, Texas, Final Report no. AR-802 (April, 1971).

44. Somers, J. H., and G. D. Kittredge. "Review of Federally Sponsored Research on Diesel Exhaust Odors," U.S.E.P.A., Ann Arbor, Mich., Report no. 71–75, for presentation at the 64th Annual Meeting of the Air Pollution Control Association, Atlantic City, N. J., June 27–July 2, 1971.

45. Spindt, R. S., G. J. Barnes, and J. H. Somers. "The Characterization of Odor Components in Diesel Exhaust Gas," SAE Paper No. 710605, (1971).

46. Stahman, R. C., G. D. Kittredge, and K. J. Springer. "Smoke and Odor Control for Diesel Powered Trucks and Buses," SAE PT-14, 533 (1967–70).

47. Stahman, R. C., and K. J. Springer. "An Investigation of Diesel Powered Vehicle Odor and Smoke," National Petroleum Refiners Association, FL-66-46, Fuels and Lubricants Meeting, Philadelphia, Pa., Sept. 1966.

48. Turk, A. "Selection and Training of Judges for Sensory Evaluation of the Intensity and Character of Diesel Exhaust Odors," U.S. Dept. of Health, Education and Welfare, PHS, Publication 999-AP-32. U.S. Dept. of HEW, Bureau of Disease Prevention and Environmental Control, National Center for Air Pollution Control, Cincinnati, Ohio, 1967.

49. Rounds, F. G., and H. W. Pearsall. "Diesel Exhaust Odor," SAE Paper No. 863 (1956).

50. Trumpy, D. K., S. C. Sorenson, and P. S. Myers. Discussion of the paper by G. J. Barnes, "Relation of Lean Combustion Limits in Diesel Engines to Exhaust Odor Intensity," SAE PT-14, 159 (1967–70).

51. DeCorson, S. M., C. E. Hussey, and M. J. Ambrose. "Smokeless Combustion in Oil-Burning Gas Turbine," paper presented at Combustion Institute, Central States Sect., March 26–27, 1968.

52. Porter, G. "The Mechanism of Carbon Formation," Advisory Group

for Aero. R&D Memo. Ag 13/M9, Scheveningen, Netherlands Conf., May 3–7, 1954.

53. Alcock, J. F., and W. M. Scott. "Some More Light on Diesel Combustion," Proceedings, Institution of Mechanical Engineers, (A.D.), London Vol. 5, pp. 179–200 (1963).

54. Behrens, H., "Flame Instabilities and Combustion Mechanism," 4th Symposium (International) on Combustion (Baltimore: Williams and Wilkins, 1953) pp 538–545.

55. Kassel, L. S.   J. Amer. Chem. Soc. **56**, 1838 (1934).

56. Golothan, D. W.   "Diesel Engine Exhaust Smoke: The Influence of Fuel Properties and the Effects of Using Barium-Containing Fuel Additive," SAE **PT-14**, 508 (1967–70).

57. Troth, K. A.   "Relationship Between Specific Gravity and Other Fuel Properties and Diesel Engine Performance," ASTM Symposium on Diesel Fuel Oils (1966).

58. McConnell, G., and H. E. Howells.   "Diesel Fuel Properties and Exhaust Gas – Distant Relations?" SAE Transactions, (1967) pp 76.

59. Khan, I. M.   "Formation and Combustion of Carbon in a Diesel Engine," Diesel Engine Combustion Symposium, Proceedings, Institution of Mechanical Engineers, London **184** (Pt 3J), 36–43 (1970).

60. Rost, H.   M.T.Z. **22**, 458 (1961).

61. Broeze, J. J., and G. Stillebroer.   "Smoke in High Speed Diesel Engines," SAE Transactions, **57** (3), 64 (1949).

62. Savage, J. D.   "The Diesel Engine Exhaust Problem with Road Vehicle," Diesel Engineers and Users Association, paper no. S. 302 (June, 1965).

63. Parks, M. V., C. Polonski, and R. Toye.   "Penetration of Diesel Fuel Sprays in Gases," SAE Paper No. 660747 (1966).

64. Burman, P. G., and F. DeLuca.   *Fuel Injection and Controls for Internal Combustion Engines* (New York: Simmons-Boardman Publishing Corp., 1962) p 135.

65. Sitkei, G.   "Beitrag Zur Theorie der Strahlzer Staubung," ACTA Tech. **25** (1–2), 81–117 (1969). German Technical Translation – F-129, NASA., "Contribution to the Theory of Jet Atomization."

66. Becchi, G. A.   "Analytical Simulation of the Fuel-Injection in Diesel Engines," SAE Paper No. 710568 (1971).

67. Wylie, E. B., J. A. Bolt, and M. F. El-Erian.   "Diesel Fuel-Injection System Simulation and Experimental Correlation," SAE Paper No. 710569 (1971).

68. Rosselli, A., and P. Badgley.   "Simulation of the Cummins Diesel Injection System," SAE Paper No. 710570 (1971).

69. Zeldovich, Ya. B., P. Ya. Sadovnikov, and D. A. Frank-Kamenetskii.   "Oxidation of Nitrogen in Combustion," Academy of Sciences, USSR, Moscow-Leningrad (1947).

70. Eyzat, P., and J. C. Guibet.   "A New Look at Nitrogen Oxides Formation in Internal Combustion Engines," SAE Paper No. 680124 (1968).

71. Heywood, J. B., J. A. Fay, and L. H. Linden.   "Jet Aircraft Air

Pollutant Production and Dispersion," AIAA paper 70-115, New York (1970).

72. Lavoie, G. A., J. B. Heywood, and J. C. Keck. "Experimental Theoretical Study of Nitric Oxide Formation in Internal Combustion and Engines," Combust. Sci. Technol. 1 313 (1970).

73. Newhall, H. K., and S. M. Shahed. "Kinetics of Nitric Oxide Formation in High Pressure Flames," 13th Symposium (International) on Combustion, The Combustion Institute, Pittsburgh, Pa. (1971), pp 381–389.

74. Starkman, E. S., and H. K. Newhall. "Direct Spectroscopic Determination of Nitric Oxide in Reciprocating Engine Cylinders," SAE PT-14, 214 (1967–70).

75. McConnell, G., "Oxides of Nitrogen in Diesel Engine Exhaust Gas: Their Formation and Control," Proceedings, IME 178, (Pt. 1, No. 38), 1001 (1963–64).

76. Fenimore, C. P. "Formation of Nitric Oxide in Premixed Hydrocarbon Flames," 13th Symposium (International) on Combustion, the Combustion Institute, Pittsburgh, Pa., 1971, pp 373–380.

77. Meguerian, G. H. "Nitrogen Oxide Formation, Suppression, and Catalytic Reduction," American Oil Company, Research and Development Dept., PD 23 (July, 1971).

78. Obert, E. F. *Internal Combustion Engines,* 3rd ed. (Scranton, Pa.: International Textbook Company, 1968).

79. Meurer, J. "Evaluation of Reaction Kinetics Eliminates Diesel Knock—The M Combustion System of M.A.N.," SAE Trans. 64, 250 (1956); 72, 712 (1962).

80. Lyn, W. T., and E. Valdmanis. "The Application of High-Speed Schlieren Photography to Diesel Combustion Research," J. Photogr. Sci. 10, 74 (1962).

81. Lewis, G. D. "Combustion in a Centrifugal-Force Field," 13th Symposium (International) on Combustion, The Combustion Institute, Pittsburgh, Pa., 1971, pp 625–629.

82. Nagao, F., and H. Kakimoto, "Swirl and Combustion in Divided Chamber Diesel Engines," SAE Trans. 70 680 (1962).

83. Bowdon, C. M., B. S. Samage, and W. T. Lyn. "Rate of Heat Release in High Speed Indirect-Injection Diesel Engine," Diesel Engine Combustion Symposium, Proceedings, Institution of Mechanical Engineers, London, 184 (Pt 3J), 122 (1969–70).

84. Downs, D. "A European Contribution to Lower Vehicle Exhaust Emissions," Conference on Low Pollution Power System Development, Eindnoven, February 23–25, 1971.

85. Abthoff, J., and H. Luther. "Die Messungen der Stickoxid-Emission von Dieselmotoren und ihre Beeinflussung durch Massnahmen am Motor," ATZ 71 (4), 124 (1969).

86. Marshall, W. F., and R. D. Fleming. "Diesel Emissions Reinventoried," RI 7530, (Washington, D.C.: U.S. Dept. of the Interior, Bureau of Mines, July, 1971).

87. Springer, K. J. "Emissions from a Gasoline and Diesel Powered

Mercedes,220 Passenger Car," Report AR-813, Southwest Research Institute, San Antonio, Texas (June, 1971).

88. Campau, R. M.   "Low Emission Concept Vehicles," SAE Paper No. 710294, (1971).

89. Meguerian, G. H., and C. R. Lang, "NO_x Reduction Catalysts for Vehicle Emission Control, SAE Paper No. 710291 (1971).

90. Valdamanis, E., and D. E. Wulfhorst. "The Effects of Emulsified Fuels and Water Induction on Diesel Combustion," SAE PT-14, 570 (1967–70).

91. Torpey, P. M., M. J. Whitehead and M. J. Wright.   "Experiments in the Control of Diesel Emissions," Conference on Air Pollution Control in Transport Engines, Institute of Medical Engineering, London, November, 1971.

92. Ohigashi, S., H. Kurodo, Y. Nakajima, T. Hayashi, and K. Sugihara.   "A New Method of Predicting Nitrogen Oxides Reduction on Exhaust Gas Recirculation," SAE Paper No. 710010 (January, 1971).

93. Quador, A. A. "Why Intake Charge Dilution Decreases Nitric Oxide Emission from Spark Ignition Engines," SAE Paper No. 71009 (1971).

9

EMISSION INSTRUMENTATION

Part I   Nondispersive Infrared Analyzer

NDIR analyzers are the standard instruments presently used for the testing and legal certification of some automotive exhaust emissions. They are used for measuring the concentration of CO and CO_2.

Principle of Operation

In the NDIR analyzer the exhaust gas species being measured are used to detect themselves. The method of detection is based on the principle of selective absorption: the infrared energy of a particular wave length, peculiar to a certain gas, will be absorbed by that gas. Infrared energy of other wave lengths will be transmitted by that gas, just as energy of the absorbed wave length will be transmitted by other gases. Therefore, in effect, certain gases match up with certain wave lengths in the infrared energy band. An example of this can be seen in Figure 9.1, where it is noticed that carbon dioxide absorbs infrared energy in the wave length band of about 4 to 4.5 microns and transmits energy of the surrounding wave lengths. This figure also shows that the carbon monoxide absorption band is between 4.5 and 5 microns.

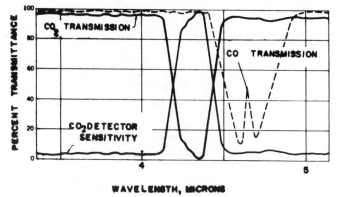

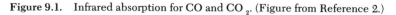

Figure 9.1.   Infrared absorption for CO and CO_2. (Figure from Reference 2.)

Construction of Instrument

The construction of the NDIR is shown in Figure 9.2. Two identical infrared sources direct infrared radiation through two separate cells, a sample cell and a reference cell. After passing through these cells the infrared radiation is received in two separate detector cells, which are full of the gas whose concentration is to be measured. The two detector cells contain equal amounts of this gas and are separated by a flexible diaphragm. This diaphragm together with a stationary metal button constitute a capacitor, whose capacitance is varied proportionally to the distance between them.

The sample cell is a flow-through tube that receives a continuous stream of the mixture of gases to be analyzed. When the particular gas to be measured is present in the sample, it absorbs the infrared radiation at its characteristic wave lengths. The per cent of radiation absorbed is proportional to the molecular concen-

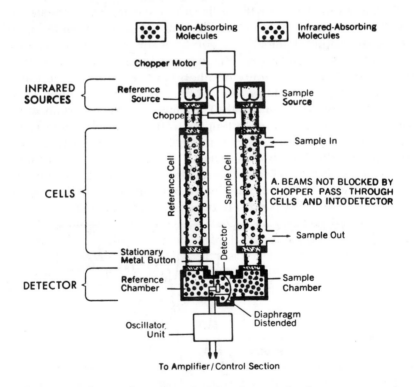

Figure 9.2. The non-dispersive infrared analyzer, with radiation transmitted to the cells. (Notice that the diaphram is deflected away from the button). (Figure from Reference 3.)

tration of the component of interest in the sample. The cells have quartz windows which do not absorb infrared energy in the region of interest. The length of the cells varies according to the application. Low concentrations are best measured by longer cells so that more molecules of interest are present.

The reference cell is sealed and is physically identical to the sample cell. It is filled with an inert gas (usually nitrogen) which does not absorb the infrared energy of the characteristic wave length of the species of interest.

The radiant energy, after passing through the cells, heats the gas in the corresponding chamber of the detector. Since no radiant energy is absorbed in the reference cell, the corresponding chamber in the detector is heated more and its pressure becomes higher than that in the other chamber. This pressure differential causes the diaphragm to move and vary the capacitance. Therefore the variation in the capacitance is proportional to the concentration of the species of interest in the exhaust sample.

A chopper is placed between the infrared source and the cells. When the chopper blocks the radiation, the pressure in the two compartments of the detector is equal because there is no energy entering either chamber of the detector. This allows the diaphragm to return to its neutral position as shown in Figure 9.3. As the chopper alternately blocks and unblocks the radiation, the diaphragm fluctuates causing the capacitance to change cyclically. This sets up an AC signal, which is impressed on a carrier wave provided by a radio-frequency oscillator. The reason for using the chopper to produce an AC signal is that the amplifiers of AC signals have better drift-free characteristics than the amplifiers of DC signals. Additional electronic circuitry in the oscillator unit demodulates and filters the resultant signal. This signal is then amplified and rectified to a DC signal which is measured by a meter or recorder. The final DC signal is a function of the concentration of the species of interest in the exhaust sample. Further details on the electronic circuits of a typical NDIR may be found in Reference 3.

Calibration

The instrument is calibrated by passing gases of known concentration through the sample cell. The zero and span controls can be adjusted so that any scale is arbitrary. With the known concentrations and their associated meter readings, a calibration curve is constructed. In practice, the curve is usually drawn between two

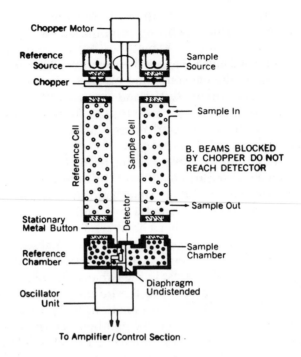

Figure 9.3. The NDIR with radiation blocked by the chopper off the cells. (Notice that the diaphragm is in its Neutral Position). (Figure from Reference 3.)

points and linearity is assumed. For linear interpolation the length of the tube should be chosen so that the readings are in the linear region of the relation between concentration and energy absorbed.

The relation between the incident energy, the absorbed energy, the length of the cell, and the concentration of the species of interest can be given by Equation 9.1:

$$E_a = E_i \left(1 - e^{-kcl}\right) \tag{9.1}$$

where:

E_a = energy absorbed
E_i = energy incident
k = absorption constant
c = concentration of species of interest
l = length of cell

Equation 9.1 can be approximated to a more simplified form if the value of kcl is very small compared to unity. Under this condition:

$$e^{-kcl} \approx 1 - kcl \qquad (9.2)$$

and Equation 9.1 becomes

$$E_a = E_i \times kcl \qquad (9.3)$$

Equations 9.2 and 9.3 show that the absorbed energy is directly proportional to the concentration c under one condition only, that is $kcl \ll 1$. This shows that if the concentration "c" is high, the length of the cell should be short and the product kcl very small compared to unity, in order that linearity of the scale could be assumed. The choice of the length of the cell should take into consideration the sensitivity of the instrument as well as the linearity of the scale. In general longer cells give better sensitivity but less linearity. On the other hand they take a longer time to purge and do not respond to transients as rapidly.

Measurement of Unburned Hydrocarbons in Engine Exhaust

The unburned hydrocarbons in the exhaust consist of about 200 different compounds, each with different composition and different number of carbon and hydrogen atoms. It is impossible to detect each of these unburned hydrocarbon compounds separately. The overall concentration of the unburned hydrocarbons may be found by measuring the equivalent concentration of n-hexane, C_6H_{14}. So the chambers of the NDIR detector are filled with n-hexane. A more accurate method for measuring the unburned hydrocarbon emissions is use of the flame ionization detector (described later in this chapter).

Interference from Other Gases

An error in the NDIR may arise if the exhaust sample contains other species which will absorb radiation at the same frequencies that the gas in the detector will absorb. For example, an infrared analyzer, equipped with a normal-hexane detector responds to gases other than n-hexane, such as CO_2, CO, and H_2O. All these gases are present in the exhaust of combustion engines. One way to minimize this interference is to place a filter containing a large concentration of the interfering gas as shown in Figure 9.4. The analyzer zero is then set with this large concentration of the interfering gas, and any interference in the sample will be a small deviation compared to the effect of the large concentrations in the filter.

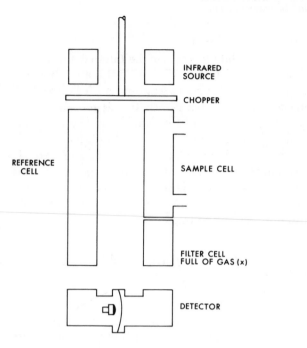

Figure 9.4.   NDIR with a filter cell to reduce the interference from gas (x).

Table 9.1 shows the readings obtained from an NDIR when samples of N_2 containing different percentages of CO, CO_2, and H_2O were tested. The highest interference is caused by H_2O and the lowest by CO. A 15.7 % CO_2 in N_2 caused an interference between 10 and 175 ppm as n-hexane. The use of CO_2 filter cell causes the interference to drop from a range of 10 to 175 ppm to a range of 1 to 15, depending on the instrument.

The effect of changing the sample cell length on carbon dioxide interference is shown in Figure 9.5. The increase in the sample cell length reduces the effect of interference caused by 15.7% CO_2. The effect of adding a CO_2 filter cell on reducing interference is shown on the same figure.

The addition of a filter containing the interfering gas is not effective in the case of H_2O. From the data of Table 9.1, we can see that water vapor interference is not lowered appreciably with a water vapor filter. The effect of the water vapor concentration on interference is shown in Figure 9.6.

One way to correct for the H_2O interference is by subtracting an appropriate value from the meter reading. A better solution is to cool the sample to 32°F where the vapor pressure of water is

Table 9.1

Interferences of the Infrared Analyzer

Sample Cell Gas	Filter Cell Gas	Interference ppm as n-Hexane		
		Minimum	Median	Maximum
7.3% CO in N_2	N_2	0	1	3
15.7% CO_2 in N_2	N_2	10	45	175
	CO_2	1	3	15
4.8% H_2O in N_2	N_2	20	32	350
(Saturated at 90°F)	CO_2	20	32	350
	H_2O in CO_2	17	28	340

Data from Reference 1.
Data for 12 n-hexane dectors
   13-1/2 inch sample cell
   1-1/2 inch filter cell

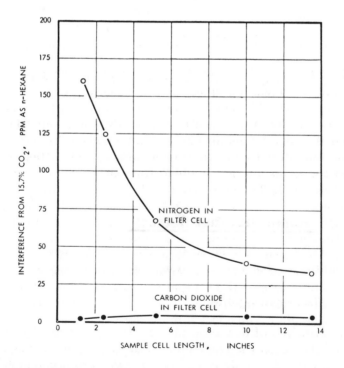

Figure 9.5. The effect of sample cell length on carbon dioxide interference (Beckman Infrared Analyzer, n-Hexane Detector 7377, 1-1/2 Inch Filter Cell). (Figure from Reference 1.)

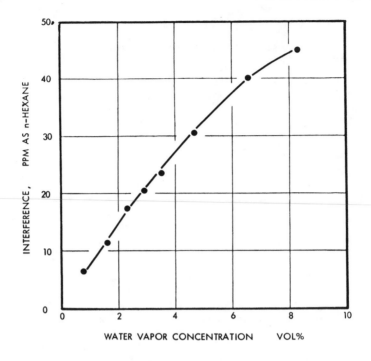

Figure 9.6. The effect of water vapor concentration on interference (Beckman Infrared Analyzer, n-Hexane Detector 7377, 13-1/2 Inch Sample Cell, 1-1/2 Inch CO_2 Filter Cell). (Figure from Reference 1.)

0.089 psia. If the sample is at 14.7 psia, the water vapor per cent will be $0.089/14.7 \times 100$ or 0.65%. This yields a constant value, (7 ppm in Figure 9.6) which can be corrected automatically if the calibrating gases are first bubbled through water, saturated, and also cooled to 32°F.

Part II   Flame Ionization Detector

The FID is one of the instruments used to measure the unburned hydrocarbon concentration in the exhaust gases.

Principle of Operation

The principle of operation of the FID is illustrated in Figure 9.7. It is based on the phenomena that pure hydrogen/air flames produce very little ionization, but if a few hydrocarbon molecules are introduced, these flames produce a large amount of ionization. The ionization is proportional to the number of carbon atoms present in the hydrocarbon molecules. All classes of hydrocar-

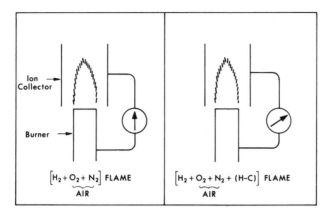

Figure 9.7. Effect of hydrocarbon compounds in sample in ionization of hydrogen-air flame.

bons (paraffins, olefins, aromatics, etc.) are measured with equal response. This conclusion does not apply to hydrocarbon molecules which contain oxygen or nitrogen atoms.

Construction of Instrument

The FID, shown in Figure 9.8, is composed of the burner assembly, the ion collector and the electric circuitry. The burner consists of a central capillary tube through which the gas sample and a mixture of nitrogen and hydrogen flow. Relatively pure hydrogen is used. The air required for combustion is introduced from around the capillary tube. The combustible mixture formed is ignited by a hot wire at the top of the burner assembly. The flame produced is of the diffusion type.

The collector and the capillary tube form part of an electric circuit. An electric polarizing battery is used to produce an electrostatic field in the vicinity of the flame. This causes the electrons to go to the burner jet and the positive ions to the collector. The DC signal produced is proportional to the number of ions formed and the number of ions formed is proportional to the number of carbon atoms in the flame. The DC signal generated is attenuated by a modulator and then fed to an AC amplifier and a demodulator.

Flow System

The sensitivity of the FID is affected by the flow rates of the sample and the hydrogen-nitrogen mixture. One of the methods used to control the rate of flow of each of these gases is to allow

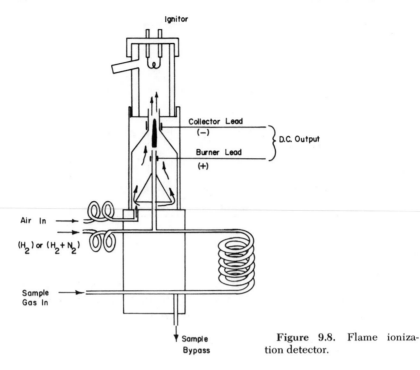

Figure 9.8. Flame ionization detector.

each to pass through a capillary as shown in Figure 9.8. The rate
of flow depends upon the cross section of the capillary, the length,
and the pressure drop across the capillary. To ensure reproducibility the capillaries should be clean and the pressure ahead of
the capillary should be regulated and kept constant.

Although the FID has a very low sensitivity to water vapor, it
is essential that condensation of H_2O in the sample system be
prevented to avoid blocking the system. This results in erratic responses in the unheated flame ionization detector. In the heated
flame ionization detector, the burner assembly and the sampling
tubes are heated to 350–400°F. This will reduce the condensation
of the heavy hydrocarbons on the walls. Probably under this condition the H_2O in the sample will pass through the system as
vapor.

Interference

For most exhaust gas hydrocarbon measurements, the presence
of other constituents does not interfere with the readings. This is

not the case with the NDIR, where CO_2 and H_2O interfere with the hydrocarbon absorbtion band, and filtering or removal is required. When oxygen is present in the exhaust sample in excess of 4 % or so, a significant response change in the FID may occur depending on the proportions of hydrogen, diluent, and burner air-fuel ratio.[1,4] Figure 9.9 shows the oxygen interference effect. In general the readings are lowered. Oxygen interference in gasoline engines arises under conditions of lean mixture operation, air injection, or dilution such as occurs in a variable dilution sampler. In heterogeneous combustion systems, mixtures leaner than stoichiometric are used and oxygen interference should be corrected.

The hydrogen to diluent ratio referred to in Figure 9.9 is defined as the hydrogen flow rate divided by the diluent flow rate. The diluent includes the sample plus any inert gas added to the fuel. Commonly a fuel with 40% hydrogen and 60% nitrogen or helium is used for safety reasons. The air-fuel ratio is defined as the air-flow rate divided by the hydrogen flow rate. These flows are suggested in Figure 9.9. A chemically correct hydrogen mixture has 2.38 volume of air per volume of hydrogen. The oxygen interference varies with the hydrogen-diluent ratio and the air-hydrogen ratio.

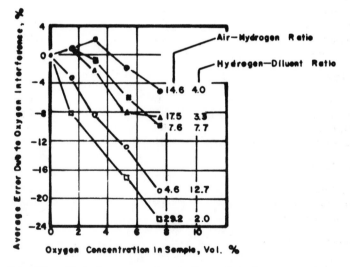

Figure 9.9. The effect of oxygen concentration and analyzer operating conditions on oxygen interference (Perkin-Elmer flame-ionization analyzer, Airflow rate: 175 ml/min, fuel hydrogen, fuel flow rate: 6 to 38 ml/min, sample: 100, 303, and 1010 ppm n-hexane in nitrogen diluted with various amounts of oxygen, sample flow rate: 3 ml/min). (Figure from Reference 1.)

FID-NDIR Response Comparison

Table 9.2 shows a relative response comparison between the FID and NDIR instruments. The FID readings were taken with pure hydrogen fuel at a 15.4:1 air/fuel ratio (lean). This is about the optimum FID operating point for uniform response to all hydrocarbons on a carbon atom basis. The FID response linearity is normally poorer at other hydrogen-diluent ratios and other

Table 9.2

Average Relative Hydrocarbon Responses
(Carbon Basis)

Hydrocarbon	NDIR (5.25″ Sample Cell)	FID (Pure Hydrogen Fuel, 15.4:1 Air/Hydrogen Ratio)
Paraffins	Hexane = 100	Hexane = 100
Methane	30	104
Ethane	100	103
Propane	103	103
i-Butane	101	—
n-Butane	106	102
i-Pentane	99	101
n-Pentane	104	102
n-Hexane	100	100
n-Heptane	97	100
Olefins		
Ethylene	9	104
Propylene	31	104
1-Butene	53	—
1-Hexene	61	—
Acetylenes		
Acetylene	1	95
Methylacetylene	16	96
Ethylacetylene	32	96
Aromatics		
Benzene	2	105
Toluene	13	105

Data from Reference 1.

air-hydrogen ratios. When a 60% N_2 – 40% H_2 fuel is used, the hydrogen-diluent ratio becomes too low for optimum linearity.

Part III   The Gas Chromatograph

Chromatography is a physical method of separating a mixture into its individual constituents so that each constituent can be analyzed separately. It is the only method by which the amount of each exhaust hydrocarbon compound can be measured. The constituents are divided or are partitioned between two phases, one of which is stationary, the other mobile and percolates through the stationary phase. This stationary phase is a solid or a liquid. With a solid stationary phase, chromatography is referred to as adsorption chromatography. With a liquid stationary phase it is referred to as partition chromatography. Exhaust gas hydrocarbon analysis involves partition chromatography.

Gas-solid chromatography and gas-liquid chromatography are conducted in separatory or fractionating columns. These are packed with the solid absorbent or with a solid supporting material impregnated with a liquid. The materials to be separated are mixed in gaseous form with the mobile inert gas phase (the carrier or effluent gas), which travels through the stationary phase. The stationary phase acts as a selective retardent for each constituent of the mixture because of the differences in solubilities (adsorption and hydrogen bonding probably contribute to the retardations). Consequently, the constituents tend to leave the column one at a time with relatively sharp separations, each constituent having a unique retention time within the column that is more or less proportional to its solubility in the stationary phase. This separation is suggested in Figure 9.10. The substances in the flowing carrier gas stream are then detected by measuring some chemical or physical property. A flame ionization detector is used to measure hydrocarbons. This measurement is continuously recorded either by direct reading or by means of a device which automatically delivers a permanent graph of the data in question. A typical gas chromatogram for some hydrocarbon species is shown in Figure 9.11.

Gas chromatography is the most effective method used for the detailed analysis of exhaust gas mixtures and for a definite identification of the different components present in the mixture. This method can be used to analyze a very small amount of the gas.

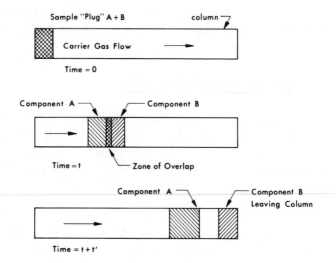

Figure 9.10. Schematic of a chromatographic process.

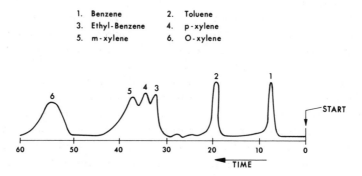

Figure 9.11. Typical gas chromatogram.

Components of the Gas-Liquid Chromatograph

A gas-liquid chromatograph is shown schematically in Figure 9.12 and is composed of:

    (1) carrier gas supplier and controller
    (2) the sample injection device
    (3) the column
    (4) the oven and thermostat
    (5) the detector
    (6) the recorder.

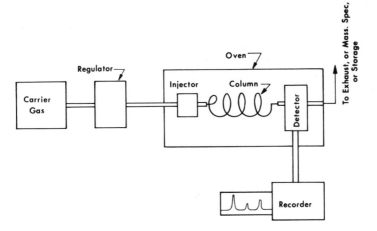

Figure 9.12.   Main components of the gas chromatograph.

Carrier Gas Supplier and Controller

The carrier gas should be an inert gas to avoid interaction with the sample or solvent. The commonly used gases are hydrogen, helium and nitrogen. The detector employed usually dictates the choice of the carrier gas. However, for highest efficiency a high molecular weight gas, such as nitrogen, should be chosen. Where rapid analysis time is required and highest efficiency is not necessary, the low molecular weight gases such as helium or hydrogen would be preferred.

The rate of flow of the carrier gas is regulated to a constant value in order to identify the components by their retention time. For quantitative analysis it is necessary for the flow to be substantially constant in order that all components recorded on the time axis may be sensed on the same volumetric basis. The flow rate is controlled by a precise regulation of the inlet and outlet pressures. Most of the gas chromatographs work at an outlet pressure of one atmosphere so that the flow rate is controlled by regulating the inlet pressure only.

The rate of gas flow can be measured by means of a rotameter, an orifice meter or a soap-film flow meter. The main advantage of the soap-film flow meter is that is is a very simple, extremely accurate device which exerts no back pressure, and whose operation does not depend on the viscosity of the gas as in the case of the rotameter or the orifice meter. The supply gas should be dry, since water vapor is not inert. A dryer may be used to reduce the concentration of the water vapor.

The Sample Injection Device

The injection system must introduce the sample reproducibly and, if the sample is a liquid, vaporize it instantly, without decomposition or pressure variations. Liquids are usually injected through self-sealing septa with syringes. The sample should be kept small in order to keep the column from reaching a saturated state.

For gaseous samples, a closed, calibrated volume loop which can be quickly switched into the carrier gas flow is used, as shown in Figure 9.13. Purging can be effected either by repeated evacuation or by excess sample flow-through.

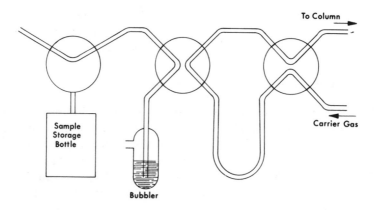

Figure 9.13.   Gas sample inlet system. (After Reference 8.)

The Column

Two types of columns can be used, capillary or packed. Capillary columns are open tubes of small diameter with a thin liquid film on the wall. Packed columns consist of an inert solid material supporting a thin film of a nonvolatile liquid. The tube may be either glass, metal or plastic, coiled to fit the chromatograph oven. Packed columns are ordinarily 1/16″ to 1/4″ O.D. tubing from 3 to 30 feet in length.

Often in a separation of two very similar materials one would have problems with overlapping peaks, as will be discussed in connection with Figure 9.15. The usual way of improving the separating ability of the apparatus is to make the column longer, that is, have more separating material for the mixture to pass over. An extreme example of this technique is the capillary column, an unpacked, very small bore tubing column of extreme length, often on the order of 100–200 meters. With these lengths of column many extremely difficult separations can be accomplished. There are drawbacks: retention time is often very long, and small samples must be used, giving minimal detector signal. Hence, one must use very sensitive detectors and live with the increase in background which often accompanies increased sensitivity.

There are many possible solid supports (stationary phases): diatomaceous earth, charcoal, clay, silica gel, firebrick, alumina, various oxides, even coffee grounds. Particle size is usually kept to about 100 mesh.

The type of liquid phase employed depends on the nature of the mixture. Table 9.3 lists typical solvent (liquid phase) and solute type (separated specie) and the maximum allowable temperature for this solvent.

There are several general criteria to be considered in choosing the liquid phase. It must be a good solvent for the components of the mixture. It must have good separating ability, be thermally

Table 9.3

Selected Solutes and Solvents

Solvent	Solute	Temp. Limit
Paraffin oils	paraffins olefins halides	150°C
Squalane	paraffins olefins	140°C
Silicone Oils	paraffins olefins esters esters	varies with molecular wgt. of oil
Polyglycols	amines nitriles ketones esters alchols ethers aromatics	100–200°C
B-Oxydipropio- nitrile	general for polar compounds	less than 100

stable and have a low vapor pressure so it does not evaporate itself.

The amount of liquid phase applied to the solid support varies from 2 to 30 % of the stationary phase weight. The liquid phase is often applied by dissolving it in a volatile solvent and pouring it through the column. The solvent then can be evaporated, leaving an even coating.

A new column, before use, must be purged by passing the carrier gas through it at operating temperatures for several hours, until the detector indicates a low background level.

The Oven and Thermostat

Precise temperature control is required for the reproducibility of the retention times. The partition coefficient (the ratio of material concentration in the liquid to that in the gas phase) is sensitive to temperature changes. It is estimated that an increase of 55°F will reduce the partition coefficient by 50%. The variation in the retention time related to temperature is illustrated in Figure 9.14. The analysis time is increased and the resolution is improved by lowering the temperature. The column temperature is usually chosen by compromise, not so high as to impair resolution and not so low as to cause long retention times.

Sometimes one or more components of a mixture may be held for a very long time on the column. The usual way to speed up the elution process is to analyze at a higher column temperature, but this has the disadvantage of spreading out each peak, which can cause overlapping of earlier peaks, i.e. fastest components. The solution to this problem is to operate the column at a lower temperature until the fast peaks have been eluted, then increase

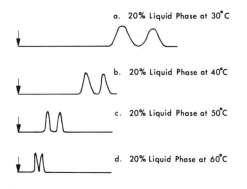

a. 20% Liquid Phase at 30°C

b. 20% Liquid Phase at 40°C

c. 20% Liquid Phase at 50°C

d. 20% Liquid Phase at 60°C

Figure 9.14.   Retention time vs. temperature. (After Reference 7.)

the temperature uniformily to elute the slower peaks. On some GC's the thermostatic control can be programmed to give a pre-determined temperature-time profile. Figure 9.15 suggests the advantage of temperature programming.

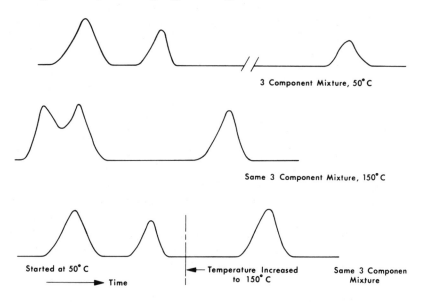

Figure 9.15. Effect of temperature programming on gas chromatogram.

The Detector

A number of different types of detectors are available, some of which are thermal conductivity, gas-density, heat of adsorption, flame temperature, and ionization types, which include flame ionization, beta-ray, and radio-frequency. The choice of detector is based on the following criteria:

applicability: must work on this sample and apparatus,
discrimination: must be able to tell carrier gas from sample,
response linearity: response must be directly proportional to component size, and
sensitivity: background and noise should be low compared to signal.

Detectors are usually limited to component concentration of 0.01 to 1 volume %. The two most widely used detectors are those using thermal conductivity and flame ionization. The thermal conductivity cell will be discussed below, and the flame ionization dilutor used for HC analysis was discussed previously.

The Thermal Conductivity Cell

Thermal conductivity detectors rely on differences in heat transfer ability of the carrier and component gases. A typical sketch is shown in Figure 9.16. Heated filaments (resistors) within the detector form a Wheatstone bridge that detects the difference between the resistance of the sample side and the reference side.[5] The filament resistance is a function of its temperature. Each filament is heated to the same temperature by a small heating current. In the reference side of the cell, the filament is cooled by the carrier gas alone. In the sample side it is cooled by the carrier gas interspersed with component peaks. When the carrier is passing through both sides, heat transfer is the same in both; the bridge is therefore balanced and no signal results. When a component peak passes through the sample side, there is a difference in heat transfer due to differing thermal conductivities. The bridge becomes unbalanced and the detector puts out a signal to the recorder amplifier. From the standpoint of heat transfer the most suitable carrier gases are hydrogen and helium because of their large thermal conductivities, although they do have low molecular weight which is a disadvantage. Thermal conductivity detectors may be used to detect small hydrocarbon molecules as well as many nonhydrocarbon exhaust gas constitutuents. These include H_2, O_2, N_2, CO_2, H_2O, CO, and NO.

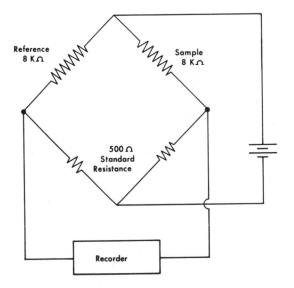

Figure 9.16.   Thermal conductivity detector.

The Recorder

The recorder is the part of the apparatus which converts the detector output into a visual display and provides a permanent record of each run. The response of the detector should be fast: less than one second to reach full deflection. It should be able to respond to currents from 10^{-6} to 10^{-13} amp, the usual range of the output of a flame ionization detector. The recorder should also have some provision for canceling background and zeroing.

The recorder gives a plot of arbitrary response vs. time (retention time) it takes the pen to reach maximum deflection for a specific component. Since this retention time is a constant for each set of operating conditions, it provides a convenient method for identifying the peaks. However, before this method of identification may be used, calibrated samples of each component must be run through the apparatus to provide a standard retention time. The conditions for this calibration must necessarily be the same as those used in the separation of the mixture.

Quantitative Aspects

As mentioned before both peak height and peak area can be used in measuring concentration or amount of each component. Peak height is more easily measured than area but it is necessary to keep all experimental variables constant, as these affect the time for the peak to emerge. One must therefore calibrate with a known amount of sample under the same conditions to be used on the unknown. Other than its relative ease in measurement, peak height has the advantage of not being affected by errors in carrier gas flow-rate.

Peak area, however, is insensitive to the variables that affect retention time because the peak area theoretically remains constant and proportional to sample size as the peak moves down the column.

Hydrocarbon Analysis

Below is a brief description of a chromatographic method used by the Ford Motor Company to separate and measure the 200+ hydrocarbons found in the exhaust of the gasoline engine. This discussion is abstrated from Reference 10. The technique is quite similar to those employed by many laboratories within the automotive and petroleum industries. Figure 9.17 shows a schematic

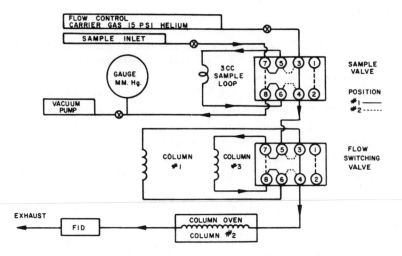

Figure 9.17. Column and valve arrangement. (Figure from Reference 10.)

of the basic system. Three columns are used. Column 1 is used to separate the lightest hydrocarbon molecules: methane, ethane and ethylene. Column 2 separates the rest and column 3 subtracts all but the paraffins.

First the vacuum pump draws the sample into the 3 cc sample loop (Figure 9.17). After the sample loop is filled the sample valve is switched allowing the sample gas to be injected directly into column 1. The flow switching valve is set in the dotted position. Column 1, which is initially placed in a dry ice slurry at −78°C, condenses all the hydrocarbons except methane. The methane passes unimpeded through columns 1 and 2 and is detected by the FID and recorded. Next column 1 is allowed to warm in air, during which time ethane and ethylene pass through and are detected. The carrier gas flow through column 1 is then reversed and the column warmed by placing it in room temperature water. By the time column 1 has reached room temperature, the remaining hydrocarbons have been flushed into column 2, a capillary column, where they are once again stopped. Column 2 is located in a temperature-programmed oven which is initially cooled to − 30°C by blowing liquid nitrogen vapor over the column.

This sequence of events is suggested in Figure 9.18, points A through G. Note that Figure 9.18 is the oven temperature program and consequently indicates the temperature of column 2 only. At point G, about 7 minutes after the analysis has started, the oven temperature is gradually raised and the remaining hydrocarbons separated.

Figure 9.19 shows an exhaust chromatogram at 30 mph cruise with Indolene fuel. Note that the complete analysis is run twice. The second time the sample is passed first through column 3 so that only the paraffins remain in the sample to be analyzed. This

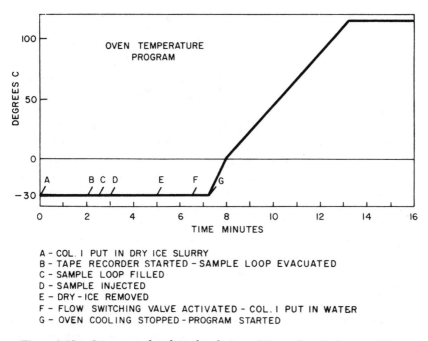

A – COL. I PUT IN DRY ICE SLURRY
B – TAPE RECORDER STARTED – SAMPLE LOOP EVACUATED
C – SAMPLE LOOP FILLED
D – SAMPLE INJECTED
E – DRY-ICE REMOVED
F – FLOW SWITCHING VALVE ACTIVATED - COL. I PUT IN WATER
G – OVEN COOLING STOPPED - PROGRAM STARTED

Figure 9.18. Sequence of analytical technique. (Figure from Reference 10.)

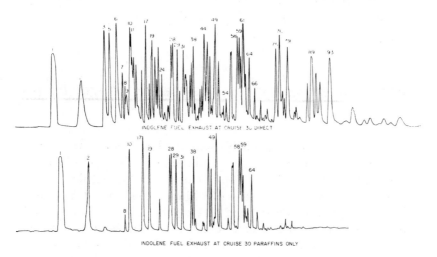

INDOLENE FUEL EXHAUST AT CRUISE 30 DIRECT

INDOLENE FUEL EXHAUST AT CRUISE 30 PARAFFINS ONLY

Figure 9.19. Gas chromatogram at 30 mph cruise. (Figure from Reference 10.)

subtractive column technique allows separation of olefins and paraffins of similar structure that have the same carbon number and about the same retention time, for example, compounds 10 and 11, butane and 1-butene.

GC Exhaust Data for Various Fuels

A series of chromatographic analyses of the exhaust of engines running on pure fuels and Indolene fuel is shown in Table 9.4 Toluene is a pure aromatic fuel, whereas propane and isooctane are straight chain and branched paraffins. The Indolene fuel had 72.2% paraffins, 7.6% olefins, and 20.1% aromatics.

It is interesting to note that the aromatic fuel, toluene had 70% by volume of the exhaust products as aromatics. These were undoubtedly toluene and benzene. Note that the exhaust composition strongly reflects the fuel composition. The same was true for propane where 56% of the exhaust was propane and other paraffins. Interestingly, the two paraffinic fuels generated about 40–50% olefins (as did Indolene) but virtually no aromatics. One might conclude that wall quenching is primarily a cracking process where larger molecules are split or partially reacted to smaller ones, with the inverse polymerization process occurring very infrequently.

A point of special interest is the average carbon number of the Indolene fuel, 6.49, and the average carbon number of the Indolene exhaust, 4.61. Based on this analysis an average fuel molecule could be thought of as

$$C_{6.49} H_{6.49 \times 1.86} \text{ or } C_{6.49} H_{12.1}$$

and an average exhaust molecule as

$$C_{4.61} H_{4.61 \times} ?$$

Part IV   Chemiluminescent Analyses of Nitrogen Oxides

Introduction

The chemiluminescent analysis method has been adopted for measurement of automotive NO_x emissions.[11] This technique was developed at both Ford Motor Company, Scientific Laboratory[12,13] and AeroChem Research.[14] The perfection of this type of exhaust analyzer permitted the establishment of a Federal NO_x standard for 1973 which heretofore has been impossible because of measurement problems in the highly diluted wet sample provided by the CVS system. Further development of a low cost

Table 9.4

GC Exhaust Data for Various Fuels

Fuel	Toluene exhaust	Indolene fuel	Indolene exhaust	Propane exhaust	Isooctane exhaust
Total hydrocarbon					
NDIR (ppm Hx)	78.5	—	195	112	281
FID (ppm Hx)	253	—	374	154	567
FID/NDIR ratio	3.26	—	1.92	1.37	2.02
Paraffins					
Mole per cent	14.0	72.2	24.5	55.9	42.7
Per cent of total reactivity	0.0	36.4	4.0	0.1	4.0
Ave. relative reactivity	0.01	0.99	0.57	0.01	0.30
Acetylenes					
Mole per cent	1.65	0	9.59	4.92	8.29
Per cent of total reactivity	0	0	0	0	0
Olefins					
Mole per cent	15.8	7.6	42.3	38.8	48.4
Per cent of total reactivity	36.0	29.5	70.8	98.8	95.5
Ave. relative reactivity	6.3	7.57	5.9	5.0	6.26
Aromatics					
Mole percent	68.6	20.1	23.4	0.36	0.63
Per cent of total reactivity	63.9	34.1	25.5	1.1	0.0
Ave. relative reactivity	2.58	3.32	3.8	5.82	0.56
GC (ppm hydrocarbon)	265	—	649	366	957
GC reactivity	734	—	2298	713	3036
GC exhaust ave. relative reactivity	2.77	—	3.54	1.95	3.17
GC fuel ave. relative reactivity	3.00	2.08	2.08	0	1.00
Mole per cent unburned fuel of exhaust hydrocarbons	55.1	—	—	43.9	12.6
GC exhaust ave. carbon number	5.74	—	4.61	2.52	3.13
GC fuel ave. carbon number	7.00	6.49	6.49	3.00	8.00

All reactivity values based on H.E.W. relative reactivity factors.
Data from Reference 10.

reliable $NO_2 \rightarrow NO$ converter made possible a measurement of NO, NO_2 and $NO + NO_2$ in combustion engine exhaust, whether at high or low concentration, wet or dry.

Principles of Operation

Figure 9.20 shows a schematic of the chemiluminescent instrument. Sample containing NO is flowed to a cylinderical plug flow reactor which is maintained at a low pressure, typically five to seven torr. Simultaneously, ozone manufactured in a built-in ozonator is introduced into the reactor and well mixed with the

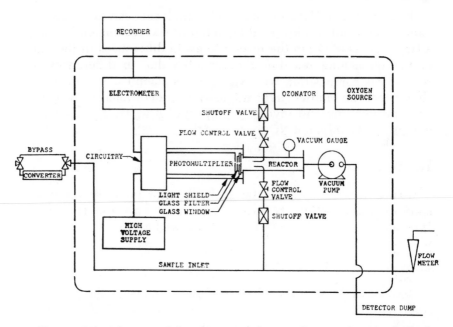

Figure 9.20. Schematic of chemiluminescent NO Analyzer as shown in Federal Register. (Figure from Reference 11.)

NO sample in the region near the detector. A reaction between NO and O_3 occurs which produces some electronically excited NO_2^* molecules. The decay to the ground state of these excited molecules emits light (photons) in the wave length region $0.6–3\mu$. This light is detected by the photomultiplier. The signal is then amplified and fed to a recorder.

The following reaction mechanism has been proposed.[13]

$$NO + O_3 \longrightarrow NO_2 + O_2 \tag{9.1a}$$

$$NO + O_3 \longrightarrow NO_2^* + O_2 \tag{9.1b}$$

$$NO_2^* \longrightarrow NO_2 + h\gamma \tag{9.2}$$

$$NO_2^* + M \rightarrow NO_2 + M^* \tag{9.3}$$

$$I = \frac{I_o[NO][O_3]}{M} \quad \text{(light intensity)}$$

Equations 9.1a and 9.1b show that only a fraction of the NO is converted to excited NO_2^*. According to Niki,[13] the excited yield is 10 % at 80°F and increases with temperature at 0.5 % per degree F. Thus calibration and operation must be at the same reactor temperature. It is also noted that deactivation of excited NO_2^* can proceed according to Equation 9.3 in which a thermal collision between NO_2 and some other molecule can cause deactivation and result in a low reading of light. Niki recommends using a large excess of O_3 in the reactor to avoid differences in the rate of the quenching reaction Equation 9.3 due to differences in reactor gas composition with varying gas samples. Equation 9.4 shows that the emitted light intensity is proportional to NO and O_3 concentration and inversely proportional to M. The analyzer measures NO only, not NO_2.

Interferences

Both Fontijn[14] and Niki[13] have checked for interferences from other exhaust constituents. Typical results are shown in Table 9.5. It is safe to assume that interferences are negligible.

Linearity and Response

Because of the operating principle, the response is theoretically linear with NO concentration as Equation 9.4 showed. Figure 9.21 shows a calibration curve. Response is limited only by the volume of the sample lines and flow rate. Two to four seconds is typical.

Range

The range of the instrument is limited by the photomultiplier tube. With a cooled tube, the range can be 10^{-2} to 10^3 ppm. Commercial units for automotive exhaust gas normally do not use cooled tubes and consequently a useful range of 1–1000 ppm is expected.

NO_2–NO Converter

By converting any exhaust NO_2 to NO, a value of total nitrogen oxides, NO_x can be attained. The technique is based upon a surface reaction in which NO_2 decomposes to NO. To accomplish this, the sample gas, before entering the chemiluminescent detector, is flowed through a stainless steel tube (316 stainless preferred) which is resistance heated to 1200°F. For a flow rate of 1.5 CFH a 6 ft tube of 1/8″ O.D. is adequate.[11] A slightly different version of the converter is shown schematically in Figure 9.22.

A point of interest is the method of checking of the converter to determine proper operation. The method suggested in the Federal Register[11] is to partially fill a clean clear sample bag with NO and

Table 9.5

Interference of Typical Gases on the
NO Determination as Measured by Chemiluminescent Analyzer

Sample flow = 32 cc/min gas composition*	O_3 = 125 cc/min interference (ppm NO)
53.5 ppm NO + 100 ppm ethylene	0
450.0 ppm NO + 100 ppm ethylene	0
53.5 ppm NO + 2.02% CO + 4.42% CO_2	− 0.2 ppm
53.5 ppm NO + 50% sat N_2	− 0.5 ppm
53.5 ppm NO + 500 ppm CH_4	0
53.5 ppm NO + 20% H_2	− 5 ppm
505 ppm CH_4 + 460 ppm NO	0
505 ppm CH_4 + 1995 ppm NO	0
500 ppm C_3H_8 + 460 ppm NO	0
500 ppm C_3H_8 + 1995 ppm NO	0
100 ppm NO_2 + 460 ppm NO	0
100 ppm NO_2 + 1995 ppm NO_2	0
50% blended air + 460 ppm NO	0
50% blended air + 1995 ppm NO	0
5.3% CO + 460 ppm NO	0
5.3% CO + 1995 ppm NO	0

*Dry N_2 was used as diluent gas. These blends of gases were flow blends and are subject to error due to gas viscosity, density and repeatability.
Data from Reference 15.

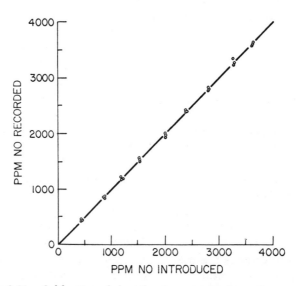

Figure 9.21. Calibration of chemiluminescent Analyzer. Response is linear to sample NO. (Figure from Reference 13.)

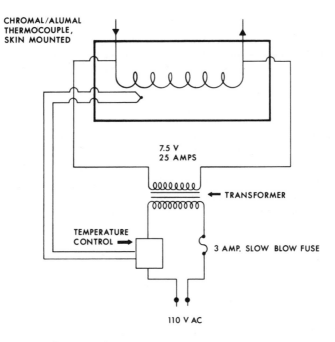

Figure 9.22. Schematic of $NO_2 \rightarrow NO$ converter proposed by Jackson.[15] Converter is 1/4 in. O.D. thin wall stainless steel tubing 6 ft. long. Overall dimensions are $8 \times 12 \times 12$ in.

N_2 calibration gas and then add hydrocarbon free air (so that no HC-NO_2 reactions occur). The NO will be converted to NO_2 in the presence of light over a period of a few minutes. Kneading the bag is recommended to initially mix the reactants. Figure 9.23 shows a typical result. Any decrease in the $NO + NO_2 = NO_x$ level indicates a failure of the converter to convert all NO_2. Ex-

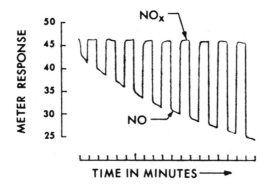

Figure 9.23. Check on converter efficiency suggested in Federal Register. (Figure from Reference 11.)

perience shows that such a failure can arise from a change in the stainless steel surface. A change can arise from contamination, oxide formation or migration of metallic constitutents to or away from the surface. If this occurs, the tube should be replaced.

REFERENCES

1. Jackson, M.W. "Analysis for Exhaust Gas Hydrocarbons: Nondispersive Infrared versus Flame-Ionization," J. APCA, 11 (12) 697 (1966). (See also Inst. Soc. of Am. Conf., October 15 – 18, 1962).
2. "Infrared Analyzers," Bulletin IR-4055, Beckman Instruments, Inc., Scientific and Process Instruments Division.
3. "Infrared Analyzers," Beckman Instructions 1307-D, Beckman Instruments, Inc., Scientific and Process Instruments Division.
4. Teaque, D. M., E. J. Lessniak, Jr., and E. H. Loeser. "A Recommended Flame Ionization Detector Procedure for Automotive Exhaust Hydrocarbons," SAE Preprint 700468 (1970).
5. Willard, H. H., L. L. Merrit, Jr., and J. A. Dean. *Instrumental Methods of Analysis* (New York: D. Van Nostrand and Company, 1968).
6. Laitinen, H. A. *Chemical Analysis* (New York: McGraw Hill Company, 1960).
7. McNair, H. M., and E. J. Bonelli. *Basic Gas Chromatography* (Oakland, Calif.: Consolidated Printers, 1957).
8. Keulemans, A. I. M. *Gas Chromatography* (New York: Reinhold Publishing Corp., 1959).
9. Bayer, E. *Gas Chromatography* (New York: Elsevier Publishing Company, 1961).
10. Lassen, H. G., et al. "Gas Chromatography and Photochemical Reactivity Factors Applied to Automobile Hydrocarbon Emissions," Ford Motor Company, Product Research Office, Report 67-20 (1967).
11. Federal Register, 36 (128), Part II (1971).
12. Stuhl, F., and H. Niki. "An Optical Method for NO in the Range 10^{-2} to 10^3 by the Chemiluminescent Reaction of NO with O_3," Ford Motor Co., Scientific Laboratory Report (March 23, 1971).
13. Niki, H., et al. "An Ozone – NO Chemiluminescence Method for NO Analyses in Piston and Turbine Engines, SAE Preprint 710072 (1971).
14. Fontijn, A., et al. Aero Chem Research Report TP-217 (September, 1969).
15. Jackson, W. E., et al. Ford Motor Co. Report, "Problems Associated with the Constant Volume Sampling Styles," presented at IIEC Technical meeting, Mobil Oil Research, June 7–9, 1971.

10

FEDERAL AUTOMOTIVE
EXHAUST EMISSIONS
TEST PROCEDURES

Introduction

Federal exhaust emission test procedures for light duty vehicles under 6000 lb GVW covering the period 1972 to 1975 assess hydrocarbon, carbon monoxide and nitric oxide emissions in terms of mass of emission emitted over a 7.5 mile chassis dynamometer driving cycle.[1,2] Results are expressed as grams of pollutant emitted per mile.

There are two procedures using the same test equipment which assess vehicle emissions. One, which we will term CVS-1, employs a single bag to collect a representative portion of the exhaust for subsequent analysis. This single bag system applies to testing of 1972, 1973, and 1974 vehicles. Based on this test, emission standards for vehicles have been set at[1]

$$
\begin{bmatrix}
\text{hydrocarbons} - 3.4 \text{ gm/mile} & (1972 \text{ to } 1974) \\
\text{carbon monoxide} - 39 \text{ gm/mile} & (1972 \text{ to } 1974) \\
\text{oxides of nitrogen} - 3.0 \text{ gm/mile} & (1973, 1974)
\end{bmatrix}
$$

The second test procedure, termed CVS-3 uses three sampling bags and is designed to give a reduced and more realistic weighing to the cold start portion of the test. This three-bag system applies to testing of 1975 and 1976 vehicles. Exhaust emission standards based on this test are[2]

$$
\begin{bmatrix}
\text{hydrocarbons} - 0.41 \text{ gm/mile} & (1975, 1976) \\
\text{carbon monoxide} - 3.4 \text{ gm/mile} & (1975, 1976) \\
\text{nitric oxide} - 3.0 \text{ gm/mile} & (1975) \\
-0.4 \text{ gm/mile} & (1976)
\end{bmatrix}
$$

The 1975 HC and CO standards are a 90% reduction from a 1970 vehicle, whereas the 1976 NO_x standard is a 90% reduction from a 1971 vehicle. This 90% reduction was called for in the Clean Air Amendments Act of 1970. Because of differences in test procedures and instrumentation prescribed for 1970/71 and 1975/76 vehicles, the baseline emissions to which the 90% reduction applies were found by averaging 1970 and 1971 vehicle emission results from the CVS-3 cycle for vehicles which meet the 1970 and 1971 emission standards. Emissions from these 1970/71 vehicles were controlled using the earlier FTP cycle and procedure[3] which is commonly termed the California cycle. Table 10.1 shows a comparison for the vehicle group tested.

Table 10.1

Exhaust Emission Comparison for a Group of Vehicles°

	HC	CO	NO$_x$
FTP	2.2 g/mile	23 g/mile	—
CVS-1 1970	4.6 g/mile	47 g/mile	—
CVS-3 1970	4.1 g/mile	34 g/mile	—
CVS-3 1971	—	—	4 g/mile

°Meeting 1970 and 1971 Federal Standards

Driving Cycle

The driving cycle for both CVS-1 and CVS-3 cycles is identical. It involves various accelerations, decelerations and cruise modes of operation. The car is started after soaking for 12 hours in a 60–86°F ambient. A trace of the driving cycle is shown in Figure 10.1. Miles per hour versus time in seconds are plotted on the scale. Top speed is 56.7 mph. Shown for comparison is the FTP or California test cycle. For many advanced fast warm-up emission control systems, the end of the cold portion on the CVS test is the second idle at 125 seconds. This occurs at 0.68 miles. In the CVS tests, emissions are measured during cranking, start-up and for five seconds after ignition is turned off following the last deceleration. Consequently high emissions from excessive cranking or dieseling are included. Details of operation for manual transmission vehicles as well as restart procedures and permissible test tolerances are included in the Federal Registers.

Fuel Specification

Table 10.2 shows the fuel specifications applicable to testing 1975 and 1976 vehicles.[2] These no longer include lead level or octane requirements which are left to the discretion of the manufacturer. Prior to 1975, 3.1–3.3 cc TEL per gallon was specified. This controlled fuel is marketed by American Oil Company under the name Indolene. It is available as clear unleaded fuel or with varying amounts of TEL (Indolene 30 has 3 g TEL/gal).

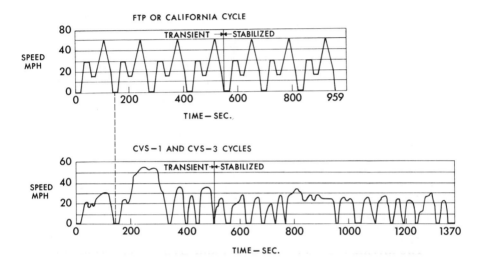

Figure 10.1. Upper-driving cycle for FTP or California Cycle Test. Lower-driving cycle for CVS-1 and CVS-3 Tests.

Table 10.2

Rules and Regulations

Item	ASTM designation	Specifications
Distillation range	D 86	
IBP, °F		75–95
10 per cent point, °F		120–135
50 per cent point, °F		200–230
90 per cent point, °F		300–325
EP, °F (max.)		415
Sulfur, wt. per cent, max.	D 1266	0.10
Phosphorous, theory		0.0
RVP, [1] lb	D 323	8, 7–9, 2
Hydrocarbon composition	D 1319	
Olefins, per cent, max		10
Aromatics, per cent, max		35
Saturates		Remainder

Dynamometer Power Absorbtion

The chassis dynamometer inertia simulation is set up according to Table 10.3. Each vehicle weight category has an equivalent inertia weight and a road power setting.

Table 10.3

Chassis Dynamometer Inertia Simulation

Loaded vehicle weight, pounds	Equivalent inertia weight, pounds	Road losd power @ 50 m.p.h. horsepower
Up to 1,125	1,000	5.9
1,126 to 1,375	1,000	6.5
1,376 to 1,625	1,500	7.1
1,626 to 1,875	1,750	7.7
1,876 to 2,125	2,000	8.3
2,126 to 2,375	2,250	8.8
2,376 to 2,625	2,500	9.4
2,626 to 2,875	2,750	9.9
2,876 to 3,250	3,000	10.3
3,251 to 3,750	3,500	11.2
3,751 to 4,250	4,000	12.0
4,251 to 4,750	4,500	12.7
4,751 to 5,250	5,000	13.4
5,251 to 5,750	5,500	13.9
5,751 to above	5,500	14.4

The Constant Volume Sampler: CVS-1 System

The CVS-1 system, sometimes termed variable dilution sampling, is designed to measure the true mass of emissions. The system is shown in Figure 10.2. A large positive displacement pump draws a constant volume flow of gas through the system. The exhaust of the vehicle is mixed with filtered room air and the mixture is then drawn through the pump. Sufficient air is used to dilute the exhaust in order to avoid vapor condensation, which could dissolve some pollutants and reduce measured values. Excessive dilution, on the other hand, results in very low concentrations with attendant measurement problems. A pump with capacity of 300–350 cfm provides sufficient dilution for most vehicles. Figure 10.3 shows the effect of dilution on dew point for varying ambient air humidity.

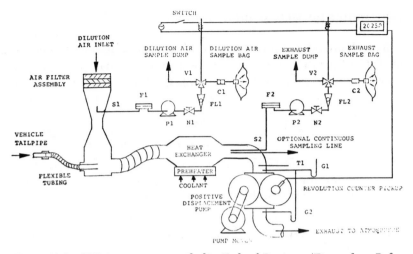

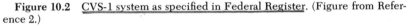

Figure 10.2 <u>CVS-1 system as specified in Federal Register</u>. (Figure from Reference 2.)

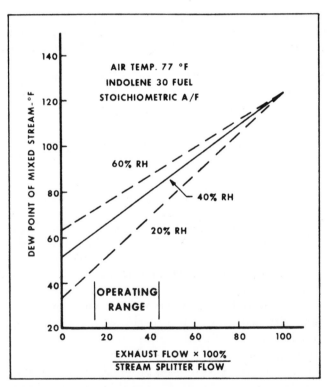

Figure 10.3. Dew point of mixture vs. dilution. To avoid condensation in the diluted sample, the temperature must be kept above the dew point of the sample. (Figure from Reference 4.)

Before the exhaust-air mixture enters the pump its temperature is controlled to within $\pm 10°F$ by the heat exchanger. Thus constant density is maintained in the sampling system and pump. A fraction of the diluted exhaust stream is drawn off by pump P_2 and ejected into an initially evacuated plastic bag. Preferably, the bag should be opaque and manufactured of Teflon or Tedlar. A single bag is used for the entire test sample in the CVS-1 system.

Because of high dilution, ambient traces of HC, CO, or NO_x can significantly increase the concentrations in the sample bag. A charcoal filter is employed for leveling ambient HC measurement. To correct for ambient contamination a bag of dilution air is taken simultaneously with the filling of the exhaust bag.

The Variable Dilution Technique

Consider a pump as in Figure 10.4 which has an output volume flow v_f constant with time. The input flow is $v_{air} + v_{exh}$. In such a system, v_{air} is decreased as v_{exh} is increased so that v_f is always the same. Let the volume fraction of HC entering the pump be F and that leaving be F'. A mass balance for HC through the pump is:

$$\text{mass flow HC in} = \text{mass flow HC out}$$

$$F \times v_{exh} \times \rho_{HC} = \text{mass flow HC in}$$

$$F' \times v_f \times \rho_{HC} = \text{mass flow HC out}$$

or

$$F' \times v_f = F \times v_{exh}$$
$$F' = \frac{F \times v_{exh}}{v_f} \tag{10.1}$$

Equation 10.1 states that the volume fraction HC leaving is proportional to the product of the volume fraction HC entering and the exhaust volume flow. Obviously if the entire volume flow v_f were trapped in a bag, the mass of HC emitted over the driving cycle would be

$$\text{mass HC in bag} = F_{bag} V_{bag} \rho_{HC} = \int_0^t F' v_f \rho_{HC} dt \tag{10.2}$$

Since collecting the entire exhaust volume is not practical, a small

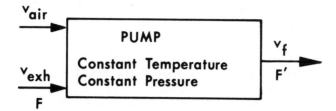

Figure 10.4. Schematic of CVS pump.

sample bag is used to get the average F_{bag} while the product of displacement per pump revolution and number of revolutions gives the total volume flow V_{bag}. To be strictly correct the volume of the sampling bag should be added to the volume drawn through the pump although this turns out to be a very small effect.

Numerical example

In a CVS-1 test, let $v_f = 350$ cfm, $v_{exh} = 50$ cfm, and $F = 210$ ppm HC for one minute and $v_{exh} = 10$ cfm and $F = 600$ ppm for one additional minute. What is average hydrocarbon concentration, F_{bag}, for this two minute test?
From Equation 10.2

$$F_{bag} V_{bag} \rho_{HC} = \int_0^{1\ min} F' v_f \rho_{HC} dt + \int_{1\ min}^{2\ min} F' v_f \rho_{HC} dt$$

Substituting F' from Equation 10.1

$$F_{bag} V_{bag} \rho_{HC} = \frac{210 \times 50}{10^6 \times 350} \times 350 \times \rho_{HC} \times 1 = 10500 \times \rho_{HC}$$

$$+ \frac{600}{10^6} \times \frac{10}{350} \times 350 \times \rho_{HC} \times 1 = 6000 \times \rho_{HC}$$

$$= 10500 \times \rho_{HC} + 6000 \times \rho_{HC}$$

and since V_{bag} for this two minute test is 350 ft³/min × 2 min = 750 ft³

$$F_{bag} = \frac{10500 \times \rho_{HC} + 6000 \times \rho_{HC}}{10^6 V_{bag} \times \rho_{HC}} = \frac{16500}{10^6 \times 750}$$

$$= \frac{220}{10^6}\ \text{or } 220\ \text{ppm}$$

Calculation of the other emission constituents would proceed in a similar manner.

Calculation of Emission Results, CVS-1

HC, CO, and NO_x measurements are made on a wet basis using FID, NDIR, and chemiluminescent detectors respectively. Instruments must be constructed to accurately measure the relatively low concentrations of the diluted exhaust. Concentration values used in the calculations are those of the dilute exhaust sample minus those of the ambient air sample. The emission mass in gm/mile is calculated as follows:

$$HC_{mass} = V_{mix} \times \rho_{HC} \times \frac{HC\ conc}{10^6} \times ppm\ C$$

$$CO_{mass} = V_{mix} \times \rho_{CO} \times \frac{CO\ conc}{10^6} \times ppm\ CO$$

$$NO_{x\ mass} = V_{mix} \times \rho_{NO_2} \times \frac{KH \times NO\ conc}{10^6} \times ppm\ NO$$

where

ρ_{HC} = density of $CH_{1.86}$ in gm*/ft^3 at 528°R and 760 mm Hg = 16.33 gm/ft^3

ρ_{CO} = 32.97 gm/ft^3

ρ_{NO_x} = 54.16 gm/ft^3 assuming NO_x is NO_2

V_{mix} = total dilute wet exhaust volume in ft^3/mile corrected to 528°R and 760 mm Hg

KH = experimentally determined humidity correction factor for NO_x

$$= \frac{1}{1 - 0.0047\ (H - 75)}, \quad H = \text{grains of water/lbm dry air}$$

Now,

$$V_{mix} = K_1 \times V_o \times N \times \frac{P_p}{T_p}$$

*calculated from Pv = mRT

where

$$K_1 = \frac{528°R}{760 \text{ mm Hg} \times 7.5 \text{ miles}} = 0.09263$$

V_o = volume pumped per one revolution of pump

P_p, T_p = pressure and temperature of dilute exhaust entering pump

N = number of revolutions of the pump per 7.5 mile test

Bags should be analyzed as quickly as possible preferably within ten minutes after the test because reactions such as those between NO, NO_2 and HC can occur within the bag quite quickly and change the test results.

CVS-3 System

The CVS-3 system is identical to the CVS-1 system except that three exhaust sample bags are used (Figure 10.5). The normal test is run from a cold start just like the CVS-1 test. After deceleration ends at 505 seconds (Figure 10.1), the diluted exhaust flow is switched from the "transient" bag to the "stabilized" bag and

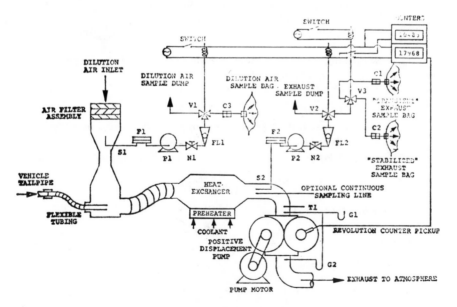

Figure 10.5. CVS-3 System as specified in Federal Register. This differs from CVS-1 in that two sample bag attachments are provided. (Figure from Reference 2.)

revolution counter no. 1 is switched off and no. 2 is activated. The transient bag is analyzed immediately. The rest of the test is completed in the normal fashion and the "stabilized" bag analyzed. However, in the CVS-3 test ten minutes after the test ends the cycle is begun again and run until the end of deceleration at 505 seconds. This second run is termed the hot start run. A fresh bag collects what is termed the hot transient sample. It is assumed that the second half of the hot start run is the same as the second half of the cold start run and is not repeated. In all, three exhaust sample bags are filled. An ambient air sample bag is also filled simultaneously.

Calculations of Emission Results — CVS-3

The calculation procedure below is abstracted from Reference 2. Compound Y may be hydrocarbons, carbon monoxide, or oxides of nitrogen.

Calculation Procedure

$$Y_{wm} = (0.43\, Y_{et} + 0.57\, Y_{ht} + Y_s)/7.5$$

where:

Y_{wm} = Weighted mass emissions of each pollutant, i.e. HC, CO, or NO_x, in grams per vehicle mile.

Y_{et} = Mass emissions as calculated from the "transient" phase of the cold start test, in grams per test phase.

Y_{ht} = Mass emissions as calculated from the "transient" phase of the hot start test, in grams per test phase.

Y_s = Mass emissions as calculated from the "stabilized" phase of the cold start test, in grams per test phase.

The mass of each pollutant for each phase of both the cold start test and the hot start test is determined from the following:

(1) Hydrocarbon Mass:

$$HC_{mass} = V_{mix} \times Density_{HC} \times \frac{HC_{conc}}{1,000,000}$$

(2) Oxides of nitrogen Mass:

$$NO_{x\,mass} = V_{mix} \times Density_{NO_2} \times \frac{NO_{x\,conc}}{1,000,000} \times K_H$$

(3) Carbon monoxide Mass:

$$CO_{mass} = V_{mix} \times Density_{CO} \times \frac{CO_{conc}}{1,000,000}$$

Meaning of symbols

HC_{mass} = Hydrocarbon emissions, in grams per test phase.

Density $_{HC}$ = Density of hydrocarbons in the exhaust gas, assuming an average carbon to hydrogen ratio of 1:1.85, in grams per cubic foot at 68°F. and 760 mm. Hg pressure (16.33 gm./cu. ft.).

HC_{conc} = Hydrocarbon concentration of the dilute exhaust sample corrected for background, in p.p.m. carbon equivalent, i.e. equivalent propane × 3.

$$HC_{conc} = HC_e - HC_d (1 - 1/DF)$$

where:

HC_e = Hydrocarbon concentration of the dilute exhaust sample as measured, in p.p.m. carbon equivalent.

HC_d = Hydrocarbon concentration of the dilution air as measured, in p.p.m. carbon equivalent.

$NO_{x\ mass}$ = Oxides of nitrogen emissions in grams per test phase.

Density $_{NO2}$ = Density of oxides of nitrogen in the exhaust gas, assuming they are in the form of nitrogen dioxide, in grams per cubic foot at 68° F. and 760 mm. Hg pressure (54.16 gm./cu.ft.).

$NO_{x\ conc}$ = Oxides of nitrogen concentration of the dilute exhaust sample corrected for background, in p.p.m.

$$NO_{x\ conc} = NO_{x_e} - NO_{x_d} (1 - 1/DF)$$

where:

NO_{x_e} = Oxides of nitrogen concentration of the dilute exhaust sample as measured, in p.p.m.

NO_{x_d} = Oxides of nitrogen concentration of the dilution air as measured, in p.p.m.

CO_{mass} = Carbon monoxide emissions, in grams per test phase.

Density $_{CO}$ = Density of carbon monoxide in grams per cubic foot at 68° F. and 760 mm. Hg pressure (32.97 gm./cu. ft.).

CO_{conc} = Carbon monoxide concentration of the dilute exhaust sample corrected for background, water vapor and CO_2 extraction, in p.p.m.

$$CO_{conc} = CO_e - CO_d (1 - 1/DF)$$

where:

CO_e = Carbon monoxide concentration of the dilute exhaust sample volume corrected for water vapor and carbon dioxide extraction, in p.p.m. The calculation assumes the hydrogen = carbon ratio of the fuel is 1.85:1.

$$CO_e = (1 - 0.01925\ CO_{2e} - 0.000323\ R)\ CO_{d\ m}$$

where:

$CO_{e\ m}$ = Carbon monoxide concentration of the dilute exhaust sample as measured, in p.p.m.

CO_{2e} = Carbon dioxide concentration of the dilute exhaust sample, in mole percent.

R = Relative humidity of the dilution air, in percent.

CO_d = Carbon monoxide concentration of the dilution air corrected for water vapor extraction, in p.p.m.

$$CO_d = (1 - 0.000323\ R)\ CO_{d\ m}$$

where:

$CO_{d\,m}$ = Carbon monoxide concentration of the dilution air sample as measured, in p.p.m.

$$DF = \frac{13.4}{CO_{2\,e} + (HC_e + CO_e) \times 10^{-4}}$$

V_{mix} = Total dilute exhaust volume in cubic feet per test phase corrected to standard conditions (528° R and 760 mm. Hg).

$$V_{mix} = V_o \times N \, (P_p/760 \text{ mm. Hg}) \, (528°R/T_p)$$

where:

V_o = Volume of gas pumped by the positive displacement pump, in cubic cubic feet per revolution. This volume is dependent on the pressure differential across the positive displacement pump.

N = Number of revolutions of the positive displacement pump during the test phase while samples are being collected.

P_p = Absolute pressure of the dilute exhaust entering the positive displacement pump, in mm. HG, i.e. barometric pressure minus the pressure depression below atmospheric of the mixture entering the positive displacement pump.

T_p = Average temperature of dilute exhaust entering positive displacement pump during test while samples are being collected, in degrees Rankine.

K_H = Humidity correction Factor.

$$K_H = \frac{1}{1 - 0.0047 \, (H - 75)}$$

where:

H = Absolute humidity in grains of water per pound of dry air.

Example Calculation

(1) For the "transient" phase of the cold start test assume V_o = 0.29344 cu. ft. per revolution; N = 10,485; R = 48 percent; H = 62 grains per pound of dry air; P_p = 692 mm. Hg; T_p = 570°R; HC_o = 105.8 p.p.m. carbon equivalent; $NO_{e\,x\,e}$ = 11.2 p.p.m.; $CO_{e\,n}$ = 306.6 p.p.m.; $CO_{2\,e}$ = 1.43 percent; HC_d = 12.1 p.p.m.; $NO_{x\,d}$ = 0.8 p.p.m.; $CO_{d\,m}$ = 15.3 p.p.m.

Then:

V_{mix} = (0.29344) (10,485) (692/760) (528/370) = 2595.0 cu. ft. per test phase.

$$K_H = \frac{1}{1 - 0.0047 \, (62 - 75)} = 0.9424$$

CO_e = (1 − 0.01925 (1.43) − 0.000323 (48)) 306.6 = 293.4 p.p.m.

CO_d = (1 − 0.000323 (48)) 15.3 = 15.1 p.p.m.

$$DF = \frac{13.4}{1.43 + (105.8 + 293.4) \times 10^{-4}} = 9.116$$

$HC_{conc} = 105.8 - 12.1\,(1 - 1/9.116) = 95.03$

$HC_{mass} = (2595)\,(16.33)\,(95.03/1,000,000) = 4.027$ grams per test phase.

$No_{x\,conc} = 11.2 - 0.8\,(1 - 1/9.116) = 10.49$

$NO_{x\,mass} = (2595)\,(54.16)\,(10.49/1,000,000)\,(0.9424) = 1.389$ grams per test phase.

$CO_{conc} = 293.4 - 15.3\,(1 - 1/9.116) = 279.8$

$CO_{mass} = (2595)\,(32.97)\,(279.8/1,000,000) = 23.94$ grams per test phase.

(2) For the "stabilizer" portion of the cold start test assume that similar calculations resulted in $HC_{mass} = 0.62$ grams per test phase, $NO_{x\,mass} = 1.27$ grams per test phase; and $CO_{mass} = 5.98$ grams per test phase.

(3) For the "transient" portion of the hot start test assume that similar calculations resulted in $HC_{mass} = 0.51$ grams per test phase; $NO_{x\,mass} = 1.38$ grams per test phase; and $CO_{mass} = 5.01$ grams per test phase.

(4) For a 1975 light duty vehicle:
$HC_{w\,m} = ((0.43)\quad(4.027) + (0.57)\quad(0.51) + 0.62)/7.5 = 0.352$ gram per vehicle mile.

$NO_{x\,w\,m} = ((0.43)\quad(1.389) + (0.57)\quad(1.38) + 1.27)/7.5 = 0.354$ gram per vehicle mile.

$CO_{w\,m} = ((0.43)\quad(23.94) + (0.57)\quad(5.01) + 5.98)/7.5 = 2.55$ grams per vehicle mile.

REFERENCES

1. Federal Register, **35** (219), Part II (1970).
2. Federal Register, **36** (128), Part II (1971).
3. Federal Register, **33** (108), Part II (1968).
4. Clark, J. B., and S. H. Mick. "Weighing Automotive Emissions," SAE Preprint 690523 (1969).

Symbols and Abbreviations

A	area; after	FTP	U.S. Federal test procedure
A_c	combustion chamber surface area	fhp	friction horsepower
A/F	air-fuel ratio	FL_i	flowmeter
ASTM	American Society for Testing Materials	fmep	friction mean effective pressure
Atm	atmosphere	fpm	feet per minute
B	before	F_r	relative fuel-air ratio; fuel equivalence ratio
BDC	bottom dead center		
bhp	brake horsepower	g	gram
bmep	brake mean effective pressure	g	acceleration of gravity
		G_i	manometer
bsfc	brake specific fuel consumption	GC	gas chromatograph
		GM	General Motor Corp.
C	Centigrade temperature scale	GVW	gross vehicle weight
		h	heat transfer coefficient; head
c	coefficient		
CA	crank angle	HC	hydrocarbon; various hydrocarbons
cc	cubic centimeter		
C_i	connector	HEW	U.S. Dept. of Health, Education & Welfare
CDS	Central daylight saving time		
		Hg	mercury
CFH	flow in cubic feet per hour	hp	horsepower
CFR	Cooperative Fuel Research Council	ID	ignition delay
		ihp	indicated horsepower
CID	cubic inch displacement	IC	intake closing
CO	carbon monoxide	IDI	indirect injection
CO_2	carbon dioxide	IO	intake opening
CI	compression-ignition	imep	indicated mean effective pressure
CID	cubic inch displacement		
CST	central standard time	in	inch
CR	compression ratio	isfc	indicated specific fuel consumption
CVS	constant volume sampler		
D	displacement volume	k	specific reaction rate; thermal conductivity
d	diameter		
DI	direct injection	K	Kelvin temperature scale
e	base of natural logarithm	l	length
E_a	activation energy	lb	pound mass; pound force
EAD	equilibrium air distillation	LBT	leanest for best torque
EC	exhaust closing	m	meter; mass
EO	exhaust opening	MBT	minimum advance for best torque
EPA	Environmental Protection Agency		
		mep	mean effective pressure
F	Fahrenheit temperature scale; volume fraction	mm	millimeter
		mpg	miles per gallon
f	exhaust residual fraction; fraction unburned fuel	mph	miles per hour
		ms	millisecond
F_i	filter	N	revolutions per unit of time
fps	feet per second		

349

n	number of moles; number of droplets	SO_2	sulfur dioxide
NA	naturally aspirated	SO_x	mixture of oxides of sulfur
N_i	needle valve	S/V	ratio of surface to volume
NO	nitric oxide	T	torque temperature
NO_2	nitrogen dioxide	t	time
NO_x	mixture of oxides of nitrogen	TC	turbocharged
		T_i	thermocouple
Nu	Nusselt number	TDC	top dead center
N/V	ratio of engine speed to vehicle velocity	TEL	tetra-ethyl lead
		V	velocity; volume; valve
ON	octane number	V_c	combustion chamber volume
O_3	ozone		
P	pressure	V_d	displacement volume
P_i	pump	V_i	valve
PAN	peroxyacylnitrates	W	work
PCV	positive crankcase ventilation	WOT	wide open throttle
		( )	concentration
PM	particulate material		
pphm	parts per hundred million by volume	*Subscripts*	
		a	air; incoming charge
ppm	parts per million by volume	B.Th.	brake thermal
		d	displacement; discharge
ppmc	parts per million as carbon	f	force; fuel
ppb	parts per billion by volume	il	illumination
		m	mass
psi	pounds per square inch	p	pressure
Q_c	heat of combustion	th	thermal
R	Rankine temperature scale		
r	radius	*Superscripts*	
$\overline{R}$	universal gas constant		
RE	Reynolds number	°	degree of temperature; crank angle degree
rpm	revolutions per minute		
RVP	Reid vapor pressure	*Greek Symbols*	
s	penetration		
S	spark	ρ	density
S_i	sample probe	δ	quench distance
SAE	Society of Automotive Engineers	η	thermal efficiency
		ϕ	fuel equivalence ratio
sfc	specific fuel consumption	μ	wave length in microns
SI	spark-ignition	μg	micrograms
SIT	self-ignition temperature	σ	surface tension

SUBJECT INDEX

Accelerating system, 86
Acceleration, 57, 79, 88, 93
Acetylenes, 52
Activation energy, 102
Additives, 64
After-fill, 182, 184
After injection, 253, 257, 262, 275
After reaction, 146, 147, 148, 149, 159, 160, 165, 201, 213
Air bleed, 89, 90
Air bleed jet, 83, 84
Air fuel ratio, 77, 89, 126, 127
Air fuel ratio
  Effect on Aldehydes, 175
  Effect on HC, CO, 144
Air injection, 143, 174, 210, 211, 213, 214, 215, 216, 220, 221, 222
Air motion in diesel engines, 241
Air pollution, 1, 5, 9, 10, 14, 15, 16
Air preheaters, 207
Air quality, 2, 3, 9, 10
Air radial flow, 242
Air swirl, 231, 241
Alcohols, 52
Aldehydes, 18, 21, 64, 139, 140, 174, 231, 250, 257, 268, 269, 293
Alkanes, 49
Ammonia, 211
Antiknock additives, 63
Aromatics, 52, 64
Aromatic hydrocarbons, 264
ASTM, 59
  Distillation curves, 53, 60
  Specifications, 53
Atomization, 235, 237, 274
Autoignition, 140, 231, 250
Automatic choke, 58
Automatic transmissions, 92
Automobile Manufacturer's Association, 2
Avogadro, 98

Back pressures, 153
Barium-type additives, 275
Benzene, 52
Benzene derivatives, 52
Blowby, 5, 15, 197, 200
Blowby losses, 72
B.M.E.P., 70
Brake horsepower, 46
Brake specific emissions, 291

Calibration, 307, 330
California, 22, 24
California cycle, 4
California Motor Vehicle Pollution Control Board, 3
Capillary, 313, 314
Carbon monoxide, 3, 5, 9, 14, 15, 132, 231, 256, 257, 267, 272, 275
Carbon particles, 257
Carburetion, 76, 126, 132, 133, 145, 221
Carburetor, 5, 80, 86, 144, 147, 151, 154, 155, 156, 157, 181, 185, 200, 204, 206, 207, 208, 215, 220, 224
Carburetor bowl volume effect on vapor loss, 183
Carburetor icing, 59, 207
Carburetor tailoring, 89
Carrier gas, 317, 319, 320, 324, 326
Catalysts, 4, 210, 211
Catalytic reactor, 210, 221, 275
Cetane number, 41, 279
Chain carriers, 102, 103
Charcoal canister, 225, 229
Charge dilution, 127, 281, 298
Chassis dynamometer, 335, 338
Chemical equilibrium, 70
Chemiluminescent, 328, 331, 342
Choke, 88
Choke system, 86
Clean Air Act, 3, 15, 335
CO emissions, 268, 295
CO, 288, 293, 294, 295
Cold starting, 56, 79
Column, GC, 317, 320, 322, 326
Combustion chamber, 97, 103, 104, 106, 107, 109, 110, 112, 158, 159, 160, 207
Combustion chamber, effect of design on HC, 161
Combustion chamber deposit buildup, effect on HC, CO, 157
Compensating jets, 83
Compression ratio, 63, 66, 67, 68, 126, 128, 232
Compression ratio, effect on HC, CO, 164
Constant volume sampling (CVS), 4
Coolant temperature, 63
Coolant temperature, effect on NO, 172
Core, 277

Crankcase blowby, 3
Crankcase dilution, 61
Crankcase vapor storage, 226, 229
Cracking, 48
Cruise, 76
CVP, 336
CVS, 328, 338, 343
Cycloparaffins, 51

Dashpots, 202
Deceleration, 125, 128
Decomposition reactions, 275, 286
Delay periods, 274
Deposits, 103, 112, 157, 158, 172,
    201, 204, 210
Design and operation variables,
    summary of effects, 177
Detonation, 61, 63
D.I., 265, 289, 297
D.I. diesel engines, 294
D.I. engine, 291, 295
D.I. engine emissions, 260
Diesel engine, 40, 43, 44, 289, 293
Diesel engine emissions, 231
Diesel odor, 269
Dieseling, 201
Diffusion-type flames, 260
Dilution, 75, 78, 79, 104, 114, 128,
    152, 154, 174, 201, 202, 338
Diolefins, 50
Direct-injection engines, 232, 251
Displacement effect on *HC* per
    cylinder, 164
Dissociation, 103
Distillation, 48, 181
Distillation curve, 55
Distribution, 150
Distributor, 155, 201, 202
Dribbling, 275
Driveability, 145, 204, 207, 208, 210
Dual induction manifold, 207, 208

Economy, 149, 153, 164
Effect of equivalence ratio, air
    fuel ratio effect on *NO*, 166
Effective pressure and efficiency, 74
Emission control, 90
Emission formation and elimination
    in D.I. and I.D.I engines, 294
Emission formation in gasoline
    engines, 117
Emissions from diesel and gasoline
    engines, 293
Engine cylinder, 100
Engine fundamentals, 39
Engine noise, 243

Engine speed, 126
Engine speed
    Effect on *HC*, *CO*, 149
    Effect on *NO*, 171
Environmental Protection
    Agency, 10, 13, 14
Equilibrium, 100, 101, 102, 104, 186
Equilibrium Air Distillation, 55
Equilibrium volatility, 53
Equivalence ratio, 100, 101, 104,
    147, 166, 168
Evaporation, 190
Evaporation loss, 60
Evaporative, 4, 5
Evaporative emissions, 15, 31, 181
Evaporative emissions-control, 224
Exhaust, 31
Exhaust back pressure
    Effect on *HC*, *CO*, 152
Exhaust emissions, 15, 97, 112
Exhaust emissions in the indirect
    injection engines, 284
Exhaust gas dilution, 125, 128
Exhaust gas recirculation, 202, 204, 297
Exhaust gas recirculation
    Effect on *NO*, 174
Exhaust residual, 126
Exhaust scavenging, 117
Exhaust smoke, 257

Federal Evaporative Test
    Procedure, 190
Federal Test Procedure (FTP), 4, 158,
    185, 210, 211, 217, 222, 335, 336
Filter cell, 309, 310
Flame front, 106, 110, 112
Flame ionization, 175
Flame ionization detector, 312, 317,
    323, 325, 326, 342
Flame propagation, 104, 106, 113, 114,
    125, 126, 145, 157
Flame speed, 41, 70
Flame travel, 110
Flame velocity, 104
Formaldehyde, 246, 270
Four-cycle engine, 117
Four-stroke cycle, 39
Four-stroke cycle engine, 40
Four-stroke engines, 129
Four-stroke gasoline, 127, 129
Friction, 149, 164
Fuels, 47
Fuel-air, 76
Fuel-air distribution in the
    spray, 251

Fuel-air ratio, 63, 68, 69, 70, 79,
  82, 83, 89, 255, 262, 269, 278
Fuel economy, 145, 151, 164, 202,
  204, 211, 214, 222
Fuel deposited on the walls, 253, 257
Fuel distribution, 58, 99
Fuel injection, 208, 210
Fuel shut off, 202
Fuel tank, 5, 185, 186, 192, 224, 229
Fuel volatility, 60
Fumigation, 275

Gas chromatograph, 317
Gas chromatographic, 177
Gas dilution, 125
Gas tank, 181
Gasoline, 53
Gasoline engine, 40, 43, 44, 293
General Motors, 22, 23, 24, 25, 32, 33

Haagen-Smit, A.J., 2
HC, 295
HC,measurement of engine exhaust,
  309, 312, 317, 325
Heat losses, 72
Heat release, 284, 260
Heat release in an I.D.I. engine, 285
Heat release rates in D.I. engines, 258
Heat rejection, 201
Heterogeneous, 97, 315
H.E.W., Dept. of, 3, 6, 32, 33
High load, 76
Homogeneous, 97
Horsepower, 90, 93
Hot soak, 181
Humidity, effect on *NO*, 173
Hydrocarbons, 3, 5, 6, 9, 10, 11, 13, 14,
  15, 17, 31, 49, 197, 288, 293
Hydrocarbon emissions, 103, 125, 129
Hydrocarbon emissions, design and
  operating variable effect-summary,
  166

I.D.I., 289, 296
I.D.I. diesel engines, 294
I.D.I. engines, 265, 291, 297
I.D.I. engine emissions, 284
Idle, 90, 125
Idle system, 87
Idling, 76
Idling system, 85
Ignitability limits, 270
Ignition delay, 41, 71, 231, 244, 245,
  246, 247, 249, 252, 266, 295
Ignition delay in D.I. engines, 243
Ignition delay period, 70

Ignition timing, 70
Incomplete combustion, 117, 125, 231,
  255
Indicated horsepower, 46
Indicator diagram, 40
Indirect injection, 265
Indirect injection engines, 232
Indirect injection engines,
  (I.D.I.), 283
Indolene, 97, 175, 190, 211, 327, 328,
  337
Injection, 231
Injection system design, 267
Injection timing, 274, 275, 280,
  281, 287, 294
Intake manifold pressure effect
  on *HC, CO*, 154
Interference, chemiluminescent, 331
Internal exhaust gas recirculation, 204
Interference, FID, 314
Interference, NDIR, 309
Isooctane, 50

Knock reactions, 112
Knock tendency, 108

Lead compounds, 64
Lean flammability limits, 270
Lean flame region (LFR), 253, 254,
  255, 259, 267, 278, 280
Lean flame-out region (LFOR), 253,
  254, 255, 262, 264, 266, 267, 268, 270,
  278, 295
Los Angeles, 1, 2, 3, 13, 14, 17, 24
Low load, 76
LRF, 268
Lubricating oil, 48, 262
Lubrication, 45

Main jet, 82
Manual transmission, 128
Manual transmission systems, 92
Mass emissions, 4, 64, 144, 148,
  149, 150, 151, 154, 157, 164, 165,
  197, 335, 342
Maximum cycle pressure, 61, 72
Maximum cycle temperature, 68, 70
Maximum temperature, 42
Maximum gas temperature, 243, 278
Mean effective pressure, 46, 66, 69, 72
Mechanisms of combustion of a
  fuel spray, 253
Mechanisms for *NO* formations,
  134, 277, 280
MBT, minimum advance for best
  torque, 74

Misfire, 127, 145
Molecular structure of the unburned
    hydrocarbon emissions, 264
Molecules, 101, 102, 103, 312, 330
M-System, 283, 289, 291, 295, 296

Naphthenes, 31, 51
NDIR, 175, 305
New York, 14
Nitric oxide (*NO*), 133, 254, 261, 277,
    278, 293, 295
NO concentration, 280, 288
Nitric oxide converter, 329, 331
NO emission, 278, 281, 295
NO emission control, 293
NO, formation in flames, 136
Nitrogen dioxide, 133
Nitrogen oxides, 61, 68, 231, 256, 279
Nondispersive infrared analyzers, 144

Octane, 112, 160
Octane number, 63, 64
Odor, 269, 270, 275, 293
Odor constituents, 231
Off-idle port, 85
Olefins, 17, 31, 33, 50, 185, 194, 328
Oxidant, 2, 3, 6, 9, 10, 11, 13, 14,
    18, 25, 28, 30, 32, 33
Oxides of nitrogen, 5, 9, 10, 11, 13,
    14, 16, 133
Oxides of sulfur, 5, 9
Oxygen interference, 315
Oxygenated compounds, 256, 270
Oxygenated hydrocarbons, 255, 257
Ozone, 1, 2, 18, 21, 24, 25, 329

Paraffins, 31, 49
Particulate, 4, 5, 9, 64, 103
Partition coefficient, 322
Penetration, 274, 275
Performance number, 63
Performance parameters, 45
Peroxides, 250
Peroxyacyl nitrates (PAN), 18, 21, 32
Photochemical, 6, 14, 16
Photochemical reaction, 21
Photomultiplier, 330, 331
Pindex, 9, 10
Polynuclear aromatics, 64
Ported spark, 201
Positive crankcase ventilation (PCV),
    198, 200, 227
Power enrichment system, 87
Power output
    Effect on *HC, CO*, 147
    Effect on *NO*, 170
Preignition, 52, 62, 108

Preignition chemical reactions, 249
Preignition reactions, 247, 250
Pressure, 104, 106, 109, 112, 148,
    168, 171, 214
Pressure rise period, 71
Public Health Service, 22, 27
Pumping loss, 42, 43, 94

Quadrajet, 206
Quench, 112, 148, 157, 159, 160, 331
Quenching, 103
    Reactions, 102

Radial flow, 241, 242, 258
Raoult's, 189
Rate of injection, 274
Reaction order, 102
Reaction rate, 102
Reactivity, 30, 31, 32, 33, 174, 185, 190,
    194
Reactivity index, 31
Reactor, 329, 330,
Reid pressure, 60
Reid vapor pressure (RVP), 53, 60, 190,
    192, 226
Relative reactivity, 31
Residence time, 148, 214, 217, 218, 221,
    293
Residual, 153, 170
    Gases, 75
Retention time, 317, 322, 325
Reynolds number, 104
Road performance, 90, 93
Roughness, 112,

Sauther Mean Diameter, 235
Scavenging, 45, 128
Second stage combustion, 270
Secondary injection, 275
Smog, 1, 13, 16, 19, 20, 21, 23, 24, 25
Smog chamber, 17, 22, 27, 30
Smog reactions, 29
Smoke, 258, 270, 273, 275, 295
Smoke intensity, 286
Smoke limit, 286
Smoke particles, 272
Smoke particulates, 231, 271
Smoke suppressant fuel additives, 275
SO_2, 2
Spark advance, 63
Spark timing, 71, 74, 75, 126
    Effect on *HC, CO*, 150
    Effect on *NO*, 168
Specific emissions, 264
Specific fuel consumption, 47
Specific reactivity, 31
Specifications for gasoline, 54

Speed, 232, 287
Spray atomization, 234
Spray core, 253, 255, 262, 272
Spray formation, 231, 232, 233, 234
   In swirling air, 241
Spray penetration, 238
Spray regions, 253
Spray tail, 253, 256, 262
Stabilized bag, 343, 344
Standards, 2, 4, 16
Stroke to bore ratio, effect on *HC*, 162
Subtractive column, 326
Surface ignition, 52
Surface temperature, effect on *HC*,
   CO, 159
Surface volume ratio, 150, 165,
   Effect on *HC*, *CO*, 160
Surge, 145, 207, 208, 217, 220
Swirl, 258, 266, 280

Techniques used to control
   NO emissions from gasoline engines
   293
TEL, 211, 224
Temperature, 104, 108, 173, 181, 202,
   214
   Distribution, 107
Temperature effect on carburetor
   vapor loss, 182, 183
Temperature effect on fuel tank
   vapor loss, 186, 189, 190, 193, 194
Temperature effect on *GC* retention
   time, 322, 323
Temperature programing, 323, 326,
   327
Temperature stratification, 106
Testing, 97
Tetraethyl lead, 63, 157, 336
Thermal conductivity detectors, 324
Thermal efficiency, 47, 66, 69, 72, 201
Thermal reactor, 210, 213, 219, 221
Throttle crackers, 202
Throttle positioner, 201
Timing and rate of injection, 267

Toluene, 52
Transient bag, 343, 344
Transmission controlled spark valve,
   202
Triple venturi, 80
Turbocharging, 265, 281
Turbulence, 104, 113, 171
Turbulent, 149
Two-cycle engine, 117
Two-cycle gasoline, 128
Two-stage combustion, 254
Two-stroke cycles, 39
Two-stroke cycle engine, 43, 44
Two-stroke engine, 39

Unburned hydrocarbons, 117, 122, 125,
   127, 129, 130, 131, 254, 255, 256, 257,
   262, 263, 264, 268, 275, 286, 294
Unburned hydrocarbon emissions, 265,
   266, 267

Valve burning, 201
Valve overlap, 126, 128
   Effect on *HC*, *CO*, 153
Valve timing, 41, 43
Vapor liquid equilibrium, 188
Vapor-lock, 59, 60
Variable valve timing, 204
Venturi, 80
Volatility, 53, 55, 56, 57, 59, 182, 190
Volumetric efficiency, 42, 45

Wall quenching, 117, 120, 125, 129, 231
Warm-up, 57, 58, 79
Water addition, 294, 296
Water injection, 202, 203, 204, 295
Wave length, 305, 306
Weber number, 234

Zeldovich, 174, 277
Zeldovich chain reaction mechanism,
   134
Zeldovich mechanism, 139